Palm Oil & Small Chop

Palm Oil & Small Chop

John Goble

Whittles Publishing

For Anne, always a generous listener,
who encouraged me to write it all down.

Published by
Whittles Publishing Ltd.,
Dunbeath,
Caithness, KW6 6EG,
Scotland, UK

www.whittlespublishing.com

ISBN 978-184995-011-4

Printed by
Short Run Press Ltd, England

Contents

Foreword

G ood handfuls of those who have been merchant seamen have written of their shipboard lives. My shelves have 25 titles published since the 1980s and several scores more running back into the 1860s. Filing cabinets harbour seamen's unpublished manuscripts and a great many transcripts of interviews recording seagoing careers. Among the latter is one from 1983 with a John Goble, a mate/chief officer/ relieving master in ships trading to West Africa.

I had interviewed John for a book I was writing on the lives of seafarers in the declining years of the British shipping industry. Purely by chance I had found one of those thoughtful and articulate people able to roll up blinds. Here was a liberal imagination, cool observation and ironic sense of humour. Close to 30 years later, the same voice has produced the book I always hoped he would.

Readers familiar with the genre of recollecting seafarers will be relieved to find not a trace of self-promotion, indeed very little of the author's doings appear at all except where they are part of a particular of the story of the fascinating West African trades and the everyday life of the merchant ship. On the one hand the book is packed with critical yet sympathetic insights and observations into the social and economic dimensions of commerce to the former colonies of Britain, France, Germany, Belgium, Spain and Portugal. On the other hand are deadly shrewd and tolerantly amused stories of shipboard discipline, 'jack' ashore and finely-drawn accounts of cargo working and sea passages.

John Goble's shipmates are sketched with a light, perceptively friendly touch even though this is a book about a trade and its actors, not about individuals and their inner life. His delightful skill at revealing character through gentle understatement especially struck me when I saw a coincidence of crossing paths about to strike. In one of the closing chapters the reader meets a difficult Polish émigré master. Although he is not named I recognised him immediately as Jan Kopec, the unsmiling, demanding mate of the *Bamenda Palm* in 1959–60, where I was fourth mate, fresh and innocent from my apprenticeship in a less exotic trade. It was my first and last ship to West Africa. Still, I saw enough of the trade to see that here was interesting country for an enquiring seafarer. John Goble's book reveals the wonderful fascination of West Africa. He does this by drawing on judicious reading on matters West African and then, as if to insist that seriousness can go hand in hand with levity, follows through with smiling observations and stories. Quite a book. Those who know ships, trades and crews will surely love it.

But so, too, will those who know also the near-impossible trials and complexities of the colonial legacy of the 'Coast'.

Tony Lane
Professor Emeritus
Cardiff University School of Social Science

Preface

It's now about a quarter of a century since the British Merchant Navy quietly lost its role of serving an island nation that depends for its prosperity on international trade. That task is now fulfilled by a global shipping industry. Within that, the Red Ensign is flown by ships whose manning and financing have little connection with Britain other than as a tax convenience. My seafaring was during the previous quarter century, a very different period indeed.

The passing of the Merchant Navy that I knew coincided with the decline of many other staple British employments. Some industries contracted with bitterness and strong political reactions. However, merchant shipping seemed to slowly expire without causing very much public interest or concern.

In contrast, many more accounts of what it was like to be a merchant seaman have been published than have appeared about being a coalminer or a worker in a shipyard or factory. These seafaring memoirs have come from a full range of writers whose experiences extended from first-trip deck boy to long-serving master. Why, then, should there be room for yet another story?

The answer is that there is an absence of published accounts of work in the West African trade, a very distinctive and fascinating corner of the shipping industry. Post-independence economic and political failures of the region strongly affected the trade and I have tried to incorporate a sense of that impact into my story.

Sailing to West Africa was never a popular choice of seafarers as it had none of the romantic or exotic connotations of the routes to Australasia or the Far East. What it offered was short voyages that principally appealed to married men, slightly better wages than in other trades and that strange attraction that made you decide to sign on for another trip to the 'Coast' rather than look for a ship sailing elsewhere.

My unique experience was to work not only for two British ship-owners serving the 'Coast' but also for the national shipping line of Nigeria. This extensive service proved to me that working with and being amongst West Africans could be taxing, frustrating and humorous in almost equal measures. In retrospect, there is a sadness that, whereas I can look back on those days from a secure retirement, those people from the West Coast of Africa that I met or sailed with, if they are still alive, are living in a part of the world that has failed its citizens most dismally.

That failure is a shadow that was gradually falling throughout my years of sailing to West Africa and which becomes apparent in this book. On a happier note, what

I associate most with the West African trade is that treat of a full 'Palm Oil Chop' accompanied by those varied side dishes of 'small chop'. Unique flavours, fondly recalled, and that's why I've chosen it as the title of this account.

I hope that a similarly satisfying flavour will come across in my words and that your reading of this memoir will therefore reflect my enjoyment in writing it. However, writing also shares with cooking the ability to convert raw materials into something subtly different. This means that, whilst places and events in this account are all sharply recalled and they occur in chronological order, the names of people, their attributed dialogue and some aspects of their personality have been gently changed or transposed as some insurance against any failure of memory.

Author's note

Some of my recollections appeared in the quarterly, *Ships in Focus Record*, during 2007. I am very grateful to both the editor, Dr Roy Fenton, and John Clarkson, the publisher of that journal, for that first opportunity to share them with an audience.

It was Professor Tony Lane, the former Director of the Seafarers International Research Centre at Cardiff University, who encouraged me to expand my memoir to book length. His invaluable critique was always available and the finished work has benefited from more than one wise application of his hand to the tiller when I was judged to be drifting off course. I hope that he now finds that his confidence in both the purposes and the final shape of this book is fulfilled.

1

The loading from Liverpool

Liverpool, early in the 1960s, was just becoming known nationally as the home of exciting new sounds in popular music. However, with the Beatles yet to make their famous impact on the United States, the name of the city was still associated globally with its status as a port and commercial centre.

That status might be declining from its zenith in the days of Empire but the port of registry of Liverpool continued to be proudly carried on the sterns of merchant ships travelling to every continent. In the ports of the West Coast of Africa, the name of Liverpool remained synonymous with sea trade. A trade that had now progressed from the shame of slavery through the rather more honourable years of colonial possession to these heady first years of African independence.

The maritime connection of the city with the world could be seen in action by anyone who used the famous electric Overhead Railway until its demolition at the end of 1956. That loss means that we must imagine ourselves onto one of those replacement green-and-cream Liverpool Corporation buses if we are to recapture the flavour of the time. So, let's board a 'Corpy' bus that proudly carries the route number 1 and which will follow the line of docks that run southwards from Seaforth.

Even if we sit on the upper deck we are unfortunately some ten metres below the vanished Overhead's level. This means that our view of ships will consist mostly of their masts and the colourful heraldry of their funnels, seen over the magnificent stone battlements of Jesse Hartley's dock architecture. The succession of variously named streets that make up the 'Dock Road' are full of goods vehicles and lorry queues whose cargoes spell out a gazetteer of the world.

We see cases that are marked for Auckland, for Buenos Aires, for Charleston, and so on through the alphabet to Wellington. Admittedly, we'll need a trip 'over the water' to Birkenhead if we want to see, say, Yokohama or Zanzibar via Mombasa.

We get off the bus outside the massive bulk of the old Cheshire Lines Railway warehouse before it grinds up the hill of Park Street, leaving the dock road behind as it heads for its Dingle terminus. As we cross the road, the time is conveniently given by the landmark clock on the end of the dock shed opposite (it still exists today).

We're heading for the gate that is between Toxteth and Brunswick Docks. If we look as though we know where we're going then the dock-gate bobby will be unconcerned. He'd be more attentive to our progress if we were leaving the estate.

Three 'south end' docks, named Brunswick, Toxteth and Harrington, are where the trade to and from West Africa is mainly conducted. The first-named is for exports, the last for imports and the middle one is for shared use. Booker Line ships trading to Demerara and Moss Hutchison ships going to the Mediterranean each have a berth in these docks but they represent a minority interest. The overwhelming flavour is West African.

There are import sheds that smell of palm kernels, groundnuts, rubber and sawn timber. Stacks of round logs lie in the open on the river side of the shed alongside sawn timber that is protected under tarpaulins. The export sheds are congested with lorries unloading bags of salt whilst others have bundles of steel angles and reinforcing rods. Cases, large and small, spell out the names of the Coast's ports and a large steel cage in the corner is filling with dutiable goods and bales of textiles.

Thirty years later, in another life, I was to revisit one of these sheds, little changed, which was then home to a bulk mail-sorting operation for Royal Mail. Another had been converted into modern accommodation for a large mailing house. But, back in time, we're able to go on board one of the ships of this trade where we'll see how this apparently chaotic collection of cargo is loaded. Then we can follow its journey from the winter drabness of the Mersey to the sunshine of West Africa.

I'm afraid that the ship that I've chosen for us to join for this voyage is not very inspiring to look at. She's short in length, with a broadness of beam that makes her dull black hull look very squat in the dock water. She has an equally squat tower of accommodation perched on top of that hull. This unpromising ensemble is completed by a foreshortened pale-yellow funnel. But, before you reject this ship on aesthetic grounds alone, let me try and explain what she is and why she looks as she does.

The ship is short because she has to be able to get along the narrow, twisting creeks of the Niger Delta. She's as wide as much longer ships because she's built to carry as much cargo as possible and speed is of less importance. The superstructure block is of an unusual height due to an additional deck that contains the cabins and public rooms for 12 passengers.

This is the maximum number that can be carried without the additional expense of employing a ship's doctor. Any passenger capacity was at a premium when she was built in the years just after the second world war, and it is also that period's austerity that largely accounts for her utilitarian look.

Ignore this visual shortcoming for a moment and instead notice the flag that flies from one of the masts. Its design combines the cross of St George with the royal crown superimposed and it's a reminder that African Royal Mail is the proud epithet of the ship's owners, Elder Dempster Lines. Thus, whilst the ship might lack the good looks of those handsome cargo liners that serve Australasia or the Far East, she yields to no one when it comes to a commercial and historical pedigree.

It's time to go up the gangway and find out more about this typical voyage from Liverpool to West Africa. We go up the wooden steps and then weave through the small throng of people that always gather near the top. Now, going carefully over the foot-high storm step that keeps the sea out of the ship's interior, the impression of dated dowdiness continues. We're in a world of wood panelling, poor lighting and the myriad smells of shipboard life. It's a distinctive blend of hot oil, old cooking, damp overcoats and tobacco smoke, accompanied by the insistent background hum of the ship's generators.

It does get better as we go up each staircase (called a 'companionway') from deck to deck and our destination, the bridge, has a reassuring calm and an ambience of polished brass and gleaming mahogany. It is from here that we can look out towards the bow and see the ship as a workplace for the Liverpool dockers.

We are level with a thicket of wires that are the means of bringing the cargo on board. There are no cranes here to assist, as we are in berths that were built for an earlier age. They suit the cargo as it is one that the fathers, even the grandfathers, of these dockers would largely recognise.

One of the ship's yellow-painted masts is but 20 feet in front of us and we can look down and see the very short number three hatch of the ship. It's short because it's just the cover for the six deep tanks that lie below, essential for carrying the vegetable oils that are one of the staples of the homeward trade. Another mast is a longer distance beyond and this lies between the two other hatches that make up the ship's forepart. Number one is a space that suffers from the narrowing of the hull as it approaches the bow; number two is the best and biggest of the holds.

If we now look aft we can see the ship's third mast and this separates the two holds that occupy the rearmost part of the ship. Number four is another large space, number five again suffers from the hull's narrowing towards the stern. Both of these holds have the disadvantage of a large duct (called the tunnel) running their length. This protects the steel shaft that transmits the engine's power to the propeller.

Every hold on the ship has a 'tweendeck that divides it horizontally. There are also separate compartments called lockers, magazines, mail or baggage rooms further subdividing these spaces. It's a far cry from today's giant open containerships but our ship is of its time and of its trade and the Liverpool dockers have the art and skill of loading it to ensure a successful voyage.

The export cargo that dominates the West African trade from Liverpool at this time in terms of volume and weight is salt for northern Nigeria. It's a historic cargo and this is evident from the proud trade marks on the white cotton bags, each holding 40 lbs of refined white Cheshire salt.

Since the contents are identical, these marks are partly for the conceit of the merchant houses but are mainly for creating some brand awareness in customers who are generally illiterate.

The leading trading organisation on the West Coast of Africa, the United Africa Company or UAC, uses a manilla (a small brass artefact that was once used as local currency), an eagle on a rock or a berewa (a type of small deer) as its trade marks. The smaller trading houses also have their brands. John Holt has a schooner on a star, G. B. Ollivant has a hunter on horseback, and you might just spot the sly humour of money-bags (three purses, all marked '£100'), or my particular favourite, a strongman and an elephant (the man is shown lifting the pachyderm).

These marks and the proud legend 'British Salt' are all in a dye that can be easily washed out because the tightly woven fabric of the bag is valuable as a recyclable textile. This means that its cleanliness must be protected, and it is being stowed by dockers who are wearing canvas overshoes. They will then enclose it in coarse hessian burlap to protect it from the rusty areas of the hold. The dockers load it, bag by bag, as it comes aboard in special canvas slings until they reach a certain height in the holds. Then it is covered with more hessian, a layer of plastic sheeting and finally by a floor of plywood boards. This makes a 'garage' space, which we will return to later.

Salt is an excellent cargo to start with as it fully occupies two or three gangs of dockers for a couple of days while the stevedore superintendent plans the more complicated parts of the cargo stowage. Loading a cargo ship in these years before the advent of the container resembles the packing of a suitcase for an extended holiday. There is, however, an important difference. The unpacking is done in every hotel of only those items needed and without disturbance to the rest of the contents.

Some voyages to West Africa only involve unloading at around half a dozen ports (typically Freetown, Takoradi, Tema, Lagos/Apapa and Port Harcourt). Other voyages might well require a ship to call at over twice that number (Dakar, Bathurst, Monrovia, Abidjan, Lomé, Cotonou, Douala, Libreville, Pointe Noire, Boma, Matadi, Luanda and Lobito, as one extreme example).

This means that successful preparation for the voyage becomes a product of the stevedores' experience and regular monitoring by the ship's officers over the next week or so. It is finally the expert eye of the individual hatch boss that is crucial to producing the nice tight seamanlike stow for which the port of Liverpool is famous.

Men such as Jimmy 'Dulux', so-called for the ex-army greatcoat that almost reaches his ankles and thus recalls the famous ICI paints advertising slogan ('One coat covers all') of the time.

'I know what they say, but it kept our kid safe and warm through Korea so it'll do me here all right,' he ruefully remarks as he goes into the shed looking to find the exact type of cargo that will fill the space in the stow that he has in mind. And there's plenty of choice for him as the cargo becomes increasingly miscellaneous with receiving approaching its closing day.

More bottom weight comes with square bulks of tinplate from South Wales for the Metal Box factory in Apapa. They join bundles of steel angles and reinforcing rods that arrive from Scotland and which will feed the building boom elsewhere in Nigeria. This weight will offset any top-heaviness effect on the ship's stability caused by a consignment of steel rails for Ghana Railways loaded in the 'tweendecks.

There's more weight up there in the form of stout wooden cases of Crocodile-brand machetes made in the West Midlands. They're placed next to black cast-iron cooking pots which have to be taken out of carriage skips and then stacked with the ample use of straw to protect them in the stow.

Nowadays these items can often be seen planted with flowers in suburban gardens; then they were the staple cooking utensil of rural West Africa. They come in various sizes and the Liverpool dockers inevitably dub them as 'quarter', 'half', 'full' or even 'double missionary'.

The British manufacturing industry is enjoying an almost unchallenged dominance of the market in our ex-colonies such as Sierra Leone, Ghana and Nigeria. Our holds will fill with crates proudly marked 'Another Ford Tractor', 'Another English Electric Transformer for...', 'Morris Motors: Made in England' and similar patriotic slogans.

It is when the larger items of cargo and the vehicles have to be loaded that the limitations of these South End docks are apparent. They were built for the sailing ship and have only a ten-foot-wide apron between the shed door and the ship's side. This helps to minimise cargo wetting when it rains but it also reduces the room to manoeuvre these bulkier cargoes.

One of the port's small fleet of floating cranes has already delivered two large packaged boilers and will return on sailing day to bring bulldozers and earthmoving vehicles. Today it is time to load some other vehicles from the quay and then roll them in on top of the salt cargo.

This calls for breasting the ship off the quay and allowing two small pontoons, called 'dummies', to be floated into the resulting gap. When the ship is then pulled hard alongside this pair, the quay apron has been doubled in width. In order not to delay the dockers, this operation takes place before the working day starts and the ship is then brought back to its original state during the lunch break. It's paid overtime for the ship's riggers and sailors and unpaid overtime for the officers.

First to be loaded are the lorries, effectively just the chassis and the engine housed in either a wooden box or under a minimal bonnet. The coachwork will be added in West Africa to form the distinctive 'mammy-wagons' that we will meet later on the coast.

These rudimentary vehicles have been driven up from factories near Crewe or in the Midlands. The delivery drivers boast a distinctive heavy-weather garb of ex-army greatcoats, flat caps, woollen mufflers and those driving goggles that recall the motoring days of Mr Toad.

The lorries retain just enough fuel to be driven over the floor of plywood sheets to their stowage places on top of the salt but this amount will have inevitably evaporated when the time comes to unload them. We can therefore look forward to a lot of pushing and curses of 'Why dis ting never go proper?' from the understandably aggrieved dockers in West Africa.

Then it is the turn of the smaller vehicles to be loaded: Land Rovers if we are bound for the francophone ports, black Morris Minors for the Nigerian taxi trade, Austins, Fords and Hillmans for the expatriate residents of these former colonies. The riggers are kept busy securing all these vehicles as they are loaded. Timber frames enclose the wheels of the larger ones, twisted rope and wire lashings for them all, completed by a short wooden stick jammed in to prevent it unravelling. This is termed a 'Spanish wind-lass', a phrase that doubtless originated as a maritime insult to that country from some long-forgotten historical conflict.

The mate works with the stevedoring superintendents to make the stowage decisions that ensure the ship's required stability, draught and trim. That means the ship will be upright, not overloaded as indicated by the famous Plimsoll marks and slightly less deep in the water at the bow than at the stern.

The hatch bosses and dockers see that all the spaces are efficiently filled. It is then the work of the junior officers and apprentices to watch the separation and security of the cargo. The former is a matter of checking that it can be unloaded in the required order with no risk of having items overcarried or inaccessibly buried. The latter is altogether more problematical because they are pitched against the Liverpool docker set on enjoying his perks of a dip into the more desirable items of cargo.

What was once a way of supplementing their poor and irregular wages has become an established and self-awarded bonus despite the dockers now sharing in the country's rising prosperity. Pilfering of the cargo can never be eradicated, only controlled. Hatch watchmen are employed but they are either elderly former dockers or poorly paid casuals. Their effectiveness is very limited, so it is the ship's staff who must get out and about around the hatches and try and minimise the larceny.

The design of the ship both helps and hinders the security of the cargo. There are six special lockers, six deep tanks, a mail room and two explosives magazines where spirits, tobacco, textiles, batteries, razor blades and similar high-value items can be put under lock and key. Unfortunately there are dark corners which are almost impossible to police. The quantity of pilferable cargo outstrips our secure capacity and so a decision must be made on what can be left in open stowage without being too severely depleted.

Wooden cases of Guinness are amongst the usual choices. Each contains a dozen quart bottles and is proudly stamped in blue with the slogan 'Guinness is Good for You'. This is a product endorsement that is shared equally enthusiastically by the dockers of Liverpool and West Africa. This desirable liquid is given stowages that can be easily viewed from the deck but the stevedores readily rise to the challenge.

A few tell-tale empty bottles begin to appear and the gang become more than usually boisterous and noisy.

'Watch out fer that hook, yer big prick.'

'Oh, aye. Your wife tell you everythin'?'

Unfortunately the full extent of their depredations will only become apparent in a few weeks' time and 3,000 sea miles away.

In the worst case that I recall a small refreshment area was made in the centre of the stow, quite invisible from the exterior and accessed via a ventilator trunking, and probably fifty cases or so were consumed. After that drink, what better than a chaser? So a case of whisky is allowed to drop on one of its corners and this produces a jangle of enamel mugs to collect the precious fluid as it pours forth. This practice is relatively harmless since the damaged case can be sent ashore for replacement and, with all the bottle necks intact, no excise duty will be levied on the shipper.

Now, to happily round off a successful day, a bale of finest Yorkshire worsted or printed cotton can be intercepted and then everybody can go home with material for a suit or a nice dress length 'for the wife'. However, this is where the dock-gate bobby who we passed earlier could spoil the whole day for the dockers.

I'm going home one evening as the day shift ends and can see a commotion up ahead. A line of policemen, all of them big old bruisers, are blocking the dock exit and shaking everyone down. Some unfortunates, obviously caught red-handed, are looking rather sheepish while loudly declaring innocence to their mates who have been allowed to pass out. Naturally the craftier dockers have diverted into the toilets nearby to divest themselves of any criminal loads. The overall result is that it'll be the bobbies who will treat themselves and their ladies to a windfall on this occasion.

With the lower holds filled with these large parcels of staple items, activity now switches to the 'tweendecks while the cornucopia of British industry still pours out of the shed in its many colours and variety: Black cast-iron Stanton & Staveley water pipes; glazed brown Staffordshire earthenware sewerage pipes; dull black drums of ICI caustic soda and small shiny brown drums of Bell-brand Buxton lime; Skeleton cases of galvanised corrugated-steel sheets and more substantial straw-stuffed cases of Pilkington's glass; small square tins of calcium carbide for the acetylene lamps of huts and bicycles, hessian bags of shiny blue copper sulphate crystals for the cocoa and banana plantations, and brightly coloured steel drums of specialist greases and lubricating oils.

More interestingly, there are large blue plastic kegs of 'pig parts' in brine that are helpfully labelled 'ears', 'cheeks' 'snouts' and 'trotters'. Then the familiar cartons of Kellogg's Corn Flakes, Kleenex tissues, HP Sauce, Heinz baked beans, Schweppes mixers, Horlicks and Ovaltine, all destined for the expatriate community.

The Creole gourmets of Monrovia are catered for by Aunt Jemima's Cabin Bread. Other West Africans are expecting the specialised products of a Blackburn firm that promises skin-lightening and hair-straightening. Alarmingly, these appear to contain some apparently lethal ingredients if any of their purchasers care to read the small print on the label.

We can smell heady fumes from bundles of knocked-down whisky barrels to be reassembled in Ghana that will then return filled with lime juice. Hundreds of bags of mail will also appear during these frantic final days before sailing, and the hatch bosses fall on them like vultures. This is because they are flexible and light, ideal for filling in any awkward holes in the stow without too much physical effort.

Alongside the paying cargo there are frequent deliveries of items for the ship itself. The main storing takes place on a Saturday when the dockers have the day off but other deliveries have to be fitted in around the ship's loading. It is then that having kept on the right side of the shed and ship foremen pays off in terms of getting some assistance in lifting them aboard.

The ship's portfolio of charts is returned to us one afternoon, corrected and updated by Sewill's or Kelvin Hughes Limited, marine services companies in Liverpool. Small anonymous cases and large pieces of metal also arrive for the engine-room. However, the final delivery of our stores of bread, milk and fresh vegetables from the ship chandlers will be on sailing day itself.

In parallel with the ship's needs come the trading goods of the West African crew, sourced either from the retail markets of Liverpool or the second-hand shops of Mill Street, just up the hill. Restrictions imposed by the British trade unions mean that the crew are limited in the work that they can do while in port and this allows them ample free time to assemble their 'loads'.

In fact, shopping is their principal leisure activity here. Our African crew have little in common with the bulk of the port's black community which is mainly West Indian and, as they have little money to spend anyway, the hunt for bargains that can be profitably sold on at home is a sensible use of what funds they have.

Their range of purchases will depend on the space available on board and the individual tolerances of the ship's senior officers. Sewing machines are a favoured item as these represent either a source of income for wives or a route to a considerable profit in West Africa. Furniture and any second-hand white goods and electric gadgetry that are disposed of by the newly prosperous British are equally acceptable.

Finding space for this booty is a problem once the spare corners of a cabin are filled and so there is fierce competition to acquire any stowage possibilities elsewhere. A noticeable collection now exists on top of the poop house but, covered by an old tarpaulin, it might just pass for ship's equipment. If not, and if entreaties to the mate do not lead to leniency, then a pair of serviceable three-piece suites and other items will soon be bobbing in the ship's wake, much to the chagrin of at least one West African entrepreneur.

The day before sailing, the dock shed is nearly empty of cargo as the final day's work will principally comprise heavy lifts to go on deck. The registered letter mails and sundry dangerous goods will be delivered directly to the ship on the day of departure. The cargo for the next sailing is therefore already arriving.

There is the ubiquitous salt from Northwich, and a little dock locomotive is shunting in several rail wagons laden with steel rails from Workington. On board, the signing of the Articles of Agreement, the legal document that ties the ship's company to the master and hence to the ship-owner, has been completed. Finally, the ship is beginning to form the little community that will inhabit it for the duration of the West African adventure.

The ship's passenger accommodation, which is not yet rendered completely redundant by the growth of air travel, has been partially booked and so we are joined by half a dozen Irish missionary priests bound for the Cameroons. Two of them look like seasoned tropical clerics; the others are much younger.

A sympathetic observer can only hope that they will retain their sense of purpose during what will undoubtedly be a testing tour of duty. For the next few weeks, however, they will be well fed with familiar food and will not fail to be generously treated by the ship's officers to cans of Guinness, if that is their tipple.

They each have only very modest amounts of cabin baggage to carry aboard. Their astute and thrifty Order has negotiated an amalgamation of their hold baggage allowances and used it to cover the freight on a second-hand but very serviceable-looking diesel-powered generating set. That is now securely lashed in one of the 'tweendecks. Will their heavenly patron arrange for us to enjoy a peaceful crossing of the wintry Bay of Biscay in return for being hospitable to his agents? We'll soon see.

2

The leaving of Liverpool

I t's now sailing day, so I drive down to the ship after a quick breakfast at home because there will be plenty for me to do today. My suitcase is in the car; it doesn't contain much because I've been bringing my seagoing inventory down in daily instalments. What it does contain is an empty additional holdall because I know from experience that this piecemeal joining of a ship can lead to a nasty surprise when it comes time to pack and return home from another port.

In fact, I'm being a bit cheeky in not severing my connection with home and getting either a taxi or the bus to the ship this morning. The tide times mean that we're not sailing until late evening and I can get home again for a while after loading is completed. It's the advantage of living only a couple of miles from the docks. It also extends the pleasure of driving my first car, bought only a few weeks ago and still a novel and satisfying possession. That's been made possible from a princely salary of about nine hundred pounds a year, no lasting romantic entanglements and free bed and board at home between voyages.

As I reach the alleyway leading to my cabin, the mate, Don, a taciturn man from the Borders, drily welcomes me with a 'Nice of you to join us at last!' and tells me to get the sailing board up. This is a small wooden panel that is tied to the rail at the top of the gangway. It bears the ship's name and renditions of both the company's house flag and the Red Ensign, and informs its readers 'Vessel sails at 2100 today. Shore leave ends at 2000'. One of the apprentices has already hoisted the Blue Peter, the white flag with the deep blue border that signifies our impending departure. Two hatches are already covered up and their derricks lowered, all of which all adds to the atmosphere of completion.

Nevertheless, there's still a lot to do yet and my first task is to go down the 'tween-deck at number five hatch in order to tally the registered mailbags. There are about 400 of these and they bear not only the livery of our own Post Office but those of several European nations that have no other surface mail route to the smaller West African ports.

Then a sling of large, pristine white canvas bags with gleaming brass eyelets is presented. Their substantial labels are addressed to HBM Embassy in either Yaoundé or Léopoldville. I also note that another label sternly advises 'Confidential Diplomatic Mails care of British Master only' and, providentially, Don is now looking over the two-foot high steel coaming that is the raised edge of the hatch:

'These mails, it says that they're care of the Old Man only.'

'Are you going to carry them up to the baggage room, then, son?'

'Not really, perhaps the apprentices…?'

'Bollocks, they're only full of goodies for the embassy staff. Sling them in with the rest of the mails and get this hatch covered, I want you up with me on the foredeck.'

Don and I arrive on the foredeck just as a Mersey Docks & Harbour Board floating crane is coming smokily alongside. It carries a colourful collection of dump trucks, earthmovers, road graders and mobile cranes. They will be put in, around and on top of our principal hatch where they can be reached by our 50 ton derrick for unloading on the Coast. Watching for damage to either the ship or these heavy lifts and then getting the hatch covered and secured takes the rest of the morning.

My lunch break is foreshortened by the need to don my lifejacket and join in the practice boat and fire drill that is witnessed by the marine superintendent and one of the company's senior managers. This is part of the customary inspection on sailing day that reassures both ship and head office that all is in good order for the imminent voyage.

The shore managers then join the master and his senior officers for a formal farewell lunch and I get back to the foredeck where the lashing and securing of the cargo is continuing. The last of the loading is completed by mid-afternoon and I get a grudging permission from Don to repatriate my car and return before we sail.

My father has not yet returned from his work in a shipping company office at Garston Dock; neither is my brother home from the local technical college where he is preparing for an engineering career at sea so I have only my mother and the family dog to say farewell to. During the six weeks that I've just spent at home on leave my mother has steadfastly refused to take any payment for board and lodging. My father disapproves of this generosity so, before leaving the house, I manage to make her accept some money for a treat for herself. I also know that she'll be able to enjoy the novelty of using my car in place of the bus while I'm away at sea.

Then it's a slightly emotional farewell and I make the brisk ten-minute walk to the Dingle where the No. 1 bus is handily waiting. I've just had time to pick up a copy of the *Liverpool Echo* from the newsagents that I pass on the way. That is one little pre-sailing ritual that marks the finality of my departure. The paper can also be saved to pass on to some exiled Liverpudlian who I'll inevitably come across on the Coast.

Strange, I think, as we rattle off towards Mill Street in the gathering dark, that only a few years previously this bus (and its Overhead Railway predecessor) was my daily form of travel to school. It was doubtless that early exposure to the apparent romance of the sea and its ships that had contributed to my choosing this career.

Off the bus, then, at the foot of Park Street and through the dock gates, it's a well-timed arrival at the ship as the Dock Board waterman is dismantling his standpipe and this means that I can tell Don that I'm going to read our departure draughts.

For this task, I need two essential tools from my cabin, a hydrometer to give to one of the apprentices so that he can discover the density of the dock water, and a torch to allow me to read the draught marks. The forward draught is an easy one, the oily dock is just lapping the foot of the painted mark '21' but down aft the numbers are harder to read as the waterline under the ship's ample stern is difficult to detect. In the end I settle for 21 feet forward and 22 feet 4 inches aft and this suits Don.

Now it can be entered on the official freeboard notice with our signatures and we are fully compliant with yet another legal obligation and so avoid a statutory £20 fine. It's time to round up the apprentices, find the electrician and the duty engineer and begin the departure ritual of 'testing the gear'.

This involves making sure that the navigation lights are working, the telegraph conveys the same order on the bridge as in the engine-room when it is moved and that the rudder moves appropriately when the steering wheel is turned. The radar is set in motion, as is the new toy of a VHF radio set. The appropriate chart is laid out on the chart table ready for use and, crucially, the bridge kettle is full and the makings for tea and coffee and enough sandwiches are present for the long night to come.

After the Mersey pilot boards, the gangway is lifted, the tugs arrive and are secured, the ship leaves the berth and suddenly the awareness strikes. We're sailing and the familiar dockside and the skyline of Liverpool will, for a few months, become just the memory of home. Two miles away, on this ordinary weekday evening, my family are watching the latest episode of *Z-Cars* on television. I would be feeling the first burst of homesickness were it not for the fact that nobody is left alone for long enough to harbour such thoughts.

A litany of shouted orders, the clanging of the telegraph, much blowing of whistles and hooting of tugs sees us pass into Brunswick Dock and then through the opened Brunswick river entrance and into the Mersey. After the restricted spaces offered by these Victorian docks, we are now safely into broad waters. We must still note that the nearby flashing buoy marking Pluckington Bank is there to discourage us from turning too eagerly towards the river's mouth. It's a brief opportunity to look back and further swallow the confused emotions of this departure from the familiar and the growing excitement of getting properly back to sea.

Out in the main stream we're soon abreast of the city's impressive waterfront although its impact is muted to brooding silhouettes. The era of stone-cleaning and facade floodlighting is still some years in the future. I glance aft from the bridge wing and the lopsided bulk of the Anglican cathedral is just about distinguishable on top of its hill. For our six clerical passengers, who are also on deck and looking outwards, their cathedral has yet to grace the city's skyline with its distinctive truncated cone.

Over to port there's a Blue Funnel Line ship leaving the Alfred Basin in Birkenhead. No mistaking that severely upright profile and, between us, one of the Manchester Liners has left her home port's canal and is surging seawards at speed. We cannot match her progress as we must find our way past the poorly lit bulk of an elderly tramp, doubtless fully laden with bulk sugar, which is being lined up for the Langton Lock.

The waters off the Gladstone Dock entrance are empty and a clear night is already revealing the winking red and white lights of the buoys and light-floats that mark the sides of the Crosby Channel. If it were daylight I would be able to see the distinctive clocktower of my old school. This was a school whose official song had a line that said 'where countless ships go by, to brave the angry sea'. However, a distinctly dim view was taken of those few of us who left at 16 to join those ships rather than staying two more years, bound for university or 'proper' careers ashore.

It's time to make a brew for the end of my watch to serve the master, the pilot and also my watchkeeping relief, Dave, the second mate. It's a welcome task that is delayed when it becomes apparent that our forward visibility is affected by a brilliant beam of light from an unshaded window. It's being reflected brightly by both the mast in front of the bridge and the gaudy yellow and green of the deck cargo on the hatchtop. An exchange ensues:

> Master: 'What stupid sod has left that bloody light on? Good Lord, Pilot, you can't trust any of them to darken ship properly these days. Find out, third mate, which imbecile it is and tell them to switch it off pronto.'
>
> Third mate: (having looked over the bridge front) 'I think it's coming from your day room, sir. Have you got the key and I'll go down and take a look?'
>
> Master: 'You cheeky young bugger, more likely it's the chief engineer's office, as usual, but get down there and sort it out. Sorry about this, Pilot'.
>
> Third mate: (returning to the bridge, which is now enjoying the prospect of total darkness, and having decided not to limit his career prospects further) 'All done, sir. It was the chief's office, as you thought. I'd not counted the windows correctly.'
>
> Master: 'I thought so. These bloody engineers can never be trusted to put the lights out properly without an engine breakdown to help them.'

That crisis over, the beverages have been circulated, the logbook is written up and it's now time to go down to my cabin and end an eventful day. When I return to the bridge at eight the next morning we will have disembarked the pilot to his cutter off Point Lynas. Then we'll have rounded the top of the island of Anglesey, taken our official passage departure as the Skerries lighthouse comes abeam, and be pointing south to sunshine and to Africa.

3

Sailing south

West Africa

Others, especially the French, would dispute it, but the sea trade of West Africa was dominated by British companies during the 1960s. Elder Dempster Lines was the 'King of the Coast', not least in its own estimation, since the company had a distinguished heritage

Although its origins lay in the granting of a Royal Charter to the African Steamship Company in 1852, it was the commercial acumen of Sir Alfred Jones towards the end of the 19th century that resulted in its maritime dominance of West Africa. Unfortunately, following his death, it became part of Lord Kylsant's shipping empire, which was broken up in the economic upheavals of 1931.

It then came into the ownership of a famous Liverpool shipping enterprise, Alfred Holt & Company, whilst retaining its separate identity. In turn, Elder Dempster in 1952 took over the fleet of an important Glasgow shipowner, the British & Burmese Steam Navigation Co. Ltd. (familiarly known as Paddy Henderson's) and traded most of those acquired ships to West Africa. Elder Dempster also provided a passenger service between Liverpool and the ports of the British possessions in West Africa.

The other British company serving the Coast was Palm Line, a subsidiary of the United Africa Company (UAC), itself a part of the Unilever organisation. There was also a small fleet belonging to the merchant house of John Holt and Co. and, later, the new national shipping companies of Ghana and Nigeria. These four lines were the partners of Elder Dempster in the shipping conference that regulated the trade.

In West Africa itself, these rankings were reversed as both UAC and John Holt had extensive business and inland waterways interests whilst Elder Dempster had only a few lighterage operations and some small river ferries at Calabar.

Elder Dempster did, however, offer both passenger and cargo services to and from the Canaries and Madeira, and its vessels were also frequent callers at the Atlantic ports of Morocco. They not only visited every accessible port in West Africa but also operated services to the United States and the company had a shared interest in trade with India, whilst Palm Line, for a while, offered a cargo service to and from Mediterranean ports.

Sénégal

The port of Dakar, like Las Palmas or Santa Cruz in the Canaries, was a popular refuelling point for ships of all trades as it always offered competitive prices. Older seafarers still remembered, with some understandable bitterness, its years as a bastion of Vichy France, its imprisonment of U-boat attack survivors, and Britain's failed attempt to occupy it during the war. By the 1960s, Sénégal was experiencing a much diminished status following the dismantling of the French West African empire, of which Dakar had been the administrative capital. Since then, its independent existence, although dependent on foreign food aid and French financial support, has proved to be one of the most stable and democratic in sub-Saharan Africa.

Sierra Leone

Founded in 1787 as a haven for freed slaves, later becoming a full British possession, this ex-colony was now enjoying a rather sleepy Independence.

The Creole minority of slave descendants enjoyed a relatively benign and corrupt dominance over members of the indigenous tribes, whilst the wealth generated by the export of diamonds and iron ore helped to pay for a leisurely and quiet existence.

Freetown, the capital, situated on the southern shore of one of the finest natural harbours in the world, was an important convoy assembly point during the Second World War. It was also the home of Fourah Bay College, famous as the oldest academic establishment in West Africa and forever associated with the name of Samuel Crowther, the first African to be ordained as an Anglican Bishop.

Sierra Leone was long eclipsed in its commercial importance by other West African countries by the 1960s and was principally valuable to the sea trade as the source of those itinerant labourers known as 'Krooboys'.

The Kroo (or Kru) people had a long and proud history of being familiar with the sea which had led to several generations being recruited by foreign mariners. It was their valuable expertise that greatly assisted the running of merchant ships along this dangerous and unhealthy coast. The horrors of a civil war that are nowadays mostly associated with the name of Sierra Leone were, happily at this time, still more than 30 years in the future.

The sea route from Europe to West Africa is a busy one because it begins by sharing the same tracks as ships bound for the Mediterranean and going on to Suez. Later its path is the same as ships bound for South Africa and it is not until some way south from Dakar that the only possible destination becomes the Coast.

The way is never far from land but the coastline is only visible in a few places and that visibility is often restricted to echoes on the radar display. With satellite navigation yet to come, the sextant becomes our principal source of navigational information although there is also the steady reassurance of finding most ships coming north to be appearing at or about dead ahead.

The sighting of ships during a watch helps to vary the bridge routine and so speed the four-hour spell of duty. In addition to keeping clear of these other ships there is the interest in identifying them and, if the ship is from our company, an opportunity to swap some messages and gossip.

It is still possible to distinguish where individual ships have been built or are owned as the shipbuilding dominance of Japan and Korea and the forced uniformity of the container ship are both facets of the future. Only a few years of working at sea are required before a British, Dutch, German or Japanese ship can be identified at quite a distance. True, that 'British' ship might turn out to be flying the Greek, Liberian or Panamanian flag because of its sale. Equally, British ships could be easily further described as a 'Bluey', a 'Clan', a 'City' or a 'Blue Star' boat when not very far above the horizon. This was not the esoteric interest of a 'ship spotter', it was yet another acquired part of being a British seaman.

Dakar will be our first port of call on this particular voyage in memory and this involves a week's sea journey from Liverpool. A relatively peaceful entrée to our time away and a chance for the shipboard company to establish relationships for the months ahead. Even this short sea passage could have been interrupted as ships bound to the West Coast of Africa very often call in at ports en route.

We might have gone to Milford Haven to load explosives, or to Safi and Agadir in Morocco to load tinned sardines, or visited the Atlantic islands of Madeira, Tenerife or Gran Canaria. It is this last island that provides our first landfall when the loom of the great light of La Isleta on the hill above Las Palmas appears just before dawn on the fifth day out. By breakfast time this mountainous island is sliding past our starboard side and by midday it is becoming just a bluish smudge astern.

The freshening north-east trade wind is now blowing on our port quarter and depositing the red sand of the Sahara on the exposed surfaces of the ship. This is the same wind that blew the first Portuguese ships south. They were looking for an alternative sea route to source the silk and spices of Asia that came to them overland, unreliably, and heavily taxed by the Venetians and other middlemen.

This evening, as usual, the Old Man has made his last brief visit to the bridge at just gone ten. I've signed his Night Order Book, which tells me the courses to steer through the night and why or when to rouse him before morning. Now I can light up a cigarette and idly look at the chart while waiting for the kettle to boil.

That part of the African coastline which it shows has few names and even fewer lighthouses or other useful navigational marks. On closer examination, some of those names provide an interesting diversion from my evening's tasks.

Here is Ifni, that obscure Spanish colonial possession that recalls my youthful stamp-collecting days because of its cheap and cheerful issues. I remember that they were forbidden to me because my father strongly disapproved of spending any money that might be of even the most marginal support to the Franco regime.

Then there is Cape Juby, where pioneer French aviators of the Aéropostale airmail services, Guillaumet, Mermoz and Saint-Exupéry, had one of their staging posts as well as numerous adventures.

Further south again are the treacherous shallows of the bay of Arguin, where the ship *Medusa* inspired a famous painting based upon the grisly legend of its raft of survivors. That incident sharply reminds me to resume my lookout duty.

The following day we change from our dark uniforms at 0800 into the 'whites' that we wear in the tropics. It's always a peculiar feeling on this first day as my watch period is right at the start and I head to the saloon for my breakfast feeling as though I've forgotten to put my trousers on. It also calls for a fine display of exposed lower limbs of all shapes and sizes. Colours range from alabaster to vestiges of the tan of last voyage. Also on show is a similarly broad range of apparel from the double waist buckles and knee length of the traditional 'empire-builder' shorts to the much briefer and altogether simpler styling of modern versions.

The heat-averse are preparing to lobby for the starting up of the ship's very minimal air-conditioning plant, and the sun-lovers will soon be prospecting for suitable spaces to spread out their afternoon towels and blankets. Overall there is a welcome feeling of airiness around the ship. Curtains flap freely in the open entrances of cabins and the sea is visible through the varnished teak weather doors which are now being kept pinned open at the end of the accommodation alleyways.

It will soon be the sapping humidity of the Coast and the necessary closing up and securing of the ship's interior in port and all the stresses and demands of cargo work. Today, however, we can enjoy an interval of pleasing seagoing and the sociable atmosphere of a small sea community.

Before I introduce them I shall explain something of the industry in which we work. The title of 'Merchant Navy' was created after the First World War to recognise the valuable part played by merchant shipping in that conflict. It supplanted the previous usage of 'Merchant Service' and 'Mercantile Marine', although an office still named for the latter issues my identity documents, and records my sea service. My certificate of competency, however, is issued by the Ministry of Transport and Civil Aviation and, at work, I am subject to provisions of the Merchant Shipping Act.

As the seagoing employee of a commercial shipping company, I'm a civilian; nevertheless I'm proud to be serving in the Merchant Navy. It has provided some of my training (by the Merchant Navy Training Board), it can offer cheap port accommodation if I need it (courtesy of the Merchant Navy Welfare Board) and it will pay my pension in the distant future (via the Merchant Navy Officers' Pension Fund). Finally, I'm a paid-up member of our trade union, which is the the Merchant Navy & Airline Officers' Association. That membership is because of my personal conviction, although it's also reassuring to know that they'll provide me with legal representation should I put the ship on the rocks or hit another one!

The titular head of our little floating world is the master, only to be called the 'Old Man' when you are safely out of his hearing. His employer and various shore officials will afford him the courtesy title of Captain but he will never refer to himself by that rank. After all, as many an official document still words it, he is much more impressively entitled to the status of 'Master under God'.

On this voyage, he's new to me but I know that he has the reputation of not suffering fools gladly so I need to concentrate on my duties when he's around. In fact he is quite a senior commander and should be on one of the 'Mail' boats. The story is that he challenged one very demanding and inquisitive female passenger of a certain age by loudly inquiring of her at the breakfast table, 'Have you shaved this morning, Madam?' This unfortunate remark reached head office via Government House and led to his being placed in this cargo ship quarantine.

At meal times in the saloon, both he and the chief engineer are the only ones with those medal ribbons on their uniform jackets that testify to a fairly recent war service. As they're both well into their fifties, they also appear ancient to most of the other officers. We know that the chief engineer's christian name is Archie and that the Old Man's is George but none of us would ever dare to address them so intimately. They are always known as 'the Old Man' and as 'the Chief' and that's it.

Next in importance for my life on board is the mate. I might just get away with calling him Don from time to time but he's supposed to be in line for promotion to master at the end of the voyage. I can expect that he'll already be preparing mentally for that essential distance from his mates that he'll need in future. In any case, as I know that he originates from a family of gentleman farmers in Teviotdale, I suspect that he considers we Scousers come from an altogether different planet.

The second mate, Dave, is a bit of an odd bugger. Apparently he served his time with a London Greek tramp shipping company. This means that he thinks that both myself and the two apprentices, Pete and Dougie, being products of liner companies, are rather too effete for his taste. He's quite happy to join me when the two of us, together with Lawrence, the radio officer (or 'Sparks') and maybe Tommy, the electrician, gather in one or other of our cabins to open a few of those distinctive red-and-yellow cans of Tennent's Lager and get down to discussing the day.

He's a very different person at midnight, when he's due to relieve me on the bridge and I barely get more than a grunted acknowledgement of the course being steered. There's an equally surly entrance in the morning when he comes up just after nine to wind the two bridge chronometers and to take his morning sight. At least he's a prompt reliever, never late on duty, but I'm glad that I'm not Dougie, who has to share two watches a day with him.

Our two deck apprentices are both Londoners but I don't hold that against them even when they keep rabbiting on about the attractions of the capital. While in Liverpool they showed me that they're both hard workers and always willing to learn or to lend a hand, the essence of a good shipmate.

It'll be later in the voyage that I'll get to know the engineers properly because cabin drinking always tends to lead to departmental segregation. It's only in port that all the off-duty officers can set up a collective bar in the smokeroom or in the vacated passengers' lounge for something like a film night or a general sociable get-together.

Our first contact with the African continent is made the next day. Although the low desert coastline remains invisible to both us and our rather puny radar the electric sounding machine is confirming that we are in water less than 100 fathoms (600 feet) in depth, a figure that is the definition of the edge of the continental shelf.

Our course conveniently follows this line of distinction from the oceanic abyss and thereby largely avoids entanglement with an armada of trawlers. There's a nice irony here, ashore is just the barren sandy wilderness of the Sahara but offshore the chilly waters of the Canary Current flowing south are teeming with marine life.

We close with one of these trawlers and here is Lawrence, out on the bridge wing looking at it through binoculars and identifying it as 'another of those Russian spy ships' which is 'photographing us'. It is USSR-owned, of course; the hammer-and-sickle emblem on its funnel confirms that. The evidence elsewhere only suggests an extremely battered and rusty hard-working farmer of the sea. Its counterpart seen in the North Sea might well be bristling with intelligence-gathering devices in support of Cold War strategies. All that this one gathers is a cloud of wheeling and screaming seabirds looking for the few scraps that are jettisoned from the trawl.

As 'Sparks' keeps a close eye on his 'spy-ship', so I am watching the horizon for other ships in the deceptive haze. I need to take my morning sight but, whilst the sun now shines brightly as it has climbed clear of the dust and into a cloudless sky, the sea beneath doesn't have the clearly defined edge required to provide a reliable measurement by my sextant.

Dave appears on the bridge a few minutes after nine, dutifully winds the chronometers and sees from the book kept with them that Lawrence has helpfully compared them with the time signal broadcast an hour earlier from Rugby. The Old Man appears and wants to know the result of my sextant work, grunting non-committally when I tell him that the horizon is still too undefined to use.

Not long after he disappears we find acceptable visibility and Dave says that he will let the Old Man know our results as he passes his cabin on the way down off the bridge. A little later Olatunde, our Nigerian officers' steward, arrives with my tray of morning coffee and the time up until midday must now be spent watching out for passing traffic. It is too busy and the visibility still too unreliable to get on with that endless chore so beloved of third mates, the correction of the Admiralty List of Lights, so I need to amuse myself elsewhere until midday.

On this rather old-fashioned ship it's possible to walk across the outside front of the wheelhouse courtesy of a narrow passageway. This allows me to make easy circuits of the bridge to pass the time. The helmsman is intent on watching the gyro-compass repeater and rotating his wooden chewing-stick in his mouth. Perhaps I can attempt to distract him from his duty to keep a straight course from time to time for our mutual amusement and to fill some of the time until midday?

Then, soon after eleven, Hugo arrives on the bridge with a bundle of papers. Hugo is a distant relative of one of the shipping company's directors and is on board to occupy some of the year in which he will decide whether his next destination after leaving public school is to be Oxbridge or Sandhurst. He wears his class advantages lightly and fits in with us well, cheerfully accepting the occasional nickname of Victor. This is because he's described on the Articles as a Writer, although the label of A/P or assistant purser is also provided for him.

Hugo's boss, Alan, the purser, is responsible for overseeing the paperwork concerning the commercial and financial aspects of the voyage. It's a job that's in decline and will disappear during the next decade but, for now, there's more than enough work to justify his having an assistant.

Hugo's bundle today consists of mail waybills, Post Office bills of lading, and he's been sent up to me for help in putting them into the correct port order. More likely, I expect, so that Alan can join his mate, the chief steward, in a little pre-lunch refreshment in the passengers' bar.

After my initial inquiry, 'Didn't they teach you any geography at Shrewsbury, then?', my prompting lets him deduce the mail destinations. He decides that those for Bamako are via Dakar, those for Niamey and Ouagadougou will be discharged at Lomé, and Fort-Lamy and Yaoundé mails should travel via Douala. Then it will be the Léopoldville and Elisabethville bags via Matadi and, finally, those for Brazzaville via Pointe Noire. A small problem here as we're not calling at the last place. Hugo duly notes that we'll have to palm them off on another ship and I say that Alan will be suitably impressed by both his grasp of West African geography and the useful work tactic of passing on a problem to someone else to solve.

That task done, we can both share the bridge walking circuit and combine our exercise with fooling about with wheelhouse windows, which are raised or lowered by leather straps in the manner of old railway carriages. Some appropriate dialogue, 'I say, Porter, does this train stop at Crewe?' together with suitably coarse references to Leatherhead, Effingham Junction and the like, adds to our amusement.

Our banter brings forth a mixture of puzzlement and disapproval from my Nigerian watchkeeper, Essien, still chewing away happily whilst standing at the wheel, until Hugo departs. I've then been left just enough time to get my logbook entries satisfactorily completed before noon.

Our noon sight is scheduled for twenty past twelve, so that means that I have to remain on the bridge with Dave until then. Armed with our sextants, we stand out on the port bridge wing and watch the sun reach its zenith. With the altitude agreed, unlike Errol Flynn, who apparently could read the information direct, we both have to go to our sight books to work out our latitude and longitude. That decided, we can calculate our average speed over the last 24 hours and the remaining distance to go to the Dakar pilot station.

That information goes on two chits, which Dave writes out and which I then take down to the saloon to give to the Old Man and the chief engineer. After lunch I consider a siesta in the sun but this also looks like a promising afternoon to tackle another set of my duties, the care and maintenance of the lifeboats. After all, while I'm doing that I can still enjoy the renewing effect of the African sun on my back.

We see the loom of another lighthouse the following morning, this time that of Cap Vert on one of its twin hills, welcoming us to the African continent at its most westerly point. In the growing light of a roseate dawn, we enter the harbour of Dakar, which lies behind the notorious Ile de Gorée. This name is not only rooted in the shameful working of the transatlantic slave trade but is also still remembered by a short stretch of the Dock Road back home in Liverpool. The green, yellow and red tricolor flag of Sénégal is flying from our foremast as the usual maritime courtesy; nevertheless it appears that 'L'Afrique Occidentale Française' continues to be the order of the day.

The pilot and the skipper of the harbour tug that provides a close escort as we pass through the breakwaters are both French although the former's apprentice is Senegalese. So too are the sundry port and customs officials who come up the gangway when we berth. Many of the dock labourers, the next group to board, are wearing those dark-blue baggy trousers that are supposed to support a religious belief in the next prophet being born of a man. To my mind, it's more likely that they have devised a sensible sartorial response to living in such a hot country.

The foreman stevedore, who is another Frenchman, arrives on board within a halo of cologne, garlic and Gauloises to say that he has only booked one gang because we have very little cargo. Work will start at eight. After reading the arrival draughts, that gives me just enough time to eat my breakfast. I use the empty duty messroom to eat as its usual engineer patrons are busy organising the fuel-bunkering operation.

When I return on deck a filthy black bunkering hose, flecked with sawdust and studded with all manner of dockside debris, is already safely connected. I see that the chief engineer and yet another Frenchman are inspecting the flow meter under the quay to agree a starting figure. This is a civilised operation compared to the one in my last ship, a war-built vessel, where the fuel connection was at the top of the engine-room.

This meant that one of the junior engineers had to move his bag and baggage up to the hospital. His bunk was then replaced by a drip tray and the bunkering hose dragged through his porthole and across his cabin. For this service to his employers he received the princely sum of 15 shillings 'disturbance money'.

The dockers, tall thin men from the desert regions of the country's interior, have already stripped number four hatch of its coverings. Their baggy trousers seem ungainly and their plastic sandals inadequate for their protection as they make an orderly stack of the heavy wooden hatchboards on the crowded deck. The foreman and I agree that this hatch only contains ten Land Rovers for discharge, and the unloading is discussed in a combination of language that stretches broken English, my schoolboy French and his thick Marseille accent to the limit. Fortunately he is accompanied by a bespectacled Ghanaian clerk who is fluent in both languages. He will note any damage to the vehicles and will agree a condition report for each one with Pete, the apprentice.

A very smart new set of padded slings is hoisted off the quay and all ten of these popular exports are soon safely landed ashore. The hatch is covered and the sailors are called to replace the tarpaulins; the best of the three that we normally use can now be stored away for our sojourn in the tropics, only being restored before the ocean passage home.

The gang now move on to number five hatch, where a further six Land Rovers are unloaded. Then it's on to the whisky, about 200 cases in open stow, and this clears the way for one of our special cargo lockers to be opened. First out will be 50 bales of textiles.

These are termed 'coded bales'; each one is clearly marked with a serial number, and a portion of the attached cardboard ticket has to be removed and retained on board. The first ticket portion has already been taken and kept in Liverpool and this process is designed to track and trace these desirable items. Some bales contain West Yorkshire worsted suiting, others are of colourfully printed Lancashire cottons and, as we've already seen in Liverpool, all are highly pilferable. Like the whisky, many bales are marked for Bamako and thus face a long rail and road journey to the interior. How many will arrive at that distant destination intact?

A couple of slings of registered mail follow the coded bales and then the steel doors of the locker can be locked shut again. The cargo plan indicates a few odds and sods plus twenty pallets of fire bricks and these are soon swinging ashore. So I'm off to tell the mate that we're nearly finished. It's timely news as the heavy fuel is all received and the engineers now have only the diesel oil to accept, from a battered road tanker already manoeuvring into position by the gangway.

I get back to the hatch to find that a pallet has collapsed and word has been sent ashore to find some means of discharging a couple of hundred loose bricks. At least this delay allows me time to make sure that we don't commit the sin of overcarrying any Dakar items, with all the professional shame and bureaucratic follow-up that entails.

I find nothing overlooked and tell Pete to fetch a couple of brooms so that we can sweep the debris off the hatch square. In reply to his implied query, I remind him that more vehicles are stowed below in the hold and I don't want this rubbish to be the cause of agreeing damage reports for them when we reach Lomé.

The hatches are secured and locked, the derricks that we have used remain raised but are safely stood off by tightening their rope guys and wires. The draughts are read and port officials and stevedores have received their paperwork, completed and signed. The pilot boards and our cast-off mooring ropes and wires splash into the oily waters as we take our leave of Dakar.

Our sailing is witnessed by those few who have been using the shadow cast by the ship as their shelter from the fierce sun, a disappointed dockside pedlar who found us all too busy to trade, a few optimistic fishermen and one man vigorously and a little pointedly urinating into the harbour. The ship and Africa have barely been in contact today so it seems an appropriately dismissive *bon voyage* to receive.

Later, I overhear one of our passengers remarking that he was sorry not to have been able to stretch his legs ashore and I think to myself that he needn't have worried too much. My only Dakar excursion was while calling here in an oil tanker some time earlier. Tanker men will always try and get ashore in port, however unpromising the prospect, because they spend so much time at sea.

Dakar does offer a taste of metropolitan France with its shops and pavement cafés, and its beaches are also clean and welcoming. In contrast, the railway station, its entrance flanked by the warning *Defense d'uriner* painted in six-foot-high letters, rather blunts any tourist appeal.

It is many years later that I find an account of a train journey to Bamako from this station by Ryszard Kapuscinski. A notable foreign correspondent whose writings on Africa are always worth reading, he recounts an incident on his way out of Dakar. A ride through pleasant city suburbs is dramatically interrupted when the train goes through a shanty town and a market that has encroached on the rails. The anarchy that permitted this trespass is now responsible for the panic and impromptu looting that follows. Kapuscinski skilfully uses this incident to explain the reasons behind this 'bidonville' and why such settlements now disfigure so many African cities.

We make our progress southwards from Dakar more peacefully. To port the coastline still remains invisible although not far away. At night, the Southern Cross climbs higher in the sky as our own hemisphere's Great Plough fades from view. The magnificent Milky Way spans the heavens to remind us of both the planet's and our own insignificance in galactic terms.

Early the next day we reach the 'corner' off the Casamance archipelago and turn southeastwards. Now we are in a sealane leading only to West Africa and the first ship we see is one of our own company. We pass at a respectable distance, the Red Ensigns are dipped in salute, whistles are blown and greetings and crew lists are exchanged over the VHF.

There is little breeze in this area, and heat and humidity are both beginning to rise. The engineers frequently visit the upper deck by number four hatch to complain to all and sundry about the hell that they are supposed to call their workplace. The only air-conditioned sanctuaries on the ship are the public spaces of the saloon and the two smokerooms. Our reverend passengers are fortunate to have the use of an airy veranda abaft their accommodation. There, dressed in a comfortable mufti, they enjoy their deckchairs, read or chat with each other and with those passers-by willing to spare them the time.

Elsewhere about the decks the sun-worshippers are refreshing their tans. In this bygone era this practice is seen as one of the perks of the job rather than a case of unknowing victims recklessly exposing themselves to the hazards of skin cancer. Acquiring a tan and then sporting it at home in mid-winter is a prize when a summer package holiday to Spain is still a novelty. However, we also know that any incapacity for work due to sunburn is treated as a disciplinary offence so sensible precautions are urged on the ignorant.

Dedicated sunbathers can use spare deckchairs but the standard equipment is a towel spread on top of a blanket. Then it's a matter of finding a patch of wooden deck on which to lie spreadeagled and snoring, occasionally attempting to read a dog-eared paperback. A quick smear of Nivea for protection and the after-effect is, for most, just a shiny beacon of a roaring red face to either alarm or amuse the Nigerian stewards and our fellow officers in the saloon that evening.

'Tomorrow we go Freetown but we no fit go for shore,' announces Bassey, another of my three watchkeepers, as he takes the wheel at ten for the last two hours of that evening's watch. I thank him for confirming our programme for tomorrow but observe that it shouldn't bother him as he is Nigerian and the sooner we reach his home port of Lagos, the better it will be for him.

Bassey agrees but says that he 'get some sweet mammy any time for go-shore Freetown, plenty jig-a-jig', thus confirming the popular view of seamen the world over, measuring the allure of a place by the quality of the sexual entertainment known to be on offer.

Over this last week I have begun to get to know my watch companions a little better although I can still barely name the sailors on the other two watches. Even on duty it is surnames only, mainly because those are required for entry into the logbook alongside the hours that they keep the lookout. Consequently their forenames remain unknown and immaterial although we still learn much about each other even within this most simple of relationships.

Bassey is the youngest of my three watchkeepers and a real Lagos city boy. He's more trader than sailor, with a wife and 'pickin' at home and the ambition to have homes and businesses at either end of this trade route. His steering and his general attention to his duties leave much to be desired but he seems to know where he's bound in life and I've often wondered since if he eventually arrived.

The other two watchkeepers, Babatunde and Essien, are older and more taciturn although the former tells me that his family are all carpenters and he wants to get a position as such on one of the Nigerian National Line ships. All our 'chippies' in Elder Dempster are British but he does achieve this ambition. That's because I sail with him many years later when I find that his woodwork capability is more accurately described by the derogatory Scouse term 'woodspoiler'.

Essien's home is in the Ibo heartlands and I never saw him again. I suspect that his fate was subject to the disaster of the Biafran secession yet to come. These are three partially familiar African faces with whom I am sharing the ship, and my cabin steward is another. Tomorrow there will be a host of unfamiliar others to get to know over the coming weeks when the Krooboys join us in Freetown Harbour.

The following morning finds me sharing the bridge with the Old Man and Pete. Don, the mate, has gone down to collect the carpenter and then to stand-by forward for when the anchors are required. The lighthouse of Cape Sierra Leone is our guide on the starboard bow and the Fairway Buoy, just visible on the port bow, is another.

I know, from the Old Man, that the set of the tidal current must be watched as its direction is right across the harbour mouth. If we let the ship drift off its present heading, and I'm thankful that it's reliable Essien who has the wheel just now, then Carpenter Rock, to starboard, is waiting for us. The last rusty remains of the engines of one of its victims act as a salutary visual reminder. However, all is going to plan today; we sail serenely by the lighthouse and then the Old Man asks me to look and see what is happening up in the harbour.

Using the ship's trusty Barr & Stroud bridge binoculars, I tell him that I see a Palm Line ship with some smoke coming out of its funnel and what appear to be a couple of empty ore-carriers at anchor. The Old Man interprets this as the Palm boat getting ready to berth whilst the other ships are waiting to move upriver to load iron ore at Pepel.

He tells me to contact the harbourmaster on the VHF, confirm that we will be off Queen Elizabeth II Quay in twenty minutes and to find out which anchorage we have been allocated. Freetown's role as a convoy assembly point is still remembered on the chart by the numbers of the anchorages allotted to ships in those very different days. Despite the short distance, a very crackly VHF radio response from the shore is just decipherable and gives us our anchor berth number.

We press on up the harbour with the landmarks of the Kru Town radio masts and the headlands of King Tom and Falconbridge Points on our starboard side. These names remind me of Freetown's long history of British acquaintance.

King Tom was the local monarch when the first settlers arrived, not many of whom were actually freed slaves. The group mainly consisted of indigent Africans from London's streets swept up by a philanthrophic mission to put right one of the minor side-effects of slavery. They were then followed by those of African descent who had followed other refugees from the American War of Independence into Nova Scotia.

Falconbridge celebrates a pioneering official whose wife wrote the earliest account that we have of the colony and the name of Kru Town explains the purpose of our visit. We are to continue the tradition of embarking members of the Kru (or Kroo) tribe to assist with the working of a ship along the coast of West Africa.

Now the town is in view and we can hear traffic and smell woodsmoke. We see ramshackle buildings that have lived through many rainy seasons and bright new ones that have yet to be weathered by this unforgiving climate. As we approach the QE II quay, we greet its familiar backdrop of the old brick building that housed the original Fourah Bay College and its famous lofty cotton tree nearby.

This is the place where those first Nova Scotian immigrants reportedly celebrated their safe arrival. The college itself has been replaced by a new university whose glassy modern buildings sit high up on the hill behind the town. At this point, however, we must set Freetown's history aside as it's time to attend to the business of securing a safe anchorage.

The master knows this place intimately; he knew it in wartime and probably long before, so just a quick glance at the harbour chart confirms that knowledge and the ship is soon safely anchored. There are four shackles of cable out, equal to nearly the length of the ship, and the port anchor is securely buried ten fathoms down in the black harbour mud.

We have only to await our Krooboy complement, and the sooner that objective is achieved and we can resume our voyage, the happier the Old Man will be. The bridge VHF comes alive with a request to change to Channel 6 and the dulcet tones of the agency crew manager inform us that Krooboys are being embarked and will be making their way out to us 'very soon'. 'Make that "straightaway",' barks the Old Man in a typically sharp response, 'I need to be away at 1100 to make Monrovia tomorrow.'

'Of course, Captain, not a problem, we shall see you safely on your way by then. Might I ask you to take just a very few small pieces of Monrovia cargo which I have placed on the lighter with the boys? I will be much obliged if you can help us with this very small favour.'

'Mr Macaulay, please just send the boys now. We have no space available for Monrovia cargo and no time to load it and to check all the documentation.'

'Cheeky sod,' the Old Man observes as he replaces the phone in its cradle. 'The mailboat's here in a couple of days' time and she calls at Monrovia. Old Macaulay's just looking to earn some extra "dash" from someone for the cargo. You'd think that the greedy bugger gets enough in backhanders from the Krooboys as it is.'

The crew manager proves as good as his word, despite our rebuff of his cargo request, and a large flat lighter is soon being towed out from the quay bearing our Krooboys with their meagre baggage. A fast launch has brought out the port officials and we can lower our yellow quarantine request flag as they depart with their previously flat briefcases suitably inflated with whisky and cigarettes.

It is too early in the voyage to receive any letters so there are no pleasant distractions to mark our arrival but one or two canoes soon appear to investigate any trading possibilities.

One canoe has some stems of tiny bananas but they look as unappealing as the few other items of fruit on offer. There are no takers either for the rather sad little monkey chained to one of the canoe thwarts and making free with a banana while the trader's attention is held elsewhere. A second canoe contains a very elderly man wearing an incredibly green and battered apology of a top hat. He is encouraging the throwing of coins into the water to be recovered by his accompanying two small boys. But he, too, has few takers for his proposition.

The battered and rusty lighter grinds noisily alongside number four hatch and, bereft of any cordage of its own, begs a couple of ropes from us in order to become secured under one of the derricks. The sailors throw down a couple of cargo nets and the Krooboys begin filling them with their 'loads'.

These comprise elderly metal cabin trunks, well-travelled cheap suitcases and shapeless bundles wrapped in scruffy cloth. They will disembark in two months' time or so with substantial personal cargo but, for now, they are the dispossessed and come aboard as the very lowest level of the ship's hierarchy.

A rope painting ladder is secured to the ship's side bulwark by the bosun for their access. First up the ladder is the second headman. I recall him from an earlier voyage by his stained and faded solar topee, once the possession of some colonial official, but cannot yet remember his name. I do remember and recognise the head man, who is overseeing things on the lighter, as Johnson. His preferred headgear is a battered officer's cap, complete with a green and ancient company badge, which nevertheless sports a commendably clean white cotton cover.

The rest of the Krooboys (or, if you prefer, Kroomen) will be a collection of Banguras, Contehs, Kamaras and Nipehs whom I shall gradually get to know over the rest of our stay on the Coast. For now, there are some angry mutterings on the lines of 'Why dis ladder? Dis no be proper for we.' and 'Dis ship, too much trouble for start.' Despite that, they know what is expected of them and so make short work of loading their possessions, then they swing in and secure the derrick. Things are a little spoilt, however, when their friends on the lighter are allowed to depart with our two good ropes that had secured it.

While the Krooboys carry their gear up to their forecastle accommodation, the mate and chippy go forward and I return to the bridge. It's not too long after the hour of eleven when the ship says farewell to Freetown with a magnificent cloud of thick black smoke. This is complemented by an equally black trail of muddy water as the anchor is washed off prior to stowage. Soon it will be lunchtime, followed by a siesta in the sun, no doubt with the accompaniment of the traditional Krooboy chorus caused by them busily chipping the rust off the ship's ageing steelwork.

In the relatively recent past it was common to carry up to a hundred of these men. Their numbers declined as local workforces became available, a development that was accelerated when colonies became countries and therefore wanted to preserve employment for their own nationals.

Our present complement consists of a head man, second headman, cook, two laundrymen and 14 labourers. Their principal occupation will be scaling rust but they will also clean the hatches, assist with derrick work and either provide a logging gang at one of the 'bush' ports further south or, more likely, be used to tidy up the efforts of some of the local loading gangs.

Their cook will feed them and the two laundrymen will not only attend to the ship's domestic requirements but will take in (for payment) any washing that the ship's officers and passengers put out for them.

It is this arrival of a large number of unfamiliar black faces that provides an appropriate point at which to recollect shipboard attitudes to the inhabitants of the Coast among whom we now had to live and work. Naturally there were racist aspects in our relationship which must seem deplorable to a reader of today but they were the product of our society and of that time.

Attitudes had already changed since the later days of empire. Ralph Eyre-Walker, who like me began his sea career as an apprentice in The New Zealand Shipping Company, recalled meeting Krooboys for the first time in a 1938 memoir:

> I had never worked Krooboys before, but it did not take long to become convinced
> of the necessity of maintaining that racial superiority claimed by the white man.
> The Freetown boys were if anything more amenable to discipline than those from
> further south, but even so, they were as quick as the next to profit by weakness on
> the part of those who employed them.

I have always thought that racism stands as a very good illustration of the Christian concept of 'original sin' since it exists in all people and in all societies. So we should be judged by how much as individuals and as groups we try to expiate the sin of racism in our behaviour.

Whilst West Africans were still collectively referred to in our conversation with each other as 'nig-nogs', 'coons', 'gollies' or 'jungle bunnies', these demeaning titles were never used directly or individually. This was not necessarily through cowardice or fear of the consequences although that was a factor to consider. I prefer to believe that a certain notion of politeness demanded that we used the arguably gentler prejudices of class and of hierarchy.

Nobody who comprehensively disliked Africans would choose to work on a ship in our trade although the extent of contact with the inhabitants of the Coast was more limited for the engineers than for those of us in the deck department. We generally adopted a policy that used a range of behaviours.

I personally very much enjoyed the possibilities of speaking the pidgin dialect, which could be as inventive and entertaining as one chose. Admittedly, I wouldn't dream of addressing a pilot or an agency manager in this rather condescending variety of language that I used with the dock labourers.

Similarly, I much preferred to be working with Ghanaians rather than Nigerians but that was a variant on, say, preferring the French to the Italians. And, naturally, our Nigerian sailors and our Sierra Leonian Krooboys were treated as being on our side on board ship, as distinct from shore invaders, whether officials or labourers, who most definitely were not.

Any of my frustration with African visitors to the ship had two causes: either their newly acquired identity as citizens of an independent nation exercised as petty arrogance towards anyone identified with a former colonial power, or their indolence and ignorance due to poor pay, poorer conditions or inadequate skills. Nevertheless, any visible anger and frustration had to be curbed if you didn't want to face some serious legal consequences.

The worst acceptable scolding was to accuse someone of being 'a very beast of no nation', this phrase being spat out and accompanied by a vigorous tooth-sucking grimace. Overall, and in not too rose-tinted retrospect, matters of difference in skin colour were not that pervasive. I know that I felt more real anger at some of the behavioural hoops that I was put through in later years by stroppy dockers in New York or Sydney, or political ideologues in Shanghai.

Now we sail back out into the Atlantic, round the treacherous shoals off Cape St Ann, with its habitually missing or out-of-position light float, and turn to follow the coast down to Monrovia. This will be our second port of discharge and the start of the real work of the Coast as we continue ticking off our ports of call, none of which will be separated by more than a brief sea passage.

The peace and routine orderliness of our voyage south is now changing to the chaos and unpredictable workload of the Coast proper. This will be our stage where we will act out our roles, get to know our shipmates well and start accumulating the stories that we'll tell each other, with increasing elaboration and distortion, over the coming years.

4

First ports of call down the Coast

Liberia

Liberia was created by American and British philanthropists as a home for those Africans released from their overseas bondage by the abolition of slavery. But the law of unintended consequences soon made an impact on this high ideal. To build settlements, the indigenous inhabitants of what was originally known as the 'Grain Coast' (so-called from the grains of the pepper that flourished there) were either tricked into selling their land cheaply or were forcibly evicted.

The capital, Monrovia, was named for an American president and the country always had a strong American orientation. However, it never enjoyed even the limited social and economic development of its colonial neighbours. Between the wars, its government was implicated in the supply of virtual slave labour to the Spanish island of Fernando Póo and its post-war administrations became a byword internationally for corruption and kleptocracy.

This was especially true of President Tubman and the senior members of his gloriously named True Whig party. He was protected by his staunch anti-communism and a genial reputation that he promoted abroad. It was Sir Ludovic Kennedy who recalled him in 1962 as being 'a jolly little soul, a great womaniser'. This latter attribute caused Malcolm Muggeridge to suggest that Tubman was 'quite literally, the father of his people'.

This ascendancy of the Americo-Liberians ended bloodily in 1980 and the country then descended into a savage and anarchic civil war that horrified the world. That horror also spilled over into its closest neighbour, Sierra Leone, causing the end of the Creole oligarchy there. It is only very recently that any semblance of normality and stability has reappeared in either country.

Ghana

As the first African nation to emerge from the colonial era, Ghana enjoyed the support of the world's liberal intelligensia and it seemed to justify all of their hopes during the first years of independence. Kwame Nkrumah, who had embodied the African desire to be rid of colonialism, appeared to be leading his country into a prosperity based on social justice and economic growth.

Sadly, the country was really too small to support the grand ventures planned to convert it from a primary producer into an industrial power. As a consequence, rising debt, allied to the grandiose pan-African plans of its leader, led to a military putsch. That promised renewal soon deteriorated into the kind of blatant government theft and corruption that was later emulated elsewhere in West Africa.

Fortunately for Ghana, one military leader, Jerry Rawlings, broke the pattern and he eventually allowed the return of a multi-party democracy that appears to be a route towards the future envisaged at independence. Nkrumah, who fled to safety in Guinea, died later in some obscurity. He continues to be remembered as a tragic yet sympathetic figure in modern African history.

Togo

A glance at the atlas shows that this country is a peculiar shard of territory, its shape being the product of its unusual colonial past. Once a German possession, one of the scraps taken away from the imperialist carving-up of the continent during the last decades of the 19th century, it became an Anglo-French trust territory after the First World War.

As with the one other such West African former colony of Kamerun (Cameroun), independence led to a separation of those areas of previously predominant British or French influence. Ghana was the beneficiary of the former secession although the independent remnant still suffers from a tribal north–south enmity.

The first president, the charismatic Sylvanus Olympio, was replaced by a military man, Gnassingbé Eyadema. He became West Africa's longest-serving head of state, presiding over a fairly benevolent dictatorship. In terms of overseas trade, the principal role of Togo is to act as an entrepôt for the new nations created from the French colonial possessions of the continental interior.

We enter the port of Monrovia under a leaden sky. Although it's not the official rainy season, exposure to moist Atlantic winds means that rain is never far from this stretch of the Coast. Monrovia is an undistinguished place of low-rise buildings that feature a lot of corrugated iron and concrete that is stained black and green by the fetid humidity. Even the roads cannot restrain the exuberance of tropical greenery with vegetation thrusting through large cracks in their thin tarmac covering.

Our six passengers are at the rail to see us enter the harbour breakwaters, dressed in their 'go-ashore rig' of short-sleeved shirts in suitably restrained colours and light trousers paired with sensible brogues. This obviously keen anticipation of their first shore excursion is clear and understandable, it's just a pity that it has to be this rather unprepossessing place to provide it.

For now, I hope that some exercise and recreation away from the enclosure of the ship will satisfy them. Certainly they won't disgrace themselves as I did on my first visit here. Alcoholic exuberance led our shore party to climb to the top of the stumpy lighthouse of Cape Mesurado, from where we were humiliatingly chased by the security guards from the nearby hotel.

The port is modern but it lacks the impressiveness that one might expect of being the home port name carried by the world's biggest fleet, including most of the largest vessels afloat. That is because the Liberian flag registration of ships is managed from offices in New York. Monrovia does not even supply the corporate fig-leaf of a brass plate. All registration revenues remain on the other side of the Atlantic.

The port officials and other Liberian citizens mimic American dress styles and have a tendency to put Hollywood-inspired features into their language and attitudes. This was a facet of even pre-war Monrovia remarked upon by Eyre-Walker, who, after finding 'insolence more than one could tolerate', went on:

> Being a black republic peopled originally by ex-slaves, and later pampered by emancipation, the place was alive with big-headed officials in gorgeous uniforms who fancied that no one knew anything except themselves.

Many of the dollars (the Liberian one is at par with US currency) supporting commerce in the town are the payment received by Liberia to host both a powerful Voice of America radio transmitter and an airfield for the US military. The latter is also one site of the LORAN network, a long-range navigation system using radio waves that will eventually be replaced by the use of space satellites.

A small crowd of labourers is soon making its way up the gangway and the Krooboys are setting up the derricks for them at the after hatches. There is much sociable chatter and backslapping going on, for the Kru tribe originated from this area and family ties cheerfully ignore the idea of separate nations called Sierra Leone or Liberia.

The Nigerian crew, meanwhile, are busy on the foredeck where the heavy-lift derrick, the 'jumbo', has to be made ready to discharge most of our deck cargo. No mail has been received here and hence no short but pleasant sampling of letters from home before the sweaty routine of the day begins. Just a quick change from the white uniforms of arrival into the khaki shirt and shorts of port attire and a meeting on deck with the two Swedish stevedore supervisors on how the unloading will be done.

The plan is to complete the work by evening but, if that fails, we will finish tomorrow morning. There will be no night work as our cargo is an attractive one for the local thieving community, who apparently have the run of the port after dark. It all depends on the weather: just now it's hot, airless and sticky but we must watch out to sea where a line of billowing cumulus that usually begins forming in the afternoon means that rain squalls will be on their way to visit us.

By the way, adds one of the Swedes, for heaven's sake make sure you don't cock up the lowering of the Liberian courtesy flag if you're still here at dusk. The dockworkers and a clutch of officials will be looking out for any perceived discourtesy such as allowing it to touch the deck or flap however fleetingly against a greasy wire. Then copious amounts of beer, cigarettes and dollars will be needed to assuage hurt feelings of national pride. And, his helpful parting shot advises, don't trust any of the watchmen that we provide, they're capable of stealing more from the cargo than those whom we are paying them to police.

Following those comforting remarks, the day's work continues. Dave will look after the two after hatches because of his seniority privilege. This means that he can keep an eye on things while leaning over the rail at the end of the passenger deck with the statutory cigarette and cup of coffee. Dougie will do his legwork and I take our other novitiate, Pete, up to the foredeck where the mate joins us to make sure that our heavy lifts are discharged without damage to themselves or the ship.

The first lift is a Euclid road-grader, 26 tons of steel painted a rather sickly pale green that droops alarmingly at each end when it is first lifted from its secure wooden bed on top of hatch two. Ropes have been secured to each end of its 30 foot length and these help to keep the load steady as it is slewed across the hatch.

The winch-drivers are making a very competent fist of the job, orchestrated by their head man, whose jaunty German skipper's cap probably shows that he's been a Krooman in his time. All the same, Don, still resplendent in his white uniform, is at his shoulder, just in case. The ship heels a little towards the quay as the grader passes over the side rail and then the load is being lowered rapidly, the lifting wire sluicing happily through the quadruple sheaves of its pulley block. With the load landed safely on the quay, the ship recovers its upright position.

Back on board swings the jumbo derrick for the next load, another grader. Then there are two 20 ton bright-yellow Caterpillar bulldozers and two dump trucks of a similar weight and hue to be dealt with. They're all bound for the iron-ore mines of the Bomi Hills inland. A well battered low-loader, emitting a formidable cloud of black diesel smoke, trundles along the quay to receive the first Caterpillar.

Don and the bosun are enjoying a celebratory smoke and so I nip back to see how Pete is getting on down in number three 'tweendeck. I find him content as the small consignment of whisky has gone ashore without incident. Now the labourers are busily filling cargo nets with either boxes of the mysterious Aunt Jemima's Cabin Bread or cartons of empty glass bottles designed to be filled somewhere ashore with the equally unfamiliar delights of Elephant brand African Gin.

With the heavy lifts all safely ashore, the hatch gang look around for suitable squatting or sleeping spaces while Billy the bosun and our Nigerian crew house the jumbo derrick and restore the usual arrangement of the ordinary derricks. The work of unloading carries on elsewhere but we have to wait until a quarter to one before all the dock workers stream down the gangway to enjoy their lunch break. This is because Liberia keeps its own unusual local time of forty-four and a half minutes behind the Greenwich Mean Time that is adopted by the rest of Africa westward of the prime meridian.

The break is soon over and then more cargo continues to leave the four working hatches in its glorious miscellany. But it's becoming a close race. We three mates decide, after an impromptu estimating session, that there looks to be about four or five hours' work left so I'm told to put up the sailing board by the gangway to inform everybody 'sailing at 1900'.

The Krooboys and the locals know better as they tell me repeatedly. 'Ship never go this night', 'Tonight you go for shore jig-a-jig', and the usual refrain of the Coast, 'Why this hurry-hurry, no time for life'. And it looks as though local knowledge will triumph as a line of darkening cumulus is already sending in some exploratory squalls that are visible to the north of the port.

The onshore breeze is freshening and, at nearly four o'clock, Don admits defeat and tells me to get the labour up from the hatches and to start rigging the hatch tents, those dark-green canvas pyramids that serve to protect the cargo.

There are whoops of delight from the Liberians as they make for the exit ladders. I quickly check that nobody is staying behind for a cargo rummage in the dark and then we all pull the tent edges taut as the first splashes of rain appear. From a sweaty heat to an almost chilly wet freshness doesn't take long in a Liberian downpour and it's no wonder that respiratory ailments plague so many on this stretch of the Coast.

My sanctuary on the promenade deck with a cigarette and a hot drink soon has to be left in order to go with the apprentices to check that the hatch tents are doing their job. Donning oilskins and sou'westers and carrying a bucket each, we go along the main deck and the rain does have the decency to ease a little as we bail out any puddles that have formed. We also tighten up the rope tails on each tent to prevent the pools re-forming, and look out for any evidence of opportunistic thievery.

After an hour or so, the worst of the rain has passed, leaving us with a light drizzle while the oppressive humidity begins its recovery after that brief cooling interlude. Don orders the hatch tents to be taken down but the labour shows a great reluctance to resume work. One of the Scandinavians returns and says that there is no point in resuming work as the sheds will not open since the officials in charge have departed. The labour will come back on board but only to draw the hatch beams and replace the hatchboards and will return at 8.44 and a half, Greenwich time, in the morning.

So it's up to the sailors and the Krooboys to spread the hatch tarpaulins and place the hatch-locking bars on top. Then the apprentices take their trays of padlocks around and complete the task of securing the access to the hatches. It's time for a beer, dinner in the saloon and the luxury of a night in port without any cargo work.

Our clerical contingent return in good time for their evening meal and I hear that they enjoyed their excursion and didn't even get wet. The agency boarding clerk had shown them some of the meagre 'sights' of the town before dropping them off at the Ducor hotel up by the lighthouse.

The Italian manager there had proved to be very hospitable, standing them lunch and arranging for them to spend the afternoon using the swimming pool. The only thing to mar their day's enjoyment was being ripped off by the taxi-driver bringing them back to the ship whose initial promise of a two-dollar fare became a per capita sum at the dock gates.

With the gate policeman telling them to pay up or be taken into custody, they duly shelled out the twelve dollars demanded. The four younger priests were greatly exercised by this gross act of injustice but their two seniors were more philosophical. Father

Patrick thought that they'd had quite an inexpensive day ashore anyway, whilst Father Adrian was greatly taken by the idea that they'd been successfully mistaken for a gang of genuine seafarers who could be fleeced as relatively wealthy visitors.

It appears, from the conversation over our beers before dinner, that it's too early in the voyage for most of us to consider a customary night ashore of drinking in some dive followed by the usual sexual encounters as a release from work and abstinence. This leads to the popular alternative of a 'movie-night' being proposed and organised.

There's a rectangular structure made of galvanised scaffolding that sits on top of the after masthouse and the apprentices are sent to fix a white canvas projection screen to it. Lawrence and Tommy set up the film projector at the end of the covered promenade deck and the senior officers and passengers take chairs out to enjoy the film from that level. As duty officer for the evening, I take a seat off to one side where the mate can see that I'm handy to make a turn of the decks between reels.

Otherwise, I'd be up on the deck above where behaviour can be a little less restrained because of the absence of our senior officers. The final element of the audience, our crew and the Krooboys, together with some drifters from the shore, disports itself on and around number four hatch. It's not long before we're all being transported by Hollywood into its celluloid world. Only the heavy humidity and the occasional flashes of lightning offshore remind us that we're not in a cinema back home.

The remaining cargo is despatched the next morning and we leave the port comfortably before midday. The Old Man is content; we have about five or six hours short of two days' steaming to our next port and that means an arrival in Takoradi in good time to start a full day's work. There are no squalls on the horizon today and just a refreshing breeze out of the south-west to temper the heat of the sun. I should be spending further time checking out the lifeboat equipment but that can be done tomorrow. I drag my towel and blanket into some suitable corner of the deck in order to enjoy a recreational snooze in the sun.

Our faithful Doxford diesel engine has maintained its reliable thump over the last 43 hours when I'm called to the bridge just before six in the morning. I take over the watch from Don and then I'm sent almost immediately down to the main deck to meet the smartly uniformed Takoradi harbour pilot. He's a Ghanaian who was apprenticed to this company and knows the Old Man well.

That makes for a fairly sociable and relaxed operation as we enter harbour and are turned around by a smoky old tug. This enables us to berth port-side alongside and this will be ideal for an easy departure. Takoradi is mainly an exporting port and I can see four or five ships moored to buoys that are busily loading logs from the water and sawn timber from lighters. We have only a small amount of cargo to land so time will not be tight; the relative simplicity of the harbour and the availability of pilots means that we can depart as late as ten this evening.

After their first excursion our clerics are now hungry for more. They've been correctly told that Takoradi is a friendly town and that a visit to the local market is worthwhile.

In comparison with the rather uninspiring streets of Monrovia, this part of the town will be an authentic taste of West Africa delivered with a singular Ghanaian flavour.

The traders are nearly all colourfully dressed women of a certain age, the 'market mammies', who form a tight-knit and economically powerful group. Those men accompanying them therefore keep to the margins where the political business of the day and of the nation can be volubly discussed. Many will be wearing the kind of toga that is a national dress and this sartorial display gives the market a bizarre imitation of the fora of ancient Rome.

It's here that you can buy bananas, small bitter oranges, okra, leaves, yams, rice, groundnuts, palm oil and manioc flour as well as various cooked meats wrapped in cut shards of banana leaf. Matches are sold in tiny boxes of twenty but cigarettes can be purchased individually, as can bars of soap, candles and other small domestic necessities. With colonial status being so recent, it is still the pounds, shillings and pence of the West African Currency Board that accompany any market transactions.

A tourist trade is as yet unimagined but enough resident expatriates and passing visitors exist to support a small handicrafts outlet near to the harbour. This sells some attractive wood carvings and various items that use the strikingly coloured Kente cloth.

There's no time to shop ashore for most of us; however, a trader with a few wood carvings and some pieces of Kente establishes himself in the shade of the main alleyway that faces out to the harbour. He's not in anybody's way there and he might make a few sales. I'll probably have a look at his wares later on as I did buy a nice ebony piece from him once. It has proved to be the genuine article and not some lesser timber treated with a generous veneer of black shoe polish. For now, I have the business of the foredeck to hold my attention.

All five hatches are being worked and we have the services of three dockside cranes to help matters along. Number one hatch might be a problem with whisky in open stow so I've put Pete down there. Dougie can give him a spell from time to time since he's not wanted continuously by Dave down aft.

What we're mainly unloading here in Takoradi is plain, honest 'do you good' cargo. It suits the current philosophy of the new nation of Ghana, pursuing a rapid economic development. So we have steel rails for Ghana Railways, huge tyres for the dump trucks at the Ashanti gold mines near Kumasi and a range of other similar infrastructure equipment.

Ghana is far from producing a complete nation of saints, however, and the usual anti-social port activities have to be spotted and terminated in addition to the other demands of the day's work. As in all West African ports, it's impossible to avoid some request for 'dash' from virtually everyone you encounter on deck. 'I beg you, master, just one stick (cigarette)', 'Hallo, Joe, you get any small ting for me?', 'When de ship finish, make you see me for some small dash, my fren' and so forth to form an almost continuous commentary.

There's an opportunity at some point to slip up to the forecastle head or down the offshore maindeck alleyway for a quick smoke and the usual dialogue soon ensues:

'Master, I beg you to help me with just one stick for me now.'

'Fuck off, I'm trying to have a cigarette in peace here, you bugger.'

'Ahh! Who are you to call me dat ting? You are a wicked man and God will punish you soon.'

'Piss off, my fren'. You no get savvy for any ting. Go 'way from me, now.'

'You, you…you are a very beast of no nation. You are nobody. Tchhh.'

'Go on, sod off. You be a very beast of no nation yourself.'

That last remark has really wounded his pride. Therefore he tells me that he is a citizen of Ghana and that, if he sees me ashore, he will call the police and have me thrown into jail. He storms off and I can enjoy the last few puffs of my cigarette before despatching the stub into the harbour waters. Maybe I should have given him the bloody cigarette when asked and then I could have enjoyed the total smoke in peace? Not at all. Like sharks who scent blood in the water, the dock labour would soon smell out an easy touch for a 'dash' and lobby me even more unmercifully.

The whisky stowed in number one hatch should be safe with both Pete and a pair of local watchmen in attendance, plus my frequent visits. Even so, I notice that one man standing by the open hatch, the one who directs the crane driver, has a pronounced richness of breath. No winch drivers are needed here but I also spot two or three labourers standing by the winches, being rather conspicuously idle. It doesn't need advanced detective skills to figure out that these lot are up to something.

I walk towards them to investigate, and see the distinctive shape of an empty Dimple Haig whisky bottle lying inside a coil of wire rope. 'What's this, then?' I ask one of the men but he merely grunts and turns away from me. Then I notice that one of his companions appears to be slightly stooped as he starts to move off.

I grab him by his thin and ragged shirt, turn him towards me and see that two bottles of Black & White whisky have managed to find themselves into his waistband. 'So, you be teefman?' I challenge him. 'No, no, master. Dis ting I go find, just now.' But alcohol on his breath belies that claim and my actions make his two companions more aggressive. Fortunately they back off when I call one of the watchmen up from the 'tweendeck and give him the bottles, telling him to put them back in the stow.

There's still an hour to go before midday and an official break from work. I'm in a bad mood as I go up onto the forecastle to check that all is well with the moorings and ensure that the round metal ratguards on each one are securely in place. It's not through any great need to prevent rodent access. It's more to insure against some shore official spotting them hanging free of the ropes and then coming aboard to levy some 'dash' in lieu of a fine.

There's a rich aroma up here of human excrement drying in the hot sunshine and, blow me, here's one guy actively at stool on the forward side of the windlass. 'Hey, you. Why you go kaka in dis place? You no savvy go aft for thunderbox? Wassmatter, my fren'?' Hastily he scrambles up from his crouch and tries to recover some dignity as I continue to harangue him.

I will not be denied this legitimate chance to vent some of my frustrations this hot morning so I pursue him with a symbolic boot to his backside that misses its target by yards. At least he's had the decency to evacuate onto a piece of kraft paper that he's found for the purpose. This enables me to pick up the offensive pile and drop it into the harbour waters where it peacefully sails under the wooden piles of the quay and into dark oblivion beyond.

I should introduce you at this point to the 'thunderbox' I referred to. It's a primitive lavatory that is also called, disrespectfully, the 'African ensign'. That's because it hangs over the ship's side down aft and close to where our own Red Ensign proudly flies while in port.

The 'thunderbox' is a timber box-like structure that has a floor with a circular hole and sides that are covered in hessian cloth for modesty's sake. This hessian is always best treated generously with creosote or similar to both perfume the area and prevent its theft. The screen hides the lavatory user from public view save for his head, which means that conversation with bystanders can and often does take place.

Naturally there is no toilet paper provided, but the ship can usually furnish suitable pieces of alternative material. In addition, if a ship is moored close astern, a common occurrence, one or more of its mooring ropes might pass close overhead and thus serve the purpose. Just remember not to be 'on seat' when those ropes are being handled, as they have been known to pass under the thunderbox and then, in the course of being hove tight, to lift the latrine and its occupant bodily and alarmingly, hugely entertaining those who are passing by.

It's back to work after this, so it's down the ladder to the foredeck and down another steel ladder into the 'tweendeck at number one hatch. If we can get this area completed then the hatch can be covered up. The gang can work the deck cargo of steel drums while we get the padlocks on and this removes the need to watch the whisky over the lunch break, now just forty minutes away.

Pete tells me that the two returned bottles have been put back into one of several cartons that have been broached. It's apparently the work of the Liverpool dockers but that can be sorted out at our next port of call. The task now is to find all the remaining Takoradi cargo and send it on its way.

Fortunately, despite taking a bit of a drink, the Liverpool gang have made a good clear separation of those items of cargo for here as distinct from that for other ports and so we are able to achieve our objective of clearing the hatch by midday. Then it's cover up, lock up and complete the morning by joining the crowd that is moving purposefully aft down the foredeck. The Ghanaians stream ashore or find patches of shade in which to enjoy their hour off. The ship's company look for their first beer of the day and then a quick feed in the messrooms or the saloon before resuming duty for the afternoon's toil.

After the lunch break, progress is good. The shore labour are willing and able and I know that the whisky is secure. My new concerns are checking that any other petty pilfering is controlled, that any damaged cargo is being properly recorded by the tally clerks and that no Takoradi cargo is left forgotten in amongst that for our later ports. By now a pleasant sea breeze is setting in and so a visit to the offshore rail to enjoy its cooling effect after emerging from the sweatboxes of the hatches is always welcome.

As the afternoon progresses, the individual hatches are gradually completed, checked and secured and we're left with just two gangs beavering away in number two hatch. Don asks me if we'll be finished by six. I reply that I think so but I also decide to get some hatch lighting rigged in case we do need to work on.

It's early in the voyage so we've two lockers full of these vital portable lights, called cargo clusters. They're now in pristine condition, due to Tommy's hard work on the voyage south. Later, especially once we start the all-night loading of logs, it'll be a different story.

Pete and I position a cluster at each hatch corner, lit but left lying face-down on the deck. This produces four small pools of light that slowly spread as the sun starts its descent into the red haze above the horizon beyond the breakwater and it's soon time to hang them properly over the hatch coaming. The Takoradi gangs have done well and the last sling of steel pipes and the last net of wooden boxes of machetes are safely landed on the quay not very long after the forecast hour of six.

The pilot has been called for seven and Dave tells me that he'll not only read the draughts but also test the bridge gear prior to sailing. That's uncommonly generous of him. I don't dwell on the strangeness of the gesture because I can grab some dinner in the duty mess, get properly showered and cleaned up for my position on the bridge and then keep my sea watch up until midnight. It'll have been a long day by then, eighteen hours of duty, but it's all gone reasonably well. There'll be a lot more drama, frustration and shouting matches in those ports yet to come.

From Takoradi we follow the coastline of Ghana some ten to 15 miles to port, passing through armadas of canoes fishing these rich waters and on towards the Greenwich meridian. It makes for a busy time for me during the rest of my 8–12 watch because these canoes have the unnerving habit of only displaying a light when you're nearly on top of them and then shouting curses from the blackness of the night as the wake of the ship threatens to swamp them.

Our next port of call, Lomé, is one of the last of the surf ports that once were synonymous with trading to West Africa. Our track, just before we move from west to east longitude, takes us past the most famous of them all, the port of Accra. The legendary boatmen of Accra are still recalled by the older Coast hands on board for the education of us youngsters who only know of its recent replacement, the harbour of Tema. Many tales, some of quite incredible height even by nautical West Africa standards, are told of the expertise and exploits of the canoe boatmen and the range of cargoes that went ashore in this primitive fashion.

Other hilarious stories involve the use and abuse of the 'mammy-chair'. This curious vehicle, something on the lines of an old fairground gondola that could seat two couples facing one another, is painted battleship grey and still resides in a corner of our number three 'tweendeck. This trip, it will continue to lie there. On a later voyage I was to see it used to safely send down some tremulous African deck passengers. They had proved too fearful to join their fellows who had successfully jumped from the bottom of the gangway onto a lighter in an exposed anchorage.

The anchorage we use the following day off Lomé, which lies just a mile or two from the border between Ghana and the newly independent nation of Togo, is another exposed one. The art here is to find a location that is sufficiently close to the small and rather decrepit pier to suit the surf boats. It must also be far enough out for us not to be rolling in the Atlantic swell that we can see breaking magnificently on the reddish sands of the beach. The beach is backed by palm trees and extends as far as the eye can see in both directions from the town.

The town of Lomé is all but invisible behind a cluster of waterfront go-downs save for the twin yellow spires of the cathedral, a water tower and a spindly steel latticework lighthouse. Offshore at present is a wartime-vintage Liberty ship that is loading squared logs floated off from the beach and, taking a plum position off the pier, one of the German Woermann Line's grey-hulled cargo ships.

While I am both fixing our position and keeping the Old Man informed about the depth of water under us, the Krooboys are out in force and rigging the guest warp along our starboard side.

This is a dedicated length of four-inch circumference sisal rope that is led from the forecastle right along to the poop and is made fast to the mooring bitts at each end. That's the easy bit. The art now is to secure short 'lizards' of smaller-circumference rope along its length in order to support the principal line at a height that will suit the needs of the surf boats at their work. Each lizard has a metal heart thimble that allows it to slide along the guest warp and find its optimum position.

When the surf boats arrive alongside they will be secured to us by wire ropes, the guest warp is to afford them some assistance in moving around the boats as they range up and down in the swell washing against the smooth steel cliffs of our hull.

Our anchorage is found, the ship is safely moored and settles head to current and thus parallel with the beach. The gangway is lowered and the usual queue of officials boards to transact the necessary paperwork. The agency clerk brings no personal mail, much to the frustration of many. He also informs the purser that, although our passengers will not be permitted to land, he has arranged a requested visit to the doctor for two of our Nigerian stewards.

The stevedore, another burly Frenchman encased in a cloud of Gauloise fumes, finds his way up to the mate's cabin in order to plan our unloading. Our cargo is the staple one for these French ports: whisky, Land Rovers and textiles, with a light dressing of other items. There are ten vehicles to be handled, all of them in number five lower hold. The stevedore reckons that we'll be able to put them in a surf boat alongside because the ship will lie quietly during the next few hours before the afternoon sea breeze makes a more lively platform for work. He is also hoping to have the whisky in number one hatch discharged before then. It's a pity that we have cargo at both our extremities where the surf boats find it most difficult to lie alongside satisfactorily, 'mais, c'est la vie, eh?'

I take the opportunity to snatch a quick breakfast once I've enjoyed a brief spin around the ship in the agent's launch to make a stab at reading our arrival draughts, an educated guesstimate as the ship is giving itself a swishing waterline wash in the cloudy green waters of the anchorage.

Then the shore labour arrives in a larger launch, some 50 or 60 men to form our allocated three gangs. They argue noisily with our sailors and Krooboys about the positioning of the derricks before applying themselves to the business of stripping the hatches and stacking the beams and hatchboards on decks that are now relatively clear of deck cargo.

Then the surf boats are jockeying alongside for their optimum positions with more noisy exchanges between our labourers and the boat crews. Our proximity to Ghana plus the fact that Togo was an Anglo-French condominium following its demise as a German colony after the First World War means that my rusty French will not be much required today. Our isolation from the quay will also help with cargo security. That's just as well, as Dave has to attend to a problem with our ageing Sperry gyro-compass.

The deck is thus left to myself, Pete and Dougie although Hugo has been sent out to assist us with the tallying of the coded bales. Hugo then offers to help us elsewhere if required. He's spotted a chance to escape the alternative of helping Alan wade through paper in the ship's office and so we set to the day's work.

The surf boats are fairly large, about 45 feet long and 12 feet or so in the beam, made of stout timber which long ago was painted black or grey. Too large to be pro-pelled by men with paddles, they are towed around by motorboats and we soon have the first rope net of Scotland's finest landing in the bottom of the forward one while the first Land Rover is hovering over the bulwarks and ready to descend into the aftermost one.

This latter place represents the most likely source of bother so that's where I'm positioned. Happily, the stevedore has the same idea. Only a few interjections in unintelligible speech are required from him as the bulky grey vehicle, comfortably padded inside the car slings and steadied by small ropes in the hands of many, is lowered towards the surf boat. The steadying ropes are then thrown down to enable the boat crew to nurse the load until it lands safely in the bottom of the boat. A general chorus of whoops of joy, much hand- and back-slapping and a mass lobbying for cigarettes all round follows.

Some barked words from Monsieur le Chef soon get the gang's attention refocused. A second vehicle is put into the boat safely and it is then pulled along to number four hatch to await towage while a second surf boat is positioned ready for the next two unloadings. I leave Dougie to watch these proceedings, as the gang seem competent enough under the tutelage of their 'patron', and head up forward to see how the work of unloading the alcohol is getting on.

Like the whisky that we unloaded in Dakar, most of this cargo has a long way to travel once it gets ashore, in this case to the destination of Ouagadougou. It's obviously going to a discerning clientele. These are premium blended brands such as Chivas Regal, Grant's Standfast, Haig's Dimple and Johnny Walker Black Label. There shouldn't be too much of a problem with the security here – nobody can slip ashore with a concealed bottle very easily, and anyway these boys working in the hatch (and most of them are just that, teenagers) are from the Muslim northern part of the country.

To them, I am *baturay*, the white man, so they point at the whisky and make an elaborate show in mime to represent the sad effects of this foreigner's poison on *Monsieur le baturay*. It's a theatre performance that must be drawn from experience, an extremely amusing form of communication, as they convey the staggering and shouting effect that they associate with the use of alcohol by some Europeans here in the tropics. Ah, yes, communication.

You can get by here with English since the winch drivers and gang bosses are from the coastal tribes of the south and many of them are Ghanaian citizens. Equally, there's a chance here in Lomé to try to improve my nautical French before it's needed in practice south of the Equator. I don't know if there is such a variant as 'pidgin French' since the people of these former French possessions seem to speak the language in the usual way, albeit with some unfamiliar words and inflections.

Here, with the cargo moving fairly sweetly, I can make myself familiar once again with the fact that the cargo is in the *faux-pont* rather than the 'tweendeck and remind myself to *regardez le croc* rather than look out for the hook, as the load is taken up by the *mât à charge* rather than the derrick.

I can also bark at the labour not only the common expressions for here, there, up and down but also the more esoteric phrases such as *'tirez les galiots'* or *'mettez les panneaux'*, which will become 'make you draw de beams now' or 'put de 'atchboards proper' when we visit the Anglophone ports.

I love this acquisition and use of another language because I enjoyed both French and Latin at school and I'm lucky to have some ability to mimic the speech of others. It's a matter of identifying those subtle changes of inflection, those little link words, shrugs, sniffs and use of hands and shoulders that make up the total communication package and then practice, practice.

This is a very civilised port; we will actually be stopping for a 90-minute official lunch break from half-past twelve. I send the apprentices off to get changed so that they can eat properly in the saloon, and agree with Dave that he'll also eat there and then relieve me to take my meal in the duty mess at one. In the meantime I will keep a precautionary 'monkey-eye' by showing myself around the deck where the working hatches have now fallen quiet but still remain open to access. There's no call for hatch tents as no rain is threatened so, whilst most labourers will only go below to find a shaded sleeping space, some might be tempted to do a little shopping.

For now, however, each gang is squatted on its hunkers and devouring the contents of a large white enamel bowl containing some near-white rice adorned with a rather skimpy dressing of some kind of small fish in a red pepper or tomato sauce. I politely decline an invitation from the gang at number one hatch to join their repast but I'm quite happy to point the head man in the direction of the freshwater tap outside the galley where his men can draw the necessary to wash down their spartan meal.

Access to water is an ongoing minor problem everywhere along the coast of West Africa. Here we have people who are entitled to a drink from us because they are isolated from any alternative source. Elsewhere the clamour for 'water, water, give me water, my fren'' will come from every shoreside bum and stiff who can wangle his way up the gangway.

The drinking-water capacity of the ship is limited and replenishment is not possible at every port. Therefore at some point on every voyage the handy little tap on deck has to be padlocked in order to conserve a dwindling supply.

When work resumes at two the sea breeze is beginning to set in and the ship is yawing a little as she decides whether to lie to the wind from the south-west or the coastal current from the west. This in turn makes the pitching and rolling a little more pronounced and so I have to keep a closer eye on the unloading, especially as the labour sense that they are nearing the end of the job and might well get away with an early finish to their day.

I'm thankful that the fragile cargoes have now gone and it's principally large drums of oil along with smaller drums of lime and other chemicals that are being despatched to the waiting boats. It's all done and dusted by four. The initial group of Togolese officials return to give us our clearance and obtain a further tribute of beer, spirits and cigarettes while the Krooboys and the sailors secure the hatches and the derricks ready for our departure.

There's no rush because we only need ten hours or so to reach the roads off Lagos and there's no pilotage available there before six in the morning. Dave goes forward with the carpenter to pick up the anchor. Don is up on the bridge handling the ship, under the watchful eye of the Old Man, as a useful exercise for his expected promotion at the end of the voyage. To my surprise and delight, I'm therefore not needed anywhere, so I can head for my cabin. There I can grab a shower in peace and even have an hour or so of reading my book before taking the dinner meal relief followed by my bridge watch up to midnight. Only 15 hours of duty logged today, it's almost been a holiday!

5

Lagos, the capital of the Coast

Nigeria

The Independence of this country came in 1960, three years later than that of Ghana. Thus the early years of the new nation were characterised by a keen sense of its government wanting to erase this time handicap in restoring its status as the principal state in West Africa.

To help with this political and economic supremacy, Nigeria was fortunate to have ample and still largely unexploited reserves of crude oil, that golden economic asset of the late 20th century. Later years would show that a growing reliance on this single gift from nature had its disadvantages. For now, the other natural riches of Nigeria supported a varied export trade in timber, tin, cocoa, vegetable oils and a wide variety of other produce. The revenue from these many commodities paid for an equally broad range of manufactured imports and infrastructure goods.

Nigeria, however, was really an artificial state. The old colonial borders, which derived from the European powers carving out territories in the previous century, now enclosed peoples of very different cultures and levels of development. The formation of the Nigeria that was a member of the British Empire came from the amalgamation of several pre-existing crown colonies, each of which was relatively homogenous.

The north of Nigeria, the largest region in terms of area, contained a very traditional and relatively backward society, predominantly Moslem in religious belief. The area around Lagos and the south-west was the homeland of the Yoruba, and the Ibo heartland was in the south-east. There were also other important tribal groups inhabiting the riverine areas of the Niger Delta. Personal or sectarian political power was the objective of leaders of the three principal Nigerian ethnic groups although all claimed to represent the interests of the whole country.

Much of the north was semi-arid and the only source of export earnings was the annual groundnut crop plus limited amounts of cotton, hides and skins. The oil reserves lay in the Niger Delta and extended offshore, and the south of the country also provided timber and cultivated rubber, cocoa and oil palms.

Nigerian politics were endemically noisy and corrupt. One particularly potent controversy was the actual population number in each region and hence the claims to a proportional share in the national cake. The Nigerian Army proved itself to be the most effective national organisation although, here again, it contained tribalism as an important element.

It came as little surprise that, after the country had enjoyed only a few years of independence, the politicians were usurped by the military. Ryszard Kapuscincski was in Lagos in 1966 and his diary of the first week of the *coup d'état* is an admirably concise account of the course of events that clearly explains the reasons for them.

This initial seizure of power was eventually followed by a coup by dissident junior officers, then by the destructive Civil War with the secessionary eastern state of Biafra. Frederick Forsyth made his authorial reputation with his story of that war which, although biased towards the separatists, remains eminently readable.

The country was then run by a succession of military leaders of varying probity before the civilian political class were able to regain the power that they had so carelessly surrendered.

Throughout these years of power struggles, the range and volume of exports declined. Even the rapidly growing oil revenues could not fund the necessary cures for the urban chaos that followed a flight from the land as the rural population followed the mirage of a better life in the cities. Meanwhile, those former sources of export earnings, the cocoa and oil plantations, reverted to tropical jungle. The wealth that was generated from oil was also diverted by both military and civilian oligarchies into corrupt channels. What followed was an economic collapse in Nigeria that not only affected its own sea commerce but also impacted on its neighbours.

There is great excitement for our Nigerian crew as this morning will bring the reality of arrival in their home port. The unloading of their accumulated possessions will be followed by a return to their wives and families and the chance for a few days at home.

Our steward, Olatunde, offers me a big smile when he brings up the usual tray of coffee and hot buttered toast to the bridge. A similarly happy 'Tiger' (the nickname for the captain's steward on British ships) has brought the same offering to the Old Man a little earlier. We enjoy this traditional fare as we lie gently rolling in the swell under an overcast sky and await the arrival of the Lagos pilot, booked for 0600.

It's now well past seven and there's still no sight of the pilot launch heading out from between the two long stone breakwaters that are the entrance to the lagoon harbour. Don is forward with Chippy. Dave comes up to the bridge, nicks some of my toast and irritably asks what's going on. He's justifiably aggrieved, having only gone to bed after his watch three short hours ago. 'Why can't these black bastards ever get themselves organised?' he asks rhetorically before disappearing down below.

The Old Man is more than capable of taking the ship into port without any assistance from a pilot but that's not permitted by the harbour authorities and so we continue to wait. The German ship that we saw in Lomé is now heard on the VHF calling Lagos pilots and receiving confirmation that his pilot is booked for 0800. The Old Man storms out onto the bridge wing to see where this other ship is, storms back in and grabs the VHF telephone to give 'Lagos pilots' a piece of his mind. It's all so familiar, the shambolic mess that is the West Coast's allegedly premier port.

It's now nearly 0800 and the German is sitting only a couple of hundred metres off our stern when the pilot launch is seen emerging from the breakwaters. Are we now to have an undignified scramble for a pilot? Happily, no, as the launch calls on us first. The burly Egyptian who will guide us in reaches the top of the pilot ladder and I lead him through the accommodation and up to the bridge.

He heads off the Old Man's obvious anger by profusely apologising for the delay, caused by engine problems with the pilot launch. This may or may not be true. All of us up on the bridge are convinced that this whole port is run by congenital liars, but no matter, we're on the way in and so the crew can be called to their harbour stations. They're more than happy when it's confirmed by the pilot that we're headed for the number one berth on Lagos Customs Quay, starboard side alongside.

We steam up the harbour and through the Pool anchorage, where we would be held if we had any explosives to discharge. I smilingly recall this being the case on my last ship. I'm especially remembering all the precautionary fuss (red flag flying, no steel-capped boots allowed on deck, fire extinguishers and charged hoses all ready). I then find the explosives watchman in his agency uniform, sitting on top of a stack of wooden boxes of ICI Elephant-brand African gunpowder, enjoying his cigarette.

Today we press on and, as the mouth of Five Cowrie Creek and then the Ikoyi Yacht Club pass by on our starboard side, we can see the long and crowded length of Apapa Quay on the other side of the harbour. We proceed past the traffic-choked Lagos Marina, then an empty cargo ship lying at the Marina Buoys and so eventually reach our destination, bang in the centre of town.

Our Nigerian crew are delighted and it's also convenient for the rest of us as the UAC Kingsway department store is opposite. We're also under the convenient gaze of the recently built head office of our shipping company's agency. It's no real threat – it would be very different if it were the Liverpool office, variously labelled by us as the 'House of Laughter' or the 'Kremlin', when it intrudes upon shipboard affairs.

The Nigerians get busy with their paying-off, most will re-sign immediately but will also take leave while we're in Lagos. Stand-by sailors are engaged but they're not on board yet so it's down to the Krooboys, Billy the bosun and Stan the chippy to get the derricks sorted out. We're only working three gangs and we'll just be here until the next day. The bulk of our cargo must be discharged over Apapa Quay once a berth is available there.

Soon we're busy unloading textiles and consumer goods. A good many are for the account of UAC's Kingsway Stores across Nigeria. There are also substantial amounts for the other long-established merchant houses of K. C. Chellaram, A. G. Leventis, Paterson Zochonis and the Swiss UTC.

As these are mainly shipped in cardboard cartons we soon discover that some informal shopping has taken place en route and this keeps the two Nigerian discrepancy clerks busy taking note of the damage incurred. There's also registered mail to tally out of a locker and, when that's done, I hear that the arrival of other mail means that we should have letters from home.

At my mid-morning break ('smoko'), I call by Alan's office, where Hugo gives me a single letter from my parents. It's as much as I can expect on this trip. I'm currently without anyone to send me that perfumed missive which many of my shipmates are set to enjoy. Naturally, my letter is welcome although it contains little news since it had to be posted only a week after we sailed from Liverpool. However, I am pleased to learn that our dog sends me her regards.

Hugo mentions to me that he's going ashore in the afternoon with Lawrence and would I like to join them? I accept because, although we'll be working cargo up to ten that evening, Don is content that Dave and I split the deck duties between us from noon. So, after lunch, the three of us are down the gangway and across the road and into the welcome air-conditioned ambience of the Kingsway store. Our casual ignoring of the entreaties of the 'blind' beggar stationed outside with his notice soliciting alms makes him call out, 'Wassmatter, Joe, you no read English?'

Shopping is soon done and Hugo is then keen for us to take a drink up in the cafeteria because he's heard that its harbour view is matched by the panorama of expatriate wives and he needs to calm his overexcited hormones. As it turns out, the place is nearly deserted although we stay and enjoy a soft drink in the hope that a shoal of attractive local womanhood might just appear.

No such luck, so it's out onto the street again and a walk along the marina to catch the breeze while we decide what to do next. Three such obvious visitors soon attract a tail of hawkers and other hangers-on offering all manner of delights, 'Hey, Joe, you need jig-a-jig?' 'Come see my sister, she be good for you'. We pass a bar, confer, retrace our steps and escape our entourage by entering.

No air-conditioning here, just some lazily turning ceiling fans, but the tall green bottles of locally brewed Star lager are satisfyingly cold. Hugo and Lawrence start to make plans for the rest of the day but I've work to do before long and a nap to take beforehand so I'm soon steering myself back to the ship. At least I've been ashore for the first time this trip.

My two companions also return not much later but, after dinner on board, they join the two apprentices and a small posse of engineers heading ashore once again. I'll probably not see them return but will be able to take part in the inevitable post-mortem tomorrow morning.

Our passengers have also disappeared, not of course to the city's fleshpots, but to the sanctuary of the local establishment run by their order. They'll not be back until we sail three or four days from now. By that time, I bet they'll be missing their shipboard ration of three good four-course meals a day.

My duties on deck happily finish an hour early as the last of the Lagos cargo is sent ashore. I could enjoy some time in the bar once I've got all the hatches locked but, after my shower, my bed seems an altogether more appealing prospect.

At six the next morning we're all set to leave the Lagos side of the harbour but, as you might guess, there's no sign of a pilot and we can see that there's still no visible break in the mile-long row of ships that fill our Apapa Quay destination. I'm waiting by the gangway to meet the pilot and take him up to the bridge when I spot Hugo and cannot fail to notice a splendid black eye forming on his usual cheery face.

Apparently our party met up with a group of American Peace Corps members in some dive at the back of Tinubu Square. A night's sociable drinking broke up when Hugo felt it necessary to punish some derogatory reference to the British Empire made by his new-found friends. Despite this temporary disfigurement, he seems very proud of establishing his credentials as the archetype of Jolly Jack ashore.

Naturally, just as we're all making arrangements to get some breakfast, the pilot arrives. We're soon clear of the wharf with an elderly Nigerian Ports Authority (NPA) tug on hand to help us turn around, drenching us in a foul cloud of black coal smoke in the process. A Japanese cargo ship has left Apapa Quay and is out of the channel so we can now approach the berth that she's left.

That berth is a gap that measures our length plus about 50 feet or so. It means a slow, careful approach with more than a few tense moments before we're safely alongside and can think of a breakfast that's now a couple of hours overdue. The shore labour is gathered on the quay awaiting the lowering of the gangway so that means just a couple of bacon sandwiches hastily assembled before the sweaty battle that is our principal port call begins.

We'll be working around the clock here so Dave will be on night duty, the customary arrangement. Pete willl join him and so I'll have Dougie working with me for a change. For this morning, however, all four of us are on hand to ensure that the unloading gets off to a good start. After lunch, with the rhythm established, the night men will knock off and try to get some sleep amongst the heat and din before they take over at seven.

Heat and din are here in plenty because it takes until late afternoon for any sea breeze to appear and the ship is now invaded by the Coast's most effective talking machines, Yoruba men. Of course, they're not all Yoruba, neither do they all have legitimate business on the ship so I know that our stay here will be as much concerned with keeping order as with unloading cargo. It's a different experience, of course, if you're further up the hierarchical ladder on board.

For example, I've just spotted the smart agency motor launch approaching our offshore side and so I go up to warn Don. 'Yes,' he says, 'the Old Man and the Chief are going ashore. Tell the boat skipper to go along to the steps and get the lad to take the Old Man's bag down for him.' That done, I soon see our two senior officers walking along the quay with their allocated porter.

The Old Man is in the usual shoregoing off-duty outfit that is chosen by the company's Masters. It consists of blue-checked short-sleeved shirt, dark blue knee-length shorts, long white stockings and highly polished brown leather brogues.

'He'll be the first to walk the plank, come the revolution,' growls Tommy, the electrician, who's appeared besides me. 'It's only the privileges of rank,' I mutter limply in response. Politics, along with religion, is usually avoided as a conversation topic on board but I do know that Tommy is extremely keen that the next general election at home will see the resumption of the journey to the New Jerusalem that was so rudely interrupted for him back in 1951.

'At least the old Chief's carrying his own golf clubs, so we'll spare him,' is Tommy's generous parting shot as he heads up the deck to see who's currently abusing his precious cargo winches.

As this trip progresses I'll find that some of Tommy's egalitarian views might be slightly suspect. He's a born Scouser but he's careful now to live in a prosperous suburb across the Mersey in the Wirral where his two children benefit from a free education at the highly regarded local grammar school. And he's quite happy to characterise the rest of us left living in Liverpool as lounging scroungers whose principal source of income derives directly from his income tax payments.

Today is Friday and we're keen to root out any shed cargo that is readily accessible as the weekend period is notorious for finding the sheds not open to receiving. This is due to the NPA ('No Proper Arrangement' in local parlance) staff finding it inconvenient to attend on those two days. We therefore plan to work Saturday and Sunday on the salt cargo and those other items that either go straight to consignees or to outside storage. In fact we're going to begin the discharge of salt now from number four hatch, where the first lorry is waiting to receive those precious white bags.

It's a big, powerful MAN vehicle with a high metal-sided body that looks equal to the journey ahead of several hundred miles up to Kano. A rather grubby tarpaulin has been laid in the back as protection for the load. Three small boys sit on the cab roof (the two drivers are fast asleep inside) as interested spectators to see the first sling land. There are no canvas overshoes here, just bare feet, but the bags appear to keep their pristine condition as the loading slowly completes. Its successor is already providing a cloud of filthy black exhaust smoke as it impatiently awaits its turn under the hook.

Elsewhere the Krooboys have set up a swinging derrick rig at number two hatch as there are a number of electricity transformers to be unloaded. They're just under five tons each in weight, double the load that can be safely handled by the rig of two derricks worked in unison that we use elsewhere. There are three cranes on our berth but we're not using them on this occasion. In fact one of them seems to be under repair since a group of NPA employees are poking around the connections under the quay and noisily arguing the toss with each other.

As the newest arrival here, we're soon under siege from the army of itinerant pedlars, opportunists and other bums and stiffs that bluffs its way up the gangway past the uniformed agency watchman. Unlike those ships of other nationalities that can seal off their crew living areas from visitors, we have to allow a relatively open access as so many of our company are West Africans.

This means making regular sweeps of the interior alleyways to flush out those who have no legitimate business on the ship. The deck freshwater tap is locked but the labour can either get refreshment by begging at the galley or by using a leaking standpipe on the quay that Stan is using to top up our domestic tanks.

Not all visitors are unwelcome. We all know and patronise a Nigerian tailor who can be relied upon to knock up very presentable short-sleeved shirts and shorts. They're either in white or khaki, or even a striking blue which fortunately fades after the second wash into something a lot more muted. Then there's the maker of small three-legged 'kidney' tables with (alleged) ebony and ivory inlays or the man with the 'thorn' carvings.

My particular weakness is for the 'thorn wood' carvings that are traded by a man from Jos, a place far up-country. He says that he also makes them, which may or may not be true; however, he is very knowledgeable about his wares. Thorn wood is a timber that has both light and dark constituents. This allows for the carving of the faces and limbs of little figurines from the latter material, which are then clothed and given background by use of the former part of the wood.

Over the years I'll amass a diverse collection of these carvings. Villagers in canoes, in a mammy-wagon, in various domestic settings, as well as a chess set and a nativity scene. They're great dust-collectors so nowadays they fill a box kept up in the loft where they're always available for inspection if I want to recall days spent working on the Coast. For now, I promise to meet up with the carver later in the day as I can see Don is heading purposefully towards me.

He's in this sudden hurry since the NPA shed staff are now in some form of dispute and will definitely not be opening up for business over the weekend. That sounds promising, but I daren't say as much to him. Just now we're going to visit each hatch to make an estimate of what cargo we have that is either for direct delivery or which can be sent to open storage. Later on I find that, though we'll work all through tonight, it'll be day gangs only ordered for tomorrow and Sunday.

It's just a pity that this opportunity for free time has occurred when I know that my friends ashore here are back home on leave. Otherwise I could have joined them on one of their usual weekend expeditions out to the country. However, as I'll soon discover, there are plans being hatched on board to exploit this free-time bonus.

With no cargo work scheduled for Saturday night, I'm hoping that when Dave emerges in the early afternoon of that day he'll offer to complete my day shift. Then I can join the small party that's heading up to the Apapa Club for a swim but they've long gone by the time that Dave emerges.

When he does appear and I broach the subject of splitting Sunday's work, he says that he'll do up to midday so that I can go ashore this evening and 'bag off' or whatever. He flatly refuses my preferred alternative of my doing the morning and then taking the afternoon off. Sod off to him, I think, he can get his own beer for the film show this evening, the miserable bugger.

We might have watched the second of our voyage ration of four films this evening but Lawrence and Hugo, returned from their swim, generously offer to see if they can make a swap with one of the other ships alongside. This is quite a regular occurrence in West African ports, someone from one ship walking along the quay with the distinctive square brown case containing reels of film and looking to make an exchange.

Many foreign-flag ships also carry English language movies although they're sometimes subtitled, the only exception being the Soviet ships. Despite the hostile attitudes and protocols of the Cold War, Russian seamen are always welcomed on board and loaned a film although I only once saw us try and watch their exchange movie out of curiosity. Ten per cent of the first reel was quite sufficient to justify rewinding it and putting it straight back in the can.

So we enjoy, with suitably raucous comment from all seats, an over-the-top Hollywood war epic. At drinks after the showing, the conversation turns to the subject of tomorrow. Mick, the chief steward, says that we'll have our customary steaks for lunch but then he'll be laying on a self-service buffet for the evening in order to allow the catering staff to enjoy the rest of the day at home.

Eric, our second engineer, proposes a boat trip down the harbour to Tarkwa Bay. This is enthusiastically taken up until it emerges that Dave has no intention, as he says, of acting as chauffeur to a bunch of 'ginger beer' (engineer) holidaymakers.

Don, we know, wouldn't do the conducting duty so that leaves me as the only other person qualified to take the lifeboat out. And I'm booked to look after the cargo. The livelier souls declare that they're headed off for some Saturday night action with the girls ashore and the rest of us pack up rather dispiritedly and head for our beds.

Either somebody further up the shipboard candle (I suspect that it's been the chief engineer) has put the screw on dismal Dave or he's had an unlikely overnight conversion. This is because he announces early on Sunday morning that he'll do the afternoon on deck so that I can take the lifeboat away. Getting permission to do so from Don is then just a necessary formality. He tells me to be back by six at the latest and holds me and my wages responsible for any damage to the boat which he further reminds me is also an essential part of our lifesaving equipment.

Lunch is taken at the trot and it's not long after one when our little party is assembled on the boat deck. We're dressed in an assortment of beach-type gear and accompanied by half a dozen or so cases of beer straight from the cold stores. Mick has given us a couple of large orange mesh bags that onions or carrots came in as ship's stores. These will be handy keep-nets for the beer, which we can then leave under the water for coolness.

Billy is ready to lower the boat under Don's orders (with the Old Man keeping monkey-eye as further insurance from the bridge wing) when Stan comes rushing along with a case of beer and the intention of joining us. In so doing he's losing an afternoon's overtime and I welcome him coming; just the man to sort out the plugs if we start leaking on passage. Billy has already removed the two wooden skates that encircle the hull; they help the boat to launch against an adverse list but also act as very effective brakes in the water.

After a smooth descent to harbour level the reliable little Petter diesel engine comes alive without too much bother. We cast off the two lifting hooks, keep well away from the effluent of the ship's overside discharges and bear off into the stream. There are farewell waves not only from the few officers left behind but also from the shore labour. We're also saluted by two of our Krooboys on a painting stage overside where they're glad of an excuse to put down their chipping hammers for a moment.

The tide is ebbing well, which means we're making over twice our unassisted speed. This is good because then we should have some flood tide to help us on the way home. The sun is shining, we all cluster aft to keep the propeller well in the water and we soon pick up a pleasant sea breeze as we head for the sands of Tarkwa Bay. This is seafaring as it should be, plain Jolly Jack savouring the popularly imagined millionaire's life of lounging around on sunny tropical beaches.

Tarkwa Bay, which is a little sandy inlet entered on our starboard side just before reaching the harbour entrance breakwaters, is a popular Sunday destination for the expatriate population and we find several motor cruisers are already there. Some boats fly a corporate or a national flag; the UAC vessel even has a uniformed African skipper and crew but they're mostly privately owned junior gin palaces.

One or two snotty stares are directed at our rather ungainly craft but I ignore them as I look for a suitable piece of beach to run up to. With her large flat bottom, this is an ideal way to secure the boat. A rope is attached to a metal crowbar sunk into the sand, the beer nets are lowered overside in the shade and we're in business.

The seawater temperature is nicely into the eighties, albeit a bit chillier the further you swim from the beach. It's pure pleasure, especially if you lie on your back and float with the sun beating down on you and know that work is many miles away. Hugo is highly tickled by the way we rough-and-ready sailors have muscled in on the recreational destination of Lagos expatriate society. This is a chance to tell him the popular and possibly apocryphal yarn of the ship's lifeboat taken down to New York's Coney Island beach on a similar Sunday afternoon expedition.

This strange craft soon attracts attention as it approaches the shore and its complement of Scousers respond to queries of 'Where'er you guys from?' with the bald statement 'We're from Liverpool'. This immediately puts them in the middle of an enthusiastic crowd all telling each other 'Hey, these guys just crossed the Atlantic. Give 'em a big hand.' There is the offer of drinks all round and a prominent picture and story in the next day's paper.

After our initial beer break, some of the party are keen to take a walk over to the nearby lighthouse but I need to stay here and keep an eye on the boat. Stan sensibly suggests that we put up some kind of sunshade and we cobble something together from the boat's canvas cover. It's a bit Robinson Crusoe (or maybe more like his cousin Heath Robinson) and we are soon being visited by Man Friday in the shape of beach hawkers.

It's fairly easy to chase them away in order to leave us in peace to enjoy the view of the bikini-wearers as we contentedly ingest our beers. The ramblers return and then begin to notice their reddening faces and shoulders. Whereas most people have brought along some kind of protective headgear, only good old Lawrence has had the foresight to bring a tube of Nivea sun cream, which he generously shares around with the afflicted.

By five o'clock, however, the sun is noticeably lowering and, although the beer has not all been used, it's time to get everybody organised to leave. The rising tide has just about floated the boat and a bit of a push soon gets it into water deep enough to start the engine. As we're getting the interior ship-shape we're approached by another craft; it's more of a workboat than the other posh launches and carrying another bachelor party similar to ours.

They generously offer to give us a tow home and we're soon cracking along a lot faster than we could have managed under our own steam. When we reach the Apapa Channel, they indicate that they're bound for the Lagos side of the harbour so they cast us off but wait nearby until they see that we have the engine successfully started. There are friendly waves all round and we chug up the channel to our destination.

We've been spotted by Dave in our approach. He's gone up to the boat deck and has a couple of Krooboys ready with the portable electric winch to hoist us out of the water once we've sorted out the usual twists in the lifeboat lifting wires. We take the plugs out to drain the bottom of the boat as we rise and then stop at boat-deck level. Everybody and the balance of the beer comes out and four of us set happily to the donkey work of winding in the davits. Then all hands join in making the boat secure, properly covered and restored to its normal condition.

There are still a few minutes wanting before six when I report to Don, with all back safely and the boat secured. Then it's just time to relieve Dave on deck to allow him to take a shower while I see the cargo work finished and that all the hatches are secured. After my own wash and brush-up, I've a healthy appetite for the evening's ample cold buffet. It's the perfect end to a perfect day.

On Monday morning at eight the labour is streaming aboard and we're back to the reality of West Africa. It's a rather smelly reality as we're setting up quite a rival to the normal aroma of Apapa Quay and it's all due to our extended stay in the port. There's now a second 'thunderbox' installed on the forecastle head in addition to the existing 'African Ensign' hanging off the poop. Despite that extra capacity, the labour are still making use of alfresco toilet arrangements around the deck and below and aren't punctilious about the removal of the results. The Krooboys did wash down the upper decks early on Sunday morning but the rich aroma of drying excrement or fermented urine is still strong in places in the 'tweendecks.

The growing amount of domestic garbage has filled the standard set of five or six empty 40 gallon drums that are hanging over the offside bulwarks at number four hatch. There's now a growing mound on the green canvas save-alls that have been laid out on deck alongside them. Both our Krooboys and the shore labour are enthusiastic recyclers and so you'll not find any bottles, tins or other serviceable containers in the refuse but we still generate plenty of other waste material.

Billy covers the drums with hessian cloth, which is then abstracted within the hour by the labour for tailoring purposes. He renews the covering, this time drenching it in disinfectant and sprinkling the rubbish heap for good measure. That'll shut up the engineers who customarily complain that the stench prevents the enjoyment of their 'smoko' breaks on the deck overlooking the scene.

There are no organised waste disposal systems available to use ashore. This causes us a growing problem with the rubbish being brought up from the holds and 'tweendecks as they're progressively cleared of our outward cargo. This consists of a relatively odourless mixture of spoiled salt, broken glass, bits and pieces of timber, scraped rust and chemical residues.

It's been well culled for recyclables by both the Krooboys and the locals and now hangs over the offshore side of the ship where it is securely contained in a combination of canvas save-alls and bundles made from old hessian separation cloths. I'm ashamed to say that we'll begin dumping all of this festering burden, along with the other domestic garbage, just as soon as we clear the harbour breakwaters. I just hope that none of it finds its way onto the fairly pristine sands of Tarkwa Bay – that would be ingratitude indeed.

We now have several completely cleared spaces in our cargo compartments and so a background anxiety of the last few days increases as we await our loading orders. Anxiety because we're at risk of being scheduled for a visit to the United States instead of going back to Europe or the UK.

Ordinarily, I wouldn't mind a trip across to renew acquaintance with New York and the other big east-coast ports but I plan to take my new car around Scotland on my next leave. Others, especially Hugo, are keen that we do get transatlantic orders. The buzz on the 'galley radio' (the name for every ship's grapevine) is that the Old Man's gone over to Lagos to get our cargo bookings and their destination.

For once, the rumour is correct and the news becomes public very soon after he comes up the gangway. It's Avonmouth and Liverpool and our first homeward cargo is stemmed from Calabar, our next port of call.

After that, there's a change of plan as we will then sail directly to Lobito, where a consignment of copper is waiting impatiently for us. This means that our cargo for Douala will have to remain on board for longer than planned. That'll be a worry as it contains a substantial shipment of Guinness in open stow.

It also includes the diesel generator for our passengers. Will they accompany us down south or disembark elsewhere? It's Alan who wisely observes that this news is only version one of what will eventually happen to us. For the moment I'm happy that we're loading for home ports and I'm soon busy measuring up space in our lockers to see if we can move some of our vulnerable cargo into them. That'll be done at sea using our ubiquitous Krooboys.

By the afternoon of the following day it's apparent that we will be able to sail first thing the next morning and Dave will have an easy night's duty with just one gang working the last of the cargo. For now, it's my task to take the apprentices and thoroughly check all the cargo compartments. This is to ensure that any cargo still on board for either Apapa or Lagos is found and, if necessary, discharged to the shed while it is open in the remaining daylight hours.

I'm glad that Don has booked an additional discrepancy clerk and carpenter as, getting to the end of our unloading, the damaged items are beginning to pile up. The accepted practice here, as elsewhere on the Coast, is that no package will be accepted into the shed unless it is 'intact'. So any visible external damage must be repaired with either timber or heavy-duty tape.

If the contents are complete and undamaged then the package can be tallied out of the ship along with the rest of the cargo. Alan and Hugo can 'ring' it off as delivered on the ship's copy of the cargo manifest. If there are any shortages then the actual contents must be listed on a discrepancy package note which forms the evidence when the inevitable insurance claim appears back in our office in Liverpool. This process goes on each day in port but, on this last afternoon, I'm expecting an extended signing session once I've completed checking out the hatches.

I'm also keeping an eye out for the tailor, from whom I've ordered some white and khaki uniform shirts and shorts. He's not had any money from me as yet so it'll be his loss if he misses our sailing although I'll also feel the impact on my depleted wardrobe. If he does let me down then I might have to go back to a Krooboy for the return of a set of clothing that I 'dashed' him last week. They were still wearable but beginning to border on disreputability.

Our search party finds nothing of interest in the two after hatches so I tell Billy that he can bring the sailors along to batten them down and we go forward to find number one hatch also clear. Number three will be the last one to finish. It might be the smallest hatch on the ship but it's the most awkward one to work as it has very small deck openings and contains six deep tanks.

These are fine for carrying liquid cargo but now they still contain substantial heaps of rolls of wire and loose tyres. Fortunately, one of the quay cranes is now being used, which does speed things up a bit. This help also reduces the din of using the ship's winches and derricks when they struggle to work this awkward space.

We're down number two hatch to finish our inspection. The 'tweendeck is nice and tidy with the wall of Guinness cases at its after end not too obviously pillaged. Now down the vertical steel ladder into the dusty, noisy lower hold. It's dominated by two huge packing cases, heavy lifts for Calabar, rather the worse for wear as they've been used as working platforms for discharging the cargo that surrounded them. We can see loose steel piping in piles at the sides of these cases, also for Calabar and a number of white bags of salt carefully stashed.

They're damaged, but not too badly, and the Krooboy second headman is soon at my side saying 'Dis small ting be for we, chief mate he say so'. The salt lorries have all departed and this small consignment has little chance of reaching Kano now. I let sleeping dogs lie but tell the Krooboys to get in amongst the pipes as I can certainly see a couple of parcel mailbags hiding there.

As they and the two lads set about salvaging them, I look at what is being worked by the gang at the back end of the hold. I spot a skeleton case of galvanised-steel sheet lying apart from the last few items that the gang are ready to discharge.

'Dis no belong Apapa,' the young Nigerian tally clerk tells me helpfully. Dis no belong dis ship at all, I think, as I see that it's consigned to some place via Freetown. God only knows how it's appeared in our ship, some minor oversight in Liverpool. When we return to the deck I go and tell Don that we've checked out the cargo and just have this Freetown item to dispose of. 'Well,' he says, 'with no documentation we can't land it here for transhipment. Better get it on deck and we might be able to get rid of it when we land the Krooboys on the way home.'

I'm called out from my bunk by Dave the next morning about four. This shake is an hour earlier than I expected but the thunderous look on his face discourages my inevitable query and I soon find out what's up. Drums of lubricating oil are still being landed from number three hatch as I crunch through the quay cockroaches on my way to read our departure draughts. Dave has told me to call everybody ready for our planned sailing at six and that involves a range of communications.

The Old Man gets a blow down his voicepipe from the bridge; Don receives a polite knock on his cabin door; louder knocks for Billy and Stan; louder still for the African sailors down aft, and finally, there is the kicking of an empty biscuit tin around the fetid quarters of our two apprentices. As I'm on the bridge doing the usual preparations and boiling up the kettle for a brew I notice that the dockside crane is in parked mode and, looking over the bridgefront, I see the hatches are being covered up.

With mugs of coffee and cigarettes to hand as we lean over the rails awaiting the pilot, I learn from Dave what's been going on. Apparently the gang were taking their full time instead of going for a quick finish, probably not wanting to go home in the small hours. They needed frequent waking and cajoling, the usual story of night work on the Coast. Dave was therefore employing the usual tactic of throwing small bits of scrap timber down the deep tank to liven up the occupants.

Then the crane driver started playing up so Dave improvised a 'knocker-up' using empty beer cans on the end of a long painting bamboo. He used this to rattle the cab windows of the crane by standing on deck as we're naturally quite high out of the water now. Unfortunately the driver eventually took exception to this interruption of his slumbers and walked off 'to the latrine', as he shouted to the NPA supervisor. It was well over an hour before he returned and then he caused more palaver because a temporary replacement had been found for his driving duty.

'Why for dis place be too much palaver?' I enquire of Dave. 'Dis no be proper palaver, my fren,' he responds, 'dis be WAWA, West Africa Wins Again.' But our casual dismissal of the efficiency of the Coast's principal port is soon contradicted. The NPA mooring gang arrive and are accompanied by the pilot stepping onto the gangway at six o'clock to the minute. The ship springs into life and we're all more than ready, perhaps even those of us who live here, to shake off the dust of Apapa Quay and get on with the most important part of the voyage, the loading for home.

6

Up the creeks and then across the Equator

We're sailing out into the placid waters of the Bight of Benin, where 'few come out, many go in' according to the ancient rubric of West Africa as the White Man's Grave. That's all ancient history to us, although few still have any good words to say about this 'armpit of Africa' that is the vast delta of the many branches of the River Niger. Our course is south-eastwards to the 'corner' of Cape Formoso where the lighthouse on Palm Point, if it's lit, will give us the cue to turn eastwards into the Bight of Biafra.

This morning the sun has hidden itself behind a layer of grey stratus and this means that the prospects of an afternoon's 'bronzy' don't look too good. It also feels as if a post-Lagos and mid-voyage fatigue and ennui are beginning to set in. A full 'deckhead inspection' of my cabin after lunch seems to be an attractive prospect.

I watch the last of our debris being shoved overside and disappearing in our wake. The Krooboys have the mucky job of actually dumping it, and the Nigerian sailors get the relatively clean task of washing out the grubby minor litter from all those corners where it's accumulated. That's the usual pecking order on board.

Now I'm interested to see Don, along with Stan and Billy, standing next to the Freetown case lying on deck. I'm further intrigued as two wrecking bars are produced and a gleaming silver sheet of corrugated steel is pulled out for inspection. What's going on here, then? I find out when Don appears on the bridge and says that we (not including him, of course) are going to make a temporary bulkhead in number two 'tweendeck. It will keep that stow of Guinness cases for Douala invisible from nosy folk during what it seems will be its extended stay on board.

Answering my unspoken query about the Krooboys, he says that they'll be busy down on another 'tweendeck shifting cargo to make space for loading rubber in Calabar. So it's down to me, the apprentices and Stan to use some of this windfall sheeting material this afternoon to build a suitable barrier for our vulnerable cargo. Pete and Dougie are content to be doing this job as they're currently not keeping watches, and

Hugo also volunteers to join us. He should be busy in the purser's office helping to check the Apapa tallyslips against the cargo manifest but Alan seems happier working on his own today.

We open the hatch sufficiently to get some daylight in and find that there's a good supply of four-by-four timber to hand. Stan, with his trademark canvas bumbag full of six-inch nails, is soon hammering together a suitable framework from pieces that I hold up for him after he's cut them to length. I offer to help with the sawing but he wisely declines, 'Do 'em quicker meself, pal, thanks all the same.' Hugo and the other two are making a good fist of sending down the sheets of contraband steel and the shiny bulkhead soon begins to take shape.

Even with our taking of the traditional afternoon 'smoko' at half-past two, we're all done and dusted just before four. I catch Don on his way up to his bridge watch to tell him that we've satisfactorily screened the Guinness stow. I get a grunted and perfunctory acknowledgement of my unpaid overtime in return; obviously he's practising his command skills for his forthcoming promotion. How many years will it be before it's my turn to be a right bastard to my juniors? Such is the way of the hierarchy of mates in the British Merchant Navy.

Our Calabar destination, although it's reached via some challenging shallows, is not classed as a true 'creek' port. Those places are just below the horizon over to port from our current position. It's a suitable point at which to divert this recollection to pay them a remembered visit, since 'going up the creeks' is such an essential West African experience.

The way in is via the Escravos river where there's only about seventeen feet depth of water over a shifting sandbar. Despite the construction of two lengthy breakwaters to encourage a natural scouring, constant dredging of this entrance remains essential. Once inside, it's time to look out for the canoe of our creek pilot, who belongs to one of the two families of local fishermen (they're called the Kalaroos and the Gulas) who know these tortuous inland waterways intimately.

On this occasion it's Friday Kalaroo who we spot up ahead. His boat displays a faded Elder Dempster houseflag and he's accompanied by his boarding party of helmsman and 'small boy'. Their craft is lifted out of the water by one of our derricks, and Friday and his small entourage are soon installed on the bridge, where he greets all and sundry as long-lost friends before taking charge of the pilotage.

A knowledgeable guide is essential in the complicated network of creeks that are used to reach those ports still used by seagoing ships, currently Warri and Sapele. The river entrances from the sea were named by early Portuguese navigators; however, the waterways within bear a mixture of local names and those that reflect the British dominance of the last century.

Here you will find both Elder Point and Dempster Point but Elder Dempster's hegemony of Anglophone West Africa's sea trade lapses temporarily over this part of the Coast. This is the undisputed territory of the United Africa Company, whose great fleet of inland water craft use the River Niger and its partner, the River Benue, to reach destinations that are very distant from the sea. The company's headquarters are at Burutu; its sawmill and plywood factory dominates Sapele, and its palm-oil plantations line the banks of many of the rivers.

Warri is the home of John Holt, a historic merchant house with its own small fleet of ocean ships and that port is our first destination, to be followed by the trek up to Sapele. The passage to Warri is relatively uncomplicated but the challenge begins when the ship then has to go on to Sapele. The journey begins by retracing part of the inward route and then continues through the winding Chanomi and Nana Creeks, passing the delightfully named Joetown on the way.

The most challenging feature of Nana Creek is a place we call 'The Fork'. A tricky course alteration is necessary here because the creek not only bends sharply, it also narrows to a width of no more than 300 feet, only about five times the width of the ship.

Negotiating The Fork usually requires the running of the bow of the ship into the soft mud and mangroves of one riverbank and then allowing the tide to swing the stern outwards until it is feasible to move astern out of the mud and go ahead in the desired new direction. There is no other way to insert the ship into such a paltry gap and this manoeuvre dictates the length of the vessels (around 470 feet at most) that are called upon to visit Sapele.

Once past this obstacle the next excitement, after removing any vegetation and even any jungle livestock that has come aboard, is five miles later at Youngtown Crossing. Here we enter the Benin River, not a true daughter of the Niger but a wide river in its own right.

A pair of white triangular beacons standing on the opposite riverbank give the direction to aim for. However, a good turn of speed is needed to get the ship across without being swept too far seawards. This means giving the full ahead order while the ship is still within Nana Creek and it unavoidably produces a wash that cascades through some of the waterside huts of Youngtown. This is understandably to the vocal and visible annoyance of the inhabitants.

Now we follow a river that eventually has two channels formed by three large islands. We pass the very minor port of Koko and banks that are increasingly laid out to regimented rows of oil palms. Finally we come to our destination of Sapele where the rivers Ethiope and Jamieson combine to form the Benin river.

If the ship is favoured then it turns to starboard by the manicured lawns of the general manager's mansion and reaches the wharf adjacent to the factory of African Timber & Plywood Ltd, called AT & P by old coast hands. If that is not the destination then the ship is moored between two buoys in the river and Sparks is lumbered with the duty of 'guard ship' which means he has to keep radio watch for all the ships in port until he is relieved by another ship's arrival.

The keeping of radio watches is necessary within the creeks not only to receive messages from owners and agents but also to keep in touch with other ships on the move. You wouldn't care to meet a ship coming in the other direction at The Fork, for example. It's equally essential to keep a visual lookout within the creeks for logs that have escaped from the beach or holding ponds and, waterlogged, lie just below the surface. Many a bent propeller blade has resulted from such encounters.

Needless to say, movement within the creeks is restricted to daylight hours and this might mean a night spent at anchor in the jungle somewhere. Being miles from the nearest habitation means that flocks of bats, moths and other exotic or just tiresome insects are inevitably attracted to the ship's floodlights, while strange cries, chirps and croaks emanate from the nearby mangroves. Not for long are you left bereft of human company, however.

Word soon gets around and it's the old familiar cries of 'Hello, Joe. Anyting for me? You need any kind business?' emerging from the sultry darkness. The British crew are sitting on the midships accommodation decks, hoping that the mosquitoes will leave them alone to enjoy their beer and tobacco. It's the Africans down aft who will soon have the lines of communication open with the creek people.

A rope ladder allows some of the female company aboard and the usual nautical evening entertainment ensues. By morning all the visitors have disappeared. Everybody aft seems pretty cheerful and it's only later that the chief steward will find out just how many bars of soap, bottles of HP Sauce, bed sheets, bath towels, pillowcases and counterpanes have gone to pay for the crew's sexual athletics night.

The white men will go ashore in Sapele. There's the Ferry Inn, where you can drink tall green bottles of cold Star lager, eat fried snacks of unknown provenance and shake your bottom energetically along with the ladies of the town to the enticing rhythms of high life music.

The ladies are generally comfortably built and will look all the more attractive as the evening progresses. Later on you'll feel guilty as two or three young children are thrown out of the bed on which you will enjoy your nocturnal gymnastics. You'll be even more conscience-stricken when Comfort or Charity or Grace gives you a half-crown rebate from her fee so that you can afford the fare for a black Morris Minor taxi back to the ship. With a bit of luck you'll then get showered and shaved and ready for the day's duties without anybody being able to rib you about your evening's exertions after they saw you leaving the Ferry Inn.

Happy days, but now we must return to our present voyage of recall because, although it's not as dramatic as traversing the true creeks, getting a ship to Calabar is still a stiff test of nautical expertise.

There's no pilot to assist us here; it's all down to the accumulated knowledge of the Old Man and whatever we can provide as his support. When we reach the substantial fairway buoy of the Calabar river, visibility is good enough to make out the slopes of the distant volcanic mountains of Cameroon and Fernando Póo but little can be seen of the shores ahead of us. We've 40 miles to cover and we will be making our way between the splendidly named Tom Shot Bank and its Bakasi Bank neighbour.

We see lines of fishing stakes studding the latter shoal but we're looking for the channel buoys, which are not always in their charted positions. We must hope that our binoculars and our temperamental radar will allow some fixes from the unshifting land.

The situation clearly calls for the use of that staple of the days of sail, the hand lead. Our electric sounding machine is whizzing away on its maximum resolution but it tells us little when the waters are so shallow. Billy is called forward to do his duty.

Standing on a little wooden platform, called the chains, which is mounted on the bulwarks just in front of the bridge, Billy presents a fine figure of a British seaman. Large of girth and short of stature, dressed in faded blue shorts topped by a sparkling white singlet, his balding head is protected from the sun by a piece of headgear that very loosely approximates to a cap. He is accompanied by the Krooboy second headman, who will assist in recovering the lead after it is sent into the muddy waters by Billy's surprisingly agile and accurate throw.

It's a bar lead so he'll be calling feet rather than fathoms and he roars out 'Twenty-two feet' after his first cast. All too soon, it appears, he's finding 19 and then 18 feet and then there's a definite feel of the ship sliding over mud with a fair comber following us astern as we cause the sea to pile up behind us.

I might be feeling apprehensive but the Old Man is impressively unimpressed and then Billy is shouting out figures above 20 feet again. The Old Man calls down for the Bosun to belay sounding for a while and now some better fixes from the land show that we're safely into deeper water. It's not over yet because we have Parrot Flats to cross next and there's Billy back in his pulpit and happily calling out never less than 19 feet. We push on further, the log book fills with some more atmospheric names, Smoke Point, Tobacco Head, Alligator Island and the comforting Seven Fathoms Point.

We blow our whistle loudly as we approach the last place, and a satisfyingly deep echo comes off the trees back to us. Then it's onwards to Duke Town and finally to our berth, which lies directly under the bluff that is capped by the Hope Waddell Mission Church and the Institute of the same name. These buildings are the legacy of one of those grand dames of the Victorian era, the educator and missionary Mary Slessor, who is also buried here after her 40 years of service in Calabar.

The cargo work will not start until the next morning so, after dinner, Dave is the night duty officer, which means that I can join the small party that sets off to see what Calabar has to offer by way of an evening's entertainment.

A battered old taxi grinds to a shuddering halt; the driver says that he can take us the mile or so into downtown Calabar and then act as our 'pilot' but we decline his offer. It's a sweaty stroll in the darkness that is only lit by the guttering candles and hissing gas lamps of a few roadside stalls so we're well pleased to pass through the portals of the New Excelsior Hotel and order the first round of Star lager.

Pretty soon the resident band of Prince Bassey is striking up those foot-tapping and bottom-shuffling rhythms that old Coast hands will never forget. I see from the flyers that his small boy is handing out that his most recent hit is 'Monkey dey Work, Baboon dey Chop', which is a pretty concise description of how most societies operate. It's also a shrewd commentary on how Nigeria's first years of independence are developing. When he comes to play it, the whole crowd take to the dance floor. It's a great piece of music and we thoroughly enjoy showing off to a bevy of the local girls.

We're doing our best impressions of stomping and bottom-grinding to half a dozen in particular and eventually manage to commandeer a table where we can all sit and order some more liquid refreshments. Our new acquaintances will only accept soft drinks; we remain faithful to Star and it turns out that they're all trainee teachers. It also emerges that, like Cinderella, they have a midnight curfew, which rather curtails our evening.

Once they depart it should be the signal to look out for the attentions of some of the other girls but the rain has now started and, as the New Excelsior lacks a roof, dancing under the stars has lost its viability. We decide to leave; more decrepit taxis are waiting outside but we decline the offer to take us to other nightspots in favour of returning to the ship.

The next day it's back to work, which for me means accompanying Don at number two hatch, where we have our last two heavy lifts to discharge. They're both packaged Cochrane boilers weighing nearly 20 tons (or precisely 19 tons, 11 cwt. and 2 qtrs, according to a stencil on the side of the case). They must be brought up from the bottom of the lower hold and then landed onto low-loaders. They're headed for an oil mill upcountry and a British expatriate engineer has joined us to witness their safe arrival.

His job out here, he tells us, is to build a new plant around these two boilers and he sincerely hopes that we've also brought out all the pipework and other fittings that he's expecting. That'll be the tangle of steelwork and wooden cases that now lies in the hatch after the second boiler has been safely lifted ashore.

There's not a lot of other cargo to unload here in Calabar so our attention soon turns to the first of our homeward load and there are two steel lighters already alongside filled with bales of rubber that have been brought downriver.

It's also time to get the ship's social life organised for the coming weekend. At 'smoko' the opinion is split into two camps. The minority view is that we go back to the Excelsior and seek out some guaranteed 'bagging-off' partners. The majority want to meet up with last night's lively sextet again, enjoy some female company and show off our dancing skills. No clear decision is made before we have to get back to work and, for me, that means getting down into two of the 'tweendecks to ensure the rubber cargo is being properly stowed.

A bale of sheet rubber is a rectangular grey lump of about two hundredweight, which owes some of its exterior colour to a coat of talcum powder. More powder has to be applied to each bale as it is stowed in order to prevent the bales sticking to each other and forming one great elephantine mass on our arrival in Avonmouth. It's a dedicated gang at work and they're doing a good job. They're all young lads from way up north, who completely fail to understand my traditional greeting of 'You be de rubber gang?' 'Yes, sah.' 'Well, bounce.'

As the work progresses and the contents of the paper sacks of talcum are generously applied, it is the gang that start to become the white men and take on an almost ghostly appearance. The other rubber gang are loading crepe rubber which is quite different. Here we have three-foot cubes that also weigh two hundredweight but which have a much better shape for making a tidy stow. However, as with the sheet rubber, timber planks (called dunnage) must still be carefully placed to give it some rigidity. If that's not done, then the whole shebang is at risk of shedding bales of rubber down into the lower hold, where they'll do some fair damage to anybody working down there.

Afternoon 'smoko' arrives and, socially, things have been moving fast. Hugo has been up to see the Old Man to persuade him that it'd be a good idea to invite our young ladies from the teacher-training college down to the ship tomorrow evening. He was turned down flat – so much for his future prospects of being suited to high office in the diplomatic service.

Our passengers are expected to return tomorrow from their extended stay in Lagos, pack up their gear and then travel overland to their Cameroons destination. So, Hugo was brutally informed by the Old Man, he did not want them coming back to see the ship's officers holding an orgy on board with a gang of native women. He remained unmoved by Hugo's protestations that this evening was to be essentially a praiseworthy form of promoting good Commonwealth relations.

Our stay in Calabar is not going to lift our wilting voyage spirits and worse is to come. I've just reached the foot of the steel ladder into the number five 'tweendeck when I realise that Don is also down here, accompanied by a very irate European. He turns out to be from the Oban Estates, the shippers of the rubber, and a very prickly Scotsman who is far from satisfied with the state of the stow.

All that bloody timber, it'll put splinters in the rubber, he rants. And there's not enough talc being used and some of these bales are already misshapen because of our sloppy work. Don patiently explains the purpose of the dunnage that we're using and also shows him that Oban's own tally clerk is giving the cargo a clean bill of lading. The man is not to be appeased and he storms off up on deck. Don lets him go but needs to work off his frustration by telling me to keep a closer eye on things.

I defend my corner and he eventually concedes that the man is a prick. It's all to do with the war, he says. When the rubber estates in Malaya were lost to the Japanese invasion, West Africa became our main source of supply. The shippers here in Nigeria gained an advantage that they were reluctant to lose in peacetime. They continued to demand a level of care and attention from the West African carriers that no other rubber exporter in the world enjoyed. That's the way it is and we have to live with it, so do whatever possible to shut the awkward little bugger up, he lamely concludes.

Come the evening and we're all back ashore again. The New Excelsior is still jumping to the sounds of Prince Bassey but our girls are not there, although we're not short of female company. So we jump about, down our icy lagers and generally enjoy ourselves under the stars but, for Hugo at least, it's clearly not the same thing. Is it true love denied? Who knows, but he's not going to be bagging off tonight with any of the more pliable girls that we're currently entertaining. So, soon after midnight, he's ready to leave and I join him. I might have stayed with the others to enjoy the usual end to such an excursion but I need to preserve my strength for that little Scots martinet when he returns to the ship tomorrow.

But he never shows, unlike the rain which visits us on and off throughout the day. We get into a repeated routine of tenting the hatches and drawing the metal covers over the lighters carrying the rubber. Loading wet bales of rubber is inviting real trouble with stickiness in the stow. There is some sawn timber and a few logs on offer and we could have worked them but they've failed to appear. We do manage to complete the unloading of all our inward cargo so, come evening, all I've got to hand on to Dave is the outstanding hundred tons or so of rubber for the two hatches. The rain is easing as darkness falls so, with a bit of luck, it'll be a short night for him.

Our passengers arrive back on board after their long overland journey and a farewell dinner has been arranged for them. Only the senior officers are invited but this will be followed by a film show open to all. Nobody seems to be in the mood for the New Excelsior again.

Pete tells me that Dougie has been in the shower three times already today scrubbing away at his genitals, using a Board-of-Trade-prescribed prophylactic after last night's excursion. They're both going to have an early night to compensate and Hugo has a single beer with me in my cabin before following the same plan. I can't be bothered with watching the film and also turn in early. Our stay in Calabar is coming to a very muted and unsatisfactory conclusion.

It's nearly seven the next morning when I hear Dave hammering on my cabin door. I open it and stand there, bollock-naked and trying to understand where I am and what's going on. Dave tells me that there was a steady heavy drizzle for most of the night and so he's handing an almost unchanged situation back to me but the labour have at least covered the hatches properly. Although there's only a hundred tons left to load, we can't leave Calabar as that would mean split bills of lading so we're a hostage to the weather.

At least I can enjoy my breakfast in peace in the saloon because there are no hatch tents to tend or vulnerable cargoes to watch. Meanwhile, the dockers find what shelter they can around the ship until the rain eases. The morning drags on as I can't get on with anything else. I can't even sit in my cabin and read a book or do my dhobi because Don or the Old Man will be hollering for action the moment the rain stops. It's just past morning 'smoko' when an agency clerk comes on board with some very welcome mail and I get another letter from home.

Before I get a chance to read it, up comes Don and tells me that our call at Douala is now back on. We're not going to Lobito but we're loading in Douala then going down to the Congo followed by Pointe Noire, Port Gentil, Abidjan, Freetown and Bathurst. I'm to tell the bosun to get the Krooboys down on number two 'tweendeck and dismantle the Berlin Wall around the Guinness stow. And he wants the rest of the rubber flying on board no later than ten minutes after the last drop of rain falls.

Now I can hear voices calling from somewhere on the offside of the ship so I go to investigate. A small motor launch is trying to get a raft of about twenty obeche logs alongside and is calling for some securing lines from us. I'd better check with Don before doing anything about this and so I call by his cabin, where he's in conversation with the agency clerk.

They both come out on deck and the clerk tells the launch skipper that we're not taking his consignment as its booking has been cancelled. The boat's crew soon put up a vigorous chorus of complaint about this: 'Why for dis trouble, wey dey no go tell we before we go pass dis wok? Too much wahalla, dis people, wey dey no get sense for we.'

Suddenly we're all aware that the rain has actually stopped so it's up to me, Pete and Dougie to get our two gangs mustered and the hatches opened. That done, there's more palaver with the overside rubber gangs, who insist that it's still too wet to start loading their precious cargo. All we need now is that little sod from yesterday putting his oar in again and my cup really will runneth over.

No irate Scotsman reappears, the lighter covers are eventually rolled back and the rubber boys set to with a will. The launch with his unwanted raft of logs is still stubbornly in the offing and very soon I'm told to get the logs secured alongside amidships. Another clerk has come on board from the agency and it transpires that, because we'll be too late to get to the fairway buoy before dark, we're in for another night alongside. It has been agreed that these logs and some sawn timber that's in a nearby go-down will be shipped after all and two night gangs have been booked for the task.

Sure enough, the rubber is all loaded just before dark and the apprentices and I set up the lights and ensure that the two cargo spaces are ready for the night gangs. Then I tell them the bad news. With the Guinness stow exposed again it'll be necessary to watch it while the logs are being loaded in the lower hold. More are yet to arrive but they'll only amount to about 50 in all so it'll not be an all-night job. I leave them to decide how they'll carve that duty up and go and put grumpy Dave in the picture.

He considers himself to be the world authority on loading logs but, like all great artistes, must have his stage fully prepared by others. Have I done this? Have I got that/ them out ready? Yes, yes, yes, I reply, and get off to eat my dinner in the duty mess and then get showered and changed and escape from all that fuss about twenty relatively tiny logs, each one under five tons in weight.

I need to get along to the passenger bar as the ship's officers are hosting a quickly organised unofficial farewell to our passengers, who are extremely happy that they, and their precious diesel generator, will soon be going ashore in Douala as planned. We might have been denied our original party yesterday but this turns out to be a splendid substitute. Our six Irish priests have been part of the ship's company for a few weeks now and we've all enjoyed their presence on board. It has also been quite apparent that they've enjoyed their sea experience in equal measure.

By way of a departure present they sing us some songs. We've never heard them rehearsing this repertoire on board so either they're all natural musicians or they've spent their time in Lagos honing their performance. If so, then I'm sure their hosts there took as much pleasure as we did in hearing their evocative rendering of 'When Irish Eyes are Smiling' but what was their reaction to a powerfully delivered 'What shall we do with the Drunken Sailor?' A great Sunday evening for us on board, but I'm not the only one to wonder where the next Sabbath will find these genial men.

There are therefore quite a few moderately sore heads on parade the next morning as we leave the Calabar river and head out over the muddy flats, where Billy reprises his virtuoso role with the bar lead. No problems are experienced as we're very little heavier than when we came in. Out to sea, we point ourselves south-east again and head for another fairway buoy and the channels up another shallow muddy inlet. This time it's the Rivière Wouri and we're tied up in Douala before dark. There's a white minibus waiting on the quay to whisk our passengers away to Customs and an overnight stay before their long journey north. They file carefully down the gangway, resplendent in their long white soutanes, waving their farewells to us.

I hope that they enjoy a welcome at their destination that is rather warmer than the one we're receiving here from the port officials. It's not so long since a plebiscite returned the southern part of what was formerly the trust territory of British Cameroons (the legacy of it originally being a German colony) to the republic that replaced the French possession of the rest of Cameroun. There are still strong feelings here that the British took far too long in allowing a reunion of brothers and sisters in a new nation. Strangely, when we visit the tiny ports of Victoria and Tiko we meet no such animosity despite the fact that they lie within the area that was handed over to Cameroun.

Fortunately we have the latest version of the national flag flying as a courtesy ensign, the one bearing a couple of additional stars to celebrate the reunion and only very recently introduced. That happily removes the opportunity to levy a fine for such a grave insult to the nation as flying an obsolete flag. These are the complications that accompany the dismantling of colonial empires and the sensibilities of the new nations that have succeeded them.

There's some benefit to us. Our cargo is considered to be too attractive to the local thieving community to be discharged overnight so we'll begin work on it in the morning. This means another welcome night in port but, after last night's celebrations, most of us opt for the opportunity of a nice long sleep. The next day we unload the Guinness and now only very little cargo remains on board. We are of course also scheduled to load here and the agency is offering us 200 tons of cotton for Liverpool.

It appears in the form of huge 400 kilogram bales that, although well pressed, are already a bit ragged at their ends following their long rail journey down from Tchad. These ragged areas are going to be a permanent fire hazard so we try and load the bales so that only their hessian-covered sides are presenting and then push in plywood sheets to cover the exposed cotton filaments. After that, we'll just have to put up 'No Smoking' signs and then watch out for sly smokers in the vicinity. Cotton and rubber, after all, are fine ingredients for a serious conflagration.

The gang loading the cotton are from the north of the country, lean young men selected for their strength and ready acceptance of sustained hard labour. The gang discharging the Guinness are just the opposite, stroppy and truculent and throwing the wooden cases around rather than carrying them to the cargo slings. There's no sign of any stevedore supervisors since the fleeting visit of a solitary Frenchman on our arrival the previous evening.

I can sense the gang's hostility and decide to tread carefully; maybe I can use my creaking French to moderate their behaviour? So I plead, *'Messieurs! Doucement, doucement. Avec soin, s'il vous plaît. Ne cassez pas les bouteilles dedans!'* My effort, however, is overriden by Don, who is roaring from the deck above 'Oi, you clumsy bush bastards! Make you take time with dis load or I come down dere quick quick and go beat you proper one time! You savvee?' It's amazing what authority comes from having twenty years' additional age, almost twice the waistline and three times the number of gold bars on the epaulettes.

Hostility to the British apparently doesn't extend to the port's hawkers, who've set up shop in the offside maindeck alleyway. I stroll by, inspecting their wares. The woodcarvings are crudely realised and you can smell the stain or the shoe polish from the 'mahogany' or 'ebony' pieces. One man is selling pictures fashioned from butterfly wings. They're quite attractive as we know little as yet about endangered species. Another man is selling pictures of African village life using minimal strokes of bright colours on black cartridge paper, which are even more attractive. But I have no walls at home to host these items and so I pass on.

We leave Douala in the late afternoon and once we're safely clear of the outer fairway buoy we set our course close to due south and towards the Equator. There's spectacular lightning on display after dark as we pass between Fernando Póo and the mainland. This, I remember from my meteorology textbook, is the area of the Intertropical Convergence Zone, where the air masses of both hemispheres collide and generate the rainy season that moves up and down the Coast throughout the year.

This is not an ordinary thunderstorm, this is sheer atmospheric exhibitionism. Thick columns of blue-white lightning that blind the retina momentarily, globes of ball lightning rushing in all directions and forked lightning that fills the sky with its veinous tracks. Yet, strangely, not a clap of thunder is to be heard or a drop of rain to be felt. But there's just that slight whiff of sulphur joining the smell of the mainland's jungle on the light breeze.

'Look what I've laid on for you,' I tell Dave as he grizzles into his mug of tea in the chartroom just after midnight. 'Thanks a bunch,' he replies, 'It'll be pissing down any minute and you've not got the bloody radar on yet.' I complete the handover and go down two decks where I join Terry, the fourth engineer, who is fresh up from the engine-room and we enjoy this spectacular show as we down our customary beers.

Normally we would enjoy this regular ritual, of post-watch gossip and mutual griping about those on board who are set over us, in one or the other of our cabins. However, this spectacular evening deserves to be enjoyed from the passenger deck veranda while reclining in steamer chairs. Before too long, however, Dave is proved right; we hear thunder and then feel and see the rain. It's soon sheeting down, gradually invading our sanctum even as it performs the welcome service of tempering the heat of the night. It's time to toss the empties overside and then head off for a quick shower and then to bed.

The Equator is crossed the next day, without any ceremony. To sustain the rituals of 'Crossing the Line' calls for a good deal of organisation and just isn't feasible on the

West African run. It's different if the crossing between hemispheres occurs during a long ocean passage when the whole business acts as a welcome antidote to some general tedium. But here we're just between another couple of ports.

My talkative watchkeeper, Bassey, has wangled his way back onto my 8–12 watch and puts me in the picture about our forward itinerary. Not going to Angola is a good thing as he is prevented from going ashore there by the Portuguese colonial authorities.

Going up the Congo is quite the opposite as, 'Dat Matadi be too good place to buy any kind beef', which translates as his opportunity to do some trading in exotic species, dead or alive. I get some detailed market intelligence on what is most worth dealing in and am informed that Bassey's target this trip will be snake and crocodile skins in Matadi to take to his 'cousin' in Manchester. Had we been going to New York, of course, he would be thinking big, maybe a chimpanzee or two ('Dat monkey wey get face of mortal man' is his striking description of the animal) and a potential windfall of several hundred dollars.

His extended discourse has naturally let his steering go to pot and so I have to sharply correct him, then go out to the bridge wing and see if his deviation is bad enough to be noticeable to anybody studying our wake. It's coming up for noon anyway and it looks as though our sextants will be required to confirm our southern latitude. After lunch, and before sunshine or siesta, I'll just have a quick look at my washbasin, maybe, and see in what direction the water circulates as it empties. On second thoughts, maybe not, as I don't actually know in the first place what direction it takes in the northern hemisphere.

7

Adventures south of the Equator

British influence in West Africa was barely apparent south of the Equator, but here we were aware of the colonial adventures of other European nations. British exports to these territories were minimal so we mainly came to a small number of ports to bring home the primary produce of Africa, principally timber and minerals.

Angola

Angola is a large country which was in the possession of the Portuguese (save a very brief Dutch occupation) since Diogo Cão brought it to European attention while seeking a sea route to the East Indies. The promenade around the bay at Luanda had monuments to this heritage and it was backed by an array of buildings ranging from a great medieval castle to impressive commercial and administrative structures.

This was a bold facade for the capital of what was a largely underdeveloped country. Portugal sent out poor emigrants seeking their fortunes and it also made the country a captive market for Portuguese goods. However, it provided little capital for investment. It was the mineral wealth of the interior, principally copper from Northern Rhodesia sent to the coast by rail that encouraged British ships to call. Revolution and then political reform in Portugal during the 1970s preceded an uneasy Angolan independence. A bitter civil war followed, which brought even that limited contact to an end.

Congo

Another huge country and one that seems doomed to fulfil the epithet 'Heart of Darkness' bestowed upon it by Joseph Conrad. Congo was originally conceived as a vast private estate for Leopold II, the King of Belgium. It was the exposure (principally by Roger Casement and Edmund Morel) of the cruelty meted out to its indigenous population as a result of its plantation for rubber that eventually led to its effective nationalisation.

Even so, it retained its reputation for ill-treatment of native labour, and the hasty departure of the colonial power led to the secession of the resource-rich province of

Katanga soon after independence in 1960. That rebellion was ended in 1963, but the presidency of Joseph-Désiré Mobutu gradually converted the country (called Zaire between 1971 and 1997) into yet another private estate that descended into further anarchy following his downfall and flight.

The name Congo has been restored but the country still suffers from a very fragile stability and a continuing reputation for internal cruelty and violence. Our contact with the vastness of the country was limited to calling at the ports of Boma and Matadi. A glance at any atlas illustrates how minimal this acquaintance was.

Gabon

Despite the fact that this one-party state has been under the personal rule of President Omar Bongo since 1967, Gabon receives little interest from the rest of the world. It has enjoyed prosperity for some and considerable foreign investment because of its large oil revenues and its small population.

Before oil, it was the wealth of the rainforest that attracted foreign commercial attention. The large plywood factory at Port Gentil and the huge rafts of logs that floated down the River Ogooué were symbols of this as early as the inter-war years. Ships of many nations carried these tropical logs to nearly every country in Europe and to North America, and the trade never appeared other than sustainable.

With hindsight, we know that we were aiding the degradation of the planet. However, we were no more culpable of this, at the time, than were the coalminers of Europe for aiding the phenomenon of global warming. It was the economic way of the world in the central decades of the 20th century.

We become aware of the Congo while still far from its mouth. The deep blue of the South Atlantic Ocean gradually becomes more and more discoloured with the debris from Africa's second-greatest river. The waters that wash down the sides of the ship attain the colour of Brown Windsor soup and are decorated with increasingly large clumps of matted vegetation.

The chart shows us that this mighty river has gouged a canyon several thousand feet in depth into the ocean's floor. This feature is our guide to making the necessary turn to port from our current southerly course that will take us towards the river's entrance. It's a morning of hazy sunshine and the coast hereabouts is low-lying, so it's a matter of hoping that we can soon catch sight of some landmark and then obtain a distance off with the help of radar echoes.

Once we've agreed on a reliable position and know the distance that we still have to run, I'm told to call up Banana pilot station on the VHF. As I attempt to raise a response, I'm also aware of the Old Man muttering behind me that my repeated request for 'Banana pilot' will probably produce just that, a tasty yellow fruit: 'The last bugger, a banana would have been more use to me. Bloody Belgians, they all just cleared out, and look at the riff-raff that call themselves pilots now.'

His gloomy predictions are to prove false since, as the ship stands off the low headland of Pointe Française with its numerous radio masts, a smart white launch comes racing out to meet us. I'm sweating freely due to the morning's rising humidity as I greet an immaculately attired and cool-looking pilot who is one of the few Belgians still serving this erstwhile colony of his country.

On the bridge, he wastes no time in ordering full ahead on the engines, raps out the course to the helmsman and briskly tells the Old Man, 'Good morning, Captain, now I take you to Boma port.' Before the Old Man can splutter his response, he hands him a telegram envelope, 'It is something from your agent; it explains everything.'

By now the mate is also up on the bridge and the Old Man, having read the telegram, says to Don, 'Here, listen to this bloody lot,' and reads out the message. 'Now uncalling Matadi stop transhipall loadall offering Boma stop Lobito advise 1500 copper Liverpool reverting stop.' Don harrumphs and says, 'Bloody multi-million-pound shipping company, saving five bob on a telegram and we're none the wiser as to what they're up to here.' The pilot helpfully intervenes to explain that Matadi is congested, a combination of troubles in the port and on the railway system meaning labour shortages and full transit sheds. So it's all change once again, more 'wawa'.

As we sail up the narrowing but still-broad Congo estuary, the latest news has gone around the ship with commendable speed. Our African crew will not be pleased with the possibility of a restored call at Lobito as they know that they'll be denied shore leave by the Angolan authorities, but the rest of us will be quite happy to visit there. It's an attractive little place with a very welcome European ambience to it. We naturally choose to ignore the cruel reality underneath the surface. But now we need to prepare to go alongside at Boma in a couple of hours' time.

It's an attractively scenic journey. The flat and featureless coast gradually gives way to a country of low, wooded hills and the river's debris becomes also more picturesque and interesting. Here are substantial islets of vegetation, some of them hosting flocks of white egrets whilst others are laying siege to the red-and-black buoys that are supposed to be marking the navigable channel.

Dave comes onto the bridge at midday and this allows me to get my lunch and then return as we come up to the landmark of Fetish Rock, a prominent ironstone monolith. The steward arrives to clear away the remains of a lunch that the Old Man and pilot have enjoyed on the bridge and then it's time to call everybody to harbour stations.

Off the unoccupied wharf at Boma, we let go our starboard anchor, which controls the rate at which we drift down onto the quay, and soon all is smoothly secured. The usual rabble of tribute collectors swarms up the gangway followed by our agent, a Congolese, and a young German who I recall from a previous visit is the stevedore supervisor. There's no sign of any other activity on the dockside and I soon learn from Dave that work will start the following morning.

Apparently we will not be able to unload any Matadi cargo of value or of a hazardous nature but the mails will be taken off. So those big white canvas bags of diplomatic mails that we loaded all those weeks back in Liverpool will get away to ensure that our Léopoldville embassy will soon have a fresh supply of breakfast marmalade and Gentleman's Relish.

An evening ashore is in prospect save for a couple of problems. The agent didn't bring any money down with him for us to draw and this admittedly pretty little former capital of the Belgian Congo also lacks any night-life that is accessible on foot from the port. The voyage's ration of just four films is exhausted and we're reaching that stage of the voyage where we've generally had enough of the coast and want to start heading for home.

As a result, it's a subdued evening of cabin drinking that peters out before midnight. I come out on deck very early the next morning to enjoy the freshness of an African dawn and to savour the day's stillness before the usual hell breaks loose. At the end of the promenade deck I find Tommy, along with two of the engineers, Eric and Terry, making a little cluster of near-white boilersuits and all nursing the statutory cigarettes and mugs of strong tea.

'I wouldn't mind if I never saw a nig-nog ever again,' Eric gloomily observes to no-one in particular and looks over the side at those few Africans we can see sitting with their backs against the wall of the shed. 'Look at that bloody monkey,' agrees Terry, pointing to one of the labourers, who was on his feet and had strolled across to the ship's side in order to urinate copiously against it, 'a right dirty black bastard.'

'Well,' says Tommy, 'who are we to complain, we drop all our crap on the wharf wherever we go. Just because we actually do the business out of sight doesn't make us any better.'

This is referring to the fact that our ship, lacking any on-board sewage treatment facilities, does empty all its waste water directly overside. 'Spoken like a true socialist and a brother to all men,' replies Eric even more gloomily, 'but I still reckon independence is wasted on these buggers. Wait until we get to Lobito, the old Portugooses have the right attitude to that sort of crap.'

'What d'you reckon, mate?' he says, bringing me into the discussion. It's far too early in the day for a contentious debate so I neatly avoid the issue by saying, fairly truthfully, that all Africans coming up the gangway are entitled to be treated decently until such time as they start pestering me for soap and cigarettes, start stealing the cargo or the ship's fittings, start wrecking the cargo gear or crap in the 'tweendecks.

'So,' Eric notes with a careful parting shot, 'it'll all be sweetness and light for the first five minutes then, typical bloody mate,' to which the only riposte can be 'Why don't you come out on deck and find out, instead of hiding down that engine-room and pretending to be working hard?' Which comment encapsulates the external black–white and internal deck–engine relationships at this social nadir of the voyage.

The German stevedore supervisor comes to me just before the two gangs of labour board at 0630 and says how pleased he is at our arrival because there are cargoes of sawn timber, rubber and plywood for Avonmouth that he's been trying to get shipped out for several weeks now.

In return, he'll take as much Matadi cargo as possible but explains that any valuable items just don't have a hope of surviving intact ashore for long. The army will convey the mails direct to Léopoldville, which is why they can be landed safely. Diplomatically, he didn't indicate why the military couldn't also be used to guard the cases of whisky and the bales of textiles.

Don has given me a rough plan of the cargo stowages that he's worked out and I send the two apprentices off to remove the padlocks that secure the locking bars to numbers three, four and five hatches. We'll start with rubber at the first of these spaces, then load the timber and plywood elsewhere after landing some drums and cases of Matadi cargo.

The rubber is scruffy stuff and won't require the delicate treatment that was demanded by our peppery Scottish friend up in Calabar. 'Stack it up with some timber between the tiers and dust liberally with talcum powder' are my orders. The sawn timber is in the form of loose planks which can be tightly stowed in their designated space but the plywood turns out to be a bit of a problem.

It's very well presented in packs that smell sweetly of their constituent timbers but, at eight feet long and four feet wide and weighing a ton apiece they cannot be handled manually and we have no spaces available into which they can be directly landed. They'll have to be handled on board by a forklift truck and that means considerable palaver.

The stevedore says that the truck that is normally used on board is out of service and the only one available is the usual quayside model that cannot be broken into two parts (body and counterweight) for ease of lifting aboard. So, out come the Krooboys to rig a swinging derrick at number four once the Matadi cargo has been unloaded. Our Nigerian sailors are taking advantage of the lack of cargo work up forward to get stages rigged for painting the bow, a business that benefits from some peace and quiet around the area of the forecastle and number one hatch.

While this is going on I'm approached by Pete and Dougie, who tell me that it has been agreed by my seniors that if I can manage the deck myself this afternoon they can go ashore. It appears to be a done deal so I can hardly deny them but I ask what are they going to use for money? Apparently good old Hugo, being the well-found gentleman that he is, has some metropolitan French francs in his possession and they've been told that they're widely accepted ashore.

The derrick is rigged, the forklift truck is swung aboard and some steel sheets laid over our wooden 'tweendeck hatchboards for their protection. After more derrick work by the Krooboys the first packs of plywood are hoisted off the quay and brought aboard. Belching copious black smoke, the machine does its job of carrying the cargo into the sides of the 'tweendeck and a smart-looking stow of plywood begins to take shape.

All is proceeding smoothly and the day has definitely taken a turn for the better. Lunch is eaten in peace, I've only been tapped a very few times for a fag or any other 'dash' so, when work resumes, I can even muster a cheery wave as our intrepid trio head off ashore to sample what daytime Boma has to offer.

Cargo work finishes at the very civilised hour of 1830 and Dave graciously takes over for the last hour so that I can get cleaned up for my dinner in the saloon. After the meal, the two of us are leaning over the rails on the promenade deck and enjoying a smoke as the tropical night descends when we spy our gallant trio of youngsters heading back to the ship. Others have also seen them so there's a good deal of good-natured ribbing of them as they come up the gangway. Later on I catch up with Hugo to hear how their excursion went; it turns out to be an interesting tale.

To start with, they were given a lift up to the administrative area of the town on a low hill overlooking the port. It was very picturesque with its elegant colonial-era buildings and broad avenues lined with flame trees, resplendent in their bright red floral display. But, critically, quite bereft of places of refreshment for our thirsty adventurers.

They then came across a young Belgian who lived nearby and invited them to take a beer at home with him. He agreed that the town was pretty dead but his job working on an aid project designed to improve the local bureaucracy gave him plenty of free afternoons, so he had few complaints about Boma.

He invited them to take a run with him out to a nearby beach for a swim. As our jolly jacks had no kit with them for such an excursion they initially declined. Their new friend, however, told them that the beach would be deserted so they could skinny-dip in peace.

Once there, Hugo went on, they found it was the stock tropical idyll of a smooth, sandy beach backed by dipping palms and quite free of any people. True, the water was murky rather than sparkling but that didn't spoil the aquatic activity. It was only after a while that their host began to lightly hint about what might make a further pleasurable activity for them all and it involved some mutual masturbation.

This, Hugo dryly observed, was a suggestion that anybody with experience of an English boarding-school would recognise as a frequently enjoyable way to waste a rainy Sunday winter afternoon. Unfortunately neither Pete nor Dougie seemed to be enamoured of the idea as being a quite normal masculine sexual release valve.

Eventually they worked out a compromise that served to repay their host's generosity. The three of them disported themselves in a number of naked poses on the sand while he fully enjoyed the sight by pleasuring himself as he stretched out on his towel. Then they packed up and drove back to the ship in a rather embarrassed silence. It had been, said Hugo, with an almost ambassadorial air, quite interesting to have had this insight into the work of Belgian development aid to their former colony.

We leave Boma the following afternoon and continue south towards Lobito, some 700-odd miles below the Equator and the normal limit of our voyaging along this coast. Beyond Lobito it is principally desert. This is the notorious 'Skeleton Coast' and contains only the fishy-smelling port of Walvis Bay before Cape Town.

The port of Lobito is close to the larger city of Benguela and is the ocean terminus of the famous railway that bears that name. This is a route that crosses the continent and brings out the minerals of Katanga, where a secession has recently ended, along with those of Northern Rhodesia, soon to achieve its independence as Zambia.

The sea watches for the sailors have changed again and, in the quiet of the last hour of my evening spell on the bridge, the helmsman offers his opinion on our destination. 'Ginger' Harrison, so-called by all on board because he sports a fine head of coppery hair streaked with grey, was born in Liberia but is now a Nigerian citizen. He probably went away to sea before anybody else on this ship, certainly before many of us were even born. 'Dis Angola be very bad place for we,' he opines, 'Dis Portugee man, he never go treat we proper, he go beat we, he no go give we proper money, he no go savee we Africa people at all. Tcchh!'

It's a succinct commentary on the current situation but things must have been more relaxed in the past because his final remark is 'Ah, one time wey dis place get plenty sweet mammy. Now we no get chance for go ashore nor anyting. Make we no stay dis place long time, make we go back Matadi or any kind place where Africa man get chance.'

I know that he speaks the truth about the Portuguese presence in Angola. Nevertheless, like most of the British on board, I'll just enjoy being in a port where things go on with minimum hassle, very little petty corruption and where I'll have the chance to walk ashore in a town with properly paved streets. I can find a verandah hung with flowering baskets and there I can eat a decent meal and enjoy a bottle or two of passable wine. That was my last visit. Will this call allow me to do the same?

In the afternoon I join the little band of sun-worshippers on deck and we snore and grill peacefully despite the din emanating from the foredeck where the Krooboys are continuing their assault on the ship's ample rust. We're all used to hearing the steady tap of their ordinary chipping hammers around the ship as they tackle the old enemy in between their sundry other duties but now scaling the foredeck needs the mechanical hammers to be brought into use.

These consist of a set of 18 small flat steel 'leaves' that are mounted on the end of a heavy drive shaft connected to an electric motor and which rotate at high speed. Two or three of these 'windy hammers' soon make a considerable impact on the rustiest of steel plates although hand hammers are used to trim up the awkward corners or to remove the loosest scale.

This is the one time during the voyage when the main deck can be easily tackled. All the outward cargo has gone and there's still time before a cargo of logs covers it for the homeward journey. Sadly, once the deck is scaled, primed and painted its usual shiny black, it will immediately start its journey back to rust once we are landing steel hatch beams and scattering wooden hatchboards across it. But it will have enjoyed its brief moment of elegance.

Early in my evening watch, a mass of bright lights appears on the port quarter and has drawn abeam by midnight when Dave relieves me on the bridge. It's either the Portuguese or the Belgian mailboat that's come out of Luanda and is now headed towards Lobito like us. She'll get priority, of course, but not, we hope, the last berth.

The next morning gets off to a very civilised start. I've had time to eat my breakfast in the saloon before going out on deck to greet the pilot and escort him to the bridge.

We're soon gliding past the narrow sandy spit that protects the bay and which is lined with elegant bungalows and sparkling white official buildings.

The mailboat is now berthed at the quay at the head of this spit. She's one of the Compagnie Maritime Belge's trio of attractive liners, and we take up a berth at right-angles to her. A perfect arrival is completed by the agent bringing an impressive amount of mail on board with him and the welcome news that work will not begin until 2 p.m. when the dockers return from their very generous two-hour lunch break.

Part of our cargo of copper ingots is already visible alongside, stacked neatly on a line of railway wagons and ready to be lifted aboard by the quayside cranes. The sailors have plenty of time to swing our derricks out of the way at the two hatches that will be worked and then the bosun takes advantage of this peaceful interlude to have a small gang down on the quay with paint-rollers attached to long bamboos to freshen up the black paint of the ship's side.

We've 1,600 tons of cargo to load; that's a good contribution towards the 5,500 tons we expect to take home and most of it just needs to be plonked down in the bottom of our two main holds. Some of it will have be loaded to the 'tweendecks as otherwise the ship will be too 'stiff' or bottom-heavy and thus be prone to violent rolling in a heavy sea.

There'll be no evening work done and we expect to sail late tomorrow afternoon so it looks as though it'll be an easy stay with the prospect of a stroll up the road if Dave agrees to keep ship tonight.

A wailing siren announces the hour of 2 p.m. and, as the two Portuguese crane drivers climb up to their eyries, two other Portuguese stevedores lead a party of African dockers up the gangway. They're wearing a kind of uniform consisting of khaki shorts and dark blue singlets bearing a white RP monogram. Rumour has it that they're all prisoners of some kind and they certainly appear quiet and almost sullen in comparison with the gangs that we've met elsewhere on the coast.

I'm certainly not brave or discourteous enough to inquire about their status. In fact I'm just grateful that nobody will be cadging cigarettes, food or water from me and that I can leave the usual palaver of stowing cargo to the Portuguese overseers.

The copper comes as cigar-shaped ingots, but flat-bottomed, each weighing around a couple of hundredweight. They're a dull shade of reddish black in colour but the occasional score marks reveal the gleaming pure metal beneath this surface patina. The crane lifts one stack of about 20 ingots at a time off the railway wagons and lowers it accurately into the bottom of the hold. Once it's safely landed, two dockers unhook the crane wire and, using short wooden poles which have a wire and a loop at one end, pick up a single ingot and take it over to the stow.

We'll be putting about a thousand tons in number two and then the balance in number four lower hold. It's a splendid cargo for the latter place, one of the most awkward cargo spaces in the ship. This is because, you will recall, the propeller shaft runs in a steel tunnel along the bottom of both it and number five lower hold. This means that on each side there is a space that narrows as it is gradually constrained by the tapering shape of the hull towards the stern. Copper ingots waste no valuable space as would logs or timber, neither will they split open and release their contents while they're being swung into these places as might be the case with hessian bags.

We could probably have loaded this amount of cargo by the following morning were it not for the fact that a steady supply of copper alongside is not feasible. That's because of the complicated shunting operations needed after each rail wagon is emptied. In fact work stops completely just after five when the shunter disappears with a rake of empty wagons and makes no sign of reappearing. The crane drivers come down onto the quay and amble off and then all the African dockworkers follow at a respectful interval, conveniently forgetting to close up the hatches after them.

Once again, our faithful Krooboys step into the breach and we're all secured on deck well before six. Time for a wash and brush up and then to join the party that is skipping dinner on board in favour of finding a change of menu ashore.

Don has conveniently agreed to keep ship, provided that one of us is back on board by midnight. That means I don't have to ingratiate myself with Dave to enjoy this stroll ashore. Naturally a bar is our first destination and we're soon looking at a table-full of nine well-chilled beers and deciding on the evening's programme. We're lucky that Eric proves to be an old Brazil hand and therefore has some knowledge of vital Portuguese words connected with food and drink.

After a second round of beers, the decision is made to make for a nearby restaurant and Eric's vocabulary is soon put to the test as he interprets the menu for the rest of us. We start with generous helpings of prawns that have been dressed in a spicy hot sauce and then, apart from two conservatives who just want the local resemblance to steak and chips, we address ourselves to some fish dishes.

This will be an education for me as the only connection I know that combines fish and Portugal is that standard Merchant Navy dish called 'cod Portugaise'. That recipe marries a lot of tomato to the fish ingredient and my personal view is still that a tomato should never be allowed an exit visa from its natural home in a salad bowl.

This evening, with expert help from our waiter, we enjoy an exceptional meal. It's accompanied by several bottles of wine and the novelty of looking out to sea from under a flowery canopy. It's noticeable also that we are surrounded only by European faces, even those of the waiting staff, for the first time this voyage. In retrospect, that's a racist observation, but the enjoyment of the evening actually owes far more to the fact that we all feel that we're doing one of the things that we came to sea to do. We're enjoying a place that we could never have visited had we been responsible for paying the cost of travelling there.

The next morning it's clear that someone in the marshalling yard has been spoken to as our two cranes are picking up slings of copper with no delay from a continuous file of rail wagons. At this rate we'll be all finished by mid-afternoon. Naturally this perfection soon begins to fray as the crane at number four fails to lift a sling and just utters a series of clunks from within its body.

I go to find the stevedore supervisor and I see him in earnest conversation with Don and someone from the agency. Before I can impart my bad news, Don tells me to get a tape measure and go down number five 'tweendeck and see what space is available in the fore-end, 'I'm looking for about five thousand cube,' he adds, but gives no further clue as to what's up.

Hugo is loitering at the end of the promenade deck as I head aft with the tape and a torch and willingly accepts my invitation to help with this latest job. 'I know what this is about,' he smugly tells me as we open up the trap hatch to get access, 'I heard the agency chap saying that there was some extra cargo on offer but Don wasn't very happy, something about it being for another port.'

It isn't too sweaty down below and our measuring, in a pungent atmosphere of rubber fumes, is soon complete. I go up to Don's cabin and tell him that I can only measure just under four thousand cubic feet in usable space where he's indicated. However, we could extend that if we used some space that is still available in the two wing sides of the 'tweendeck.

Back on deck, the moribund crane has been resurrected and the copper is flying on board again. Then I see a lorry coming around the end of the dock shed and stop, looking for some opportunity to get closer to our ship. It's loaded with some large white bales and, while I'm watching its arrival, Don has come up to me and says, 'There's 50 tons of eucalyptus pulp on offer, so get number five open and let's see if your measuring is any good.'

I ask Billy to do the honours and set the derricks to work the forward end of the hatch while I go up on the poop and try to see what this mysterious pulp cargo is all about. From what I can spy, the bales look to be of a size that can be manhandled into the space that I've measured without the palaver of getting a forklift on board.

Interestingly, I also see that both Don and the Old Man are heading towards the lorry with the agency clerk and another Portuguese man. From my vantage point I can soon see a lot of arm-waving and pointing at the bales. I should get back to seeing how the work is going on at number two hatch but this is far more interesting.

Then I spot Dougie and send him up there to do my duty and report back while I continue with my snooping. Now there's an African bloke up on the lorry with what looks like a pot of white paint and he appears to be blanking out some shipping marks on one of the bales of pulp. This is all fascinating stuff but I must get on with my proper work.

Just as well, because I see Don and the Old Man coming back on board and they're both looking extremely out of sorts. The agency clerk is giving them plenty of leeway before he steps on to the gangway. Of course I'm not going to hear the story directly from them as I'm too far down the chain of command for that. My faithful inside informant doesn't let me down and briefs us all at the lunch break.

This eucalyptus pulp (used in making security paper like banknotes, he loftily informs us) was for Leith but the shipper agreed to have it taken by us to Liverpool and the bill of lading would be amended. He also agreed to have the bales re-marked but, when Don and the Old Man went down to see the first consignment it was clearly marked for a consignee in Philadelphia.

This was too much 'wawa' and, despite the attendance of the whitewash man that I'd observed, they both decided that the bales weren't coming aboard despite any concession allegedly made by the shippers.

With all the copper loaded by three, an hour later we are bidding farewell to this very pleasant little harbour. For the first time this trip, we're heading north and thus properly homewards at last. Retracing our outward passage all the way back to the mouth of the Congo, we pass Boma at full speed this time. We continue up a river that, with its hilly well-wooded sides, looks very much like a Scottish sea loch.

We must negotiate a major obstacle just before we reach our destination of Matadi. This is the notorious 'Chaudron d'Enfer', a right-angled bend in the river which has sheer rock cliffs several hundred feet high as its outside perimeter. This allows it to generate some fearsome whirlpools from the powerful river currents.

Our faithful Doxford engine can only give us up to 15 knots of speed at best so we'd struggle against the 10 to 12 knots that the Congo can attain as it rushes through this fearsome obstacle. Fortunately, this month is a time of 'low river' and weaker currents so we successfully round the bend, pass under the slightly incongruous telephone wire that spans the river here and then we can see our objective. There is still the matter of putting the ship alongside the wharf, no simple task at any state of the river, but night is still over an hour away once we are all secured.

No work until morning is our welcome to Matadi and so both our Nigerian crew and some of the Krooboys are heading up the road towards the fleshpots of the town. I don't know what they're using for money as the agency clerk didn't bring any cash for the ship. This means that the European contingent must enjoy a quiet night on board with the pleasures of the town as tomorrow's treat.

When morning comes, the excursion of the previous night seems to have put the sailors in a good mood as they swing the ship's derricks outboard so as to allow the quayside cranes to work the ship. Our small offering of cargo for this port is soon unloaded without any problems and now we have the satisfaction of feeling even more confident that we're on our way home at last. There's a mixed bag of goods to be loaded here and the arrival of a lengthy cable from Lagos sets out what has been booked for the rest of our homeward cargo.

The content of that message keeps Don and Dave busy up in the former's cabin so I'm left on deck by myself to see to things. I despatch the apprentices to have a thorough search of all the cargo spaces to make absolutely sure that we're clear of any outward cargo. Then I break out my French to tell the two stevedore foremen, one Belgian, one Congolese, what will be loaded and where.

There's a hundred tons of Katanga copper to go on top of what is already in number four hold. I ask Billy to make up a bucket of water paint so that I can mark some lines across the top of the existing stow. That will act as a visible separation of the two shipments, which will be needed when this cargo is unloaded in Liverpool. As I explain this to him I'm overheard by Stan, who says that he's going down that hatch to look for some timber for a job and so he'll mark off the copper.

I'm grateful for this offer as this means I can get along to number two and make sure that the gang there understand that the logs we are to load there must be stowed as far forward as possible in the hatch. Logs on offer here are small by the standards of the West Coast, around two to four tons each and therefore well within the capability of the dock crane. They're dry logs brought alongside on railway wagons as the fierce river current prevents any rafting of timber, and thus are quite different from the great wet beasts that we'll be meeting later in the voyage.

With the gang headman at number two understanding what I want, it's now up the ladder and along to number five hatch, where the gang are preparing a space to load 45 gallon drums of glycerine. I explain that I want them to make a single tier of drums, standing on their ends, and then lay a good floor of dunnage before we load bales of rubber on top. Not long after, with all the loading going to plan, a dockside siren announces *déjeuner* and the loading gangs all file ashore.

The apprentices and I are enjoying a beer on deck when Dave appears to say that he'll do the rest of the day as I'm on the night shift and so I can take one of the boys with me for an afternoon off. Big deal. After our lunch, Lawrence says that he's going up the road so Pete and I decide to join him.

We'd expect Hugo to get wind of such an expedition but he's cloistered with Alan as they sort out the outward cargo documentation and then put it away ready for eventual scrutiny back in Liverpool. He does, however, persuade Alan to find time to allow us to sign for some of the limited supply of Congolese francs that the agency sent aboard earlier that morning.

We're soon off ashore and bound for a forbidding grey pile that looks like an office block that has been transplanted here from Antwerp. It's the Hotel Metropole, built to serve the needs of passengers using the Belgian mailboats. It seems an appropriate building for housing those grimly commercial colonial administrators who would have stayed here in the past.

The hotel interior is rather more welcoming and we're happily installed in front of our glasses of genuine Belgian lager in air-conditioned comfort. It's a bit tame here in the daytime; it lacks the atmosphere of my previous evening visits.

There are no flocks of elaborately coiffed and colourfully coutured prostitutes, no bunches of shaven-headed thugs who might well have been foreign mercenaries (somehow, one felt, they weren't involved in aid or development). Neither are there any itinerant Congolese traders peddling impressive ivory tusks and what might or might not be genuine gemstones. We eventually leave this air-conditioned haven and I invest my few remaining Congolese francs in some postcards and stamps to get them home.

Walking down the hill back to the port, Lawrence suddenly exclaims, 'Bloody hell, the ship's moving!' I suppress a response that he should have skipped that last round of drinks because I can see that he's quite correct. Well, there's no point in hurrying now as we'll not be able to get on board until what is obviously a change of berth has been completed.

Sure enough, when we do reach the wharf, we see that she's fallen back about a ship's length and we learn that the move was necessary to put us within reach of a palm-oil pipeline connection. We are to load 400 tons of this oil the following morning. Chippy and a couple of the Krooboys will secure the lids of the two deep tanks once they've been passed as clean. My job will be to see that I then let the duty engineer know. He can then begin passing steam into the steel heating coils of each tank.

Other than that, my night duty consists of watching the log stow at number two and keeping a general 'monkey-eye' around the decks for potential thieves and other unwelcome visitors. Naturally, the unplanned can and will occur. On this occasion, at about two in the morning, it's the arrival of a large truck on the wharf.

'What have they come to nick?' I wonder as I walk towards the gangway, because I can't see any load on it apart from a trio of desperadoes armed with some home-made metalwork resembling spears and swords. I see that the night supervisor is going down to investigate and then here he is, returning with the news that 20 tons of rutile sand have arrived and it must be loaded immediately as *'C'est bien valable et il y a beaucoup de voleurs là-bas.'*

I know about 20 tons of gum copal on our loading list but this stuff is news to me. I don't want to put Don on the shake as he'll be having a heavy day later on but there's no documentation for this stuff and I'm being pressed for a decision.

I go down to see what it comprises and find a number of small hessian bags in the lorry, each about a quarter the size of a cocoa sack but incredibly heavy to lift. There are no shipping marks to give me a clue but then neither are they marked for a consignee in Philadelphia.

What the hell, sometimes you have to take a chance and the Congolese supervisor seems to know what he's about. I tell him to put the cargo on board on the basis that we're offering free storage for now and that his firm must pay to have it taken off again if he's made a mistake.

Dawn has yet to break when the dockers hoist the tent over number two hatch and abruptly disappear. I check on our watchmen, have the gangway hoisted to deter boarders and take the coward's route to my bed by leaving Pete in charge of waking the ship and giving Don a note explaining what I've done with the unexpected cargo.

I must have got away with it because, as I head towards the shower just before noon, I come across Dave, who tells me that we're almost finished and will be sailing at one. Washed and dressed, I've just read the departure draughts when I see Stan, who tells me that he and the Krooboys have managed to abstract a few gallons of the food-grade hot orange nectar from the deep tanks before the final tonnage was agreed.

So we're guaranteed our palm-oil chop ration for the voyage and there'll be some as 'dash' to the sailors and to the Kroo team. The oil is for Unilever, whose own shipping company, Palm Line, is our principal commercial rival on the coast, so that'll add a nice taste of piracy to the flavour of the dish when we come to enjoy it.

We leave Matadi and then enjoy roaring down the Congo with the current in our favour, clocking 20 knots in places. We disembark the pilot off Banana and are heading out in the open Atlantic just after sunset. We've got well over half of our homeward lift on board and we know that almost all of the rest is booked for us at the two Gabonese ports of Port Gentil and Libreville.

At the latter place we'll be just a few miles from the hospital of the legendary Dr Albert Schweitzer, still practising at the hospital that he founded at Lambaréné half a century ago. Then we'll make a short call at Freetown for bunkers and to disembark our Krooboys. Our final stop will be at Bathurst in the Gambia before a week's run home to Avonmouth.

The voyage is, of course, still far from done but the lifting of spirits on board is apparent whenever we gather together either at work or when off-duty.

Port Gentil is just south of the Equator and Libreville is even closer to the line but to the north. There'll still be no 'crossing the line' ceremony and appeasement of the court of King Neptune as we'll be between two quite demanding port calls, neither of which will allow us to get ashore from what are just working anchorages.

8

Finding our way back up the Coast

As we make our way northwards towards Cape Lopez during my evening watch I can see several prominent orange flares making harsh silhouettes of the coastline trees and low hills. These are the product of burning gas off during oil production. Gabon is a fortunate country to have this addition to its treasure of other natural resources. However, there is little sign of this national wealth reaching the Gabonese who board the ship once we've found ourselves a suitable berth in the crowded anchorage that constitutes Port Gentil.

A launch containing the usual flock of officials wearing a variety of particularly battered uniforms is followed by another with our loading gangs, who also look spectacularly unkempt. Unlike the smartly dressed but subjugated dockers of Lobito, these men enjoy a cheerful freedom from foreign domination even though it looks as if they currently receive little other material benefit.

The boarding clerk brings a sheaf of cargo documentation with him, which is soon distributed to those on board who need it. Hugo hands me a set of cargo advice notes as I pass the ship's office. They're on that flimsy paper, characteristically French, that has both the feel and weight of an inferior toilet roll and they itemise our first tranches of cargo. Alan, the purser, has done some rapid mathematics to add the weights of each individual log, information that the shipper obviously thinks to be unimportant.

Most log weights are around the 3 to 5 ton mark but many are of double those figures. Alan's added a useful exclamation mark next to a declared 18 tonner. That monster should be quite easy to spot when it arrives alongside. It will also need to be carefully watched as our ordinary derricks can only offer a maximum lift of 20 tons. And all timber shippers, as we know from long experience, are always extremely modest declarers of their true log weights.

I'm happy to learn that Dave has to attend to our ailing gyro-compass so we're spared his usual log-loading impresario performance. I leave the apprentices at the more straightforward hatch and head up to where there might be problems. Arriving at number two hatch, I see that the *ackaway* (tally clerk) has the tools of his trade ready. He has a loading list, a hammer, a pot of galvanised nails, a set of tin-tallies and two ball-point pens pushed into his wiry hair.

I look over the ship's side and see one of the water-boys confidently padding bare-foot across the logs to meet the wire sling that is hanging from the bottom block of our derrick. Clad only in a tattered pair of swimming trunks, his first task is to secure the hefty fire-axe that we send down to him by tying its long tail rope to the log wires. Then he deftly manoeuvres the wire sling around one of the logs in the raft to a point about a third of the way along its length and shackles the wire back to itself.

A brief signal to his colleague on deck (the 'gangwayman') and the sling is hove just tight enough to lift the log a few inches above its neighbours. The water-boy picks up his axe and, with a few accurate blows, knocks out the steel fastening *pigouille* that attaches the log to the raft wires.

He's skilful and the water is relatively smooth today but the potential for a nasty accident is always present. The way in which he has slung the log cants it to a steep angle as it is lifted and the tightened wire sling displaces large shards of tree bark into the water. This releases the familiar and slightly fetid perfume of jungle decay for us to enjoy as the log comes up to deck level.

It's also being dragged clumsily up the ship's side and despoiling our paintwork. Past experience tells me that it's not worth nagging the gangwayman to keep it clear of the hull. I'll just make sure that he doesn't batter the ship too much as the log is swung across the deck and lowered into the hold. The tally clerk steps up to the top end of the log and nails in the inch-square white plastic that we still call a tin-tally in memory of its metal ancestor. I then see that he has a problem.

This log has been immersed in water for a long time. The tally clerk is forced to use his hammer to fastidiously scrape away a tidemark of greyish-green slime and reveal the remnants of an identifying shipping number. Now, is it the log on his sheet that is declared to be F3412 or the one that is E8142?

I have to agree with him that it could easily be either. Finally, as the barracking of the winchdrivers and the shouted enquiries from the raftmen start to become intolerable, we go for the first number and hope that we've guessed right.

Seven tons of prime Gabon *okoumé* (mahogany) has been given a clear new identity that it will carry to its final destination which is shown by a prominent shipping mark of 'MLM'. That will be the Bootle yard of Montague L. Meyer, a well-known firm of timber merchants.

The lifting wires run smoothly through the block sheaves as the full 20 foot length of log is lifted clear of the steel bulwark. The derrick starts to swing inboard but that action temporarily lowers the log. It strikes and scatters a neat pile of our wooden hatchboards and I shout angrily, 'Lift am! Make you lift the bloody ting!' before I remember to convert my call to 'Levez! Levez!'

My call is completely ignored by the winchdriver, who now allows the log to bang shudderingly on the steel hatch side as it completes its traverse of the deck. More of the slimy bark drops off and the impact also flushes out several small crustacean passengers who wisely scuttle for the nearest cover.

I must go down into the 'tweendeck, using a vertical steel ladder that has now been made slippery wet by the passing log, in order to see that it is properly stowed. I'm reassured when I see that the gang's headman, grey-haired but agile, is already bringing over the wire bullrope. He winds it around the log a couple of times as this action will deliver the spin that will shoot the log into its resting place.

Now it's a process of heaving carefully on the bullrope (the call for this is '*Vire! Doucement!*') while simultaneously easing off the lifting wire ('*Amène un peu.*') This causes the suspended log to take up a level horizontal position and to move forward. When all looks well, a shouted command of '*Amène! Amène! Amène!*' causes 7 tons of tropical timber to crash satisfyingly and noisily into its proper stowage place.

Happy with this performance, I leave my vantage point and go and see how the other log gang is faring. On my way aft, I bump into Dave, who tells me that he's coming out on deck now so I can go and get my head down before the night shift. He doesn't add that I'll be doing that spell of duty unaccompanied, a fact that I learn later when he hands over the deck to me. Oh, well, at least it's just the two logging gangs to supervise and the apprentices have put out plenty of portable deck lights, all lit and left in position.

I've had a quick look around and I'm with the night foreman, having a smoke, when the distinct 'twang' of a wire rope parting is followed by an avalanche of noise from down in number four hold. This means that the Krooboys and I might just be in business. I peer over the hatch side, the foreman and the labour are still having an angry exchange but it could be worse. Nobody is injured and my previous experience tells me what's happened here.

Some lazy sod has forgotten to see that the split pin has been put back in the snatch block. This is a steel pulley that the gang can position anywhere in the hold in order to provide the best direction of heave for the bullrope. It has a hinged side to allow any part of the rope to be inserted and this is secured by a steel split pin. Leave that out and the wire will spring out under the strain and seek an alternative direction. A risk of a nasty injury to anybody in the way and the snatch block becomes another item for the repairs list. On this occasion, we're soon back in business and logs continue to crash into their stowage places with satisfying bangs and solid thumps.

By midnight we're making steady progress through the rafts lying alongside; maybe the gangs are going for a 'job and finish'? About half-one in the morning, I find Terry, tonight's duty engineer, and we head for the night pantry. There we cobble up some very tasty fried-egg sandwiches and a pot of strong coffee. That accompanies half an hour of slanging off the senior officers, West Africa and its inhabitants and the shipping company that pays our wages.

Back on deck, I'm surprised to find that the normal night tempo of the coast is in progress. That is to say, both tally clerks are fast asleep, nobody is visible on the log rafts, winchdrivers and foremen are somnolent and there's just the odd clink of activity audible at the bottom of both hatches. It's time to shout, kick, cajole, insult and generally play the evil white slave-driver in order to restore the work rhythm.

I'm full of refreshment and energy, whilst everybody else is obviously tired, hungry and hoping that the frequent flashes of lightning that illuminate the port will turn the night's oppressive humidity into a work-stopping downpour.

Night working in West Africa is largely a waste of time as productivity is so low. I have some sympathy with the gangs. We have imposed this alien practice on them and they see no benefit in terms of enhanced wages. Indeed, if the port is very busy, the night gangs on one ship are most likely the exhausted day ones from another ship. Sometimes, this pretence is even dispensed with and the same set of men will work one ship around the clock.

By six, however, as the dawn starts to appear, we've only left a single log floating alongside one hatch. Mission very nearly achieved! I leave a note for Dave to tell him the state of play, dive into a hot shower and then into a relatively cool cabin and the sanctuary of my bunk. By mid-afternoon I'm as rested as I can hope to be as the cabin temperature is now back to its sweaty normality. Out of bed, across to the washroom and then a seat on deck, dressed in my bath towel and enjoying the breeze and a can of lemonade.

Dave spots me and comes up with the news that we're sailing at six so I'll be on my sea watch tonight instead of on deck. It's a nice change, but why? The logs that were on offer from Libreville cannot be cleared through Customs in time so we're loading sawn timber, plywood and veneers here and then we will be back-tracking to Pointe Noire to make up this 500 ton shortfall in our planned cargo.

It's only just after two o'clock so I could offer to relieve Dave for a while. Instead, I bury that generous idea in favour of a quiet spot on the bridge wing, where I can snooze in sunshine that is cooled by a sea breeze. From time to time I look over the wooden dodgers to watch the cargo being loaded.

The 1 ton cases of veneers are tricky brutes to handle as their packing is just a flimsy timber skeleton and the contents, if spilled, become virtually useless. That is because the sheets are packed sequentially and have the same order of importance as the numbered pages of a book.

New materials for furniture and building are being introduced at home but it appears that we still want the comforting and luxurious finish of good timber. Hence the appetite for mahogany veneers. The plywood that we load is of a marine quality and will satisfy a growing leisure interest in DIY boat-building, whilst bundles of sawn afromosia and iroko are for those who still demand good quality wooden furnishings.

There must be forklift trucks in use to handle these awkward items as I can see a smoky blue haze above two of the hatches. Then I see two dark-blue vehicles, carrying the name of Delmas (the principal French West African traders) on their masts, being swung over the side and deposited on a large flat steel barge. It's time to get below sharpish, get changed and come back to the bridge ready to test the gear prior to sailing.

But the day has one further surprise to spring on me. Don intercepts me in my clean white uniform and advises me to get back into khaki as I've been chosen to pick up the anchor in order to get some experience of that task. With Stan, Billy and a couple of Krooboys in tow, I'm soon heading up the foredeck past the sailors who are busy drawing the hatch tarpaulins into place.

The windlass is put into gear, a rubber hose is connected to the nearest fire hydrant and we're now waiting for the telephone to ring and tell us to start weighing anchor. Stan observes, 'We've not been here long enough to pick up much shite this time. I've seen some right bastard workouts in this place before. They just dump all sorts of old wires and that kind of crap here, typical Frogs.'

I'm watching the last boatload of officials leaving and wondering whether anybody remembered to read the departure draughts. Then the call to heave up the anchor arrives. The windlass starts slowly trundling away. The hose is able to spray a fat jet of water down the hawsepipe so that the normally rusty-red cable comes into view in clean, glittering wetness. This is all too soon defaced by nuggets of black and evil-smelling river mud. The windlass has to be further slowed in order to allow a proper cleaning.

I signal the direction that the cable is leading and ask those on the bridge for a touch ahead on the engine to ease the strain on the cable. A small cloud of black smoke shows this request is being actioned and then we soon have the cable up and down and emerging from the water like a monstrous trunk of liquorice.

I tell the bridge what's up after having rung the bell twice to show that we still have nearly two shackles (180 feet length) of cable to lift. In return, I'm told by Don to take my time and to make sure that it's well cleaned. What about me, I wonder, as I realise that I'm also benefiting from the muddy black spray. When it's apparent that the anchor has broken out of the silt of the harbour bottom, I ring the bell vigorously for a few seconds to signify 'anchor aweigh'. I also remember to take down the black anchor ball. That action will show other ships that we're now on the move.

Stan leaves one of the Krooboys to operate the windlass and joins me at the ship's side rail to watch for the anchor itself breaking the surface. This it does but it's not looking like an anchor. It's just a great, misshapen, stinking black lump with an impressive display of whiskery wires and ropes trailing some ten yards astern as we start to gather headway.

'Bloody hell,' says Stan, 'what the fuck have you found?' Unreasonably, I feel that's a personal slur, so I pointedly ignore him and motion for the Krooboy to lower the cable a bit so that this monster slips under the water again.

'It's come up a bit dirty with a lot of debris attached,' I primly tell the bridge. 'Biggest load of black shite in creation,' offers Stan. 'Just get it cleaned up and let me know when it's safely secured,' is all the help that I get from the bridge.

Time is pressing on and my dinner opportunity is fast disappearing so I'm duly grateful to see some massive mudslides taking place when I look back over the side. Soon it actually looks like an anchor and it's even lost most of its whiskers. Then it's not long before the two points of the anchor flukes have crunched audibly against the stops welded to the hull. Windlass back out of gear, brakes and stoppers on and the hose coiled away. 'Don't worry about the wires, son,' says Stan, 'Billy'll get one of the lads over there in port and clean them away. Go and get yer tea.'

Our stay in Pointe Noire goes well. Most of the logs are stacked on the wide quay apron when we arrive and are soon making up the cargo weight that had been denied us at Libreville. Terry and I, the two night-owls, together with Lawrence and Hugo, the two under-employed, even manage to have a great afternoon on the beach. It's a deserted strip of yellow sand nearby with seawater close to blood-heat, my favourite bathing temperature. As we leave the ship and walk past the bows, I have a wave and some friendly abuse from Stan, busy supervising two Krooboys in the task of cleaning up my anchor shame.

On our way back we take a short cut over some ore heaps and then along the manganese-loading wharf. This minor trespass causes us to be harangued by some scruffy security guards. They then start pelting us with lumps of ore, fortunately very inaccurately, when we refuse their calls for 'dash'. We're probably lucky to have gone as far ashore as we did, as the Congolese authorities here have already refused permission for one of our Nigerian stewards to visit the dentist.

In contrast, the crew of the Russian fish-factory ship berthed ahead of us seem free to come and go as they wish. It isn't difficult to see which side of the world's ideological divide of the 1960s is engaging the sympathies of those in charge here.

The labour is far less partisan and they get on with the work during the night without causing me too much bother. We make a dawn departure, which leads me directly into my morning sea watch. I thus extend my continuous hours of duty to 16 but I don't grumble too much. We are, after all, once again on our way in the right direction in this increasingly haphazard voyage home.

The next day is Sunday and it will be notable for two reasons. Principally, we will enjoy the gastronomic high point of the voyage but, additionally, we might just be passing very close to 'nowhere' during the course of the day. We are on a leg of nearly eighteen hundred miles between Pointe Noire and Freetown so it's an opportunity to slip back into the measured time discipline of being at sea after the relative chaos of our stays in port.

I'm on the bridge and getting down to the third mate's never-ending task of amending the *Admiralty List of Lights*. This consists of cutting out strips of new information, posted to us in weekly copies of Notices to Mariners, courtesy of the Admiralty's Hydrographic Office. Then, using a crusty paste pot, I'm sticking these scraps into a set of paperback volumes that live in the chartroom bookcase. As I do my messy best, I also know that the traditional Sunday inspection, beloved of all Merchant Navy skippers, is now under way.

We call it, irreverently, 'Parks & Gardens' or the 'March of the Unemployed'. It's a procession of the master and his three heads of departments around the accommodation of the ship in order to satisfy statutory requirements that these areas are being kept in a clean, tidy and hygienic state.

My cabin steward, Olatunde, will ensure that my cabin is clean as he undertakes that duty daily. I've done my bit by bunging any peripheral untidiness into the drawers and wardobe before I came on watch. So the inspection party will have to sift through my unwashed working gear if they want to amuse themselves by unearthing a couple of dog-eared issues of *Playboy* that I've been entertaining myself with for the past few weeks.

It's far more likely that they'll be terrifying the apprentices in their bespoke slum further down the alleyway. Then they'll be congratulating the Nigerians down aft on their attention to cleanliness, finally moving to the galley to see how the cook is managing the preparations for our eagerly awaited serving of the 'palm-oil chop'.

Even at a remove of so many years, my taste buds begin to react as I set down this account, so great is the remembered pleasure of this voyage ritual. I find myself back at one of the tables in the saloon that is occupied by myself, Hugo, Pete and Dougie. In front of each of us is a glass of Tennent's lager, courtesy of a special dispensation by the Old Man, since alcohol is normally not permitted in the saloon, except for the passengers.

Our saloon steward has just placed a generous helping of boiled rice into the soup plate in front of me. Now I can season it with salt, black pepper and a judicious sprinkling of fiery red pepper before he returns with the palm-oil stew itself.

This firstly comprises pieces of that famous fowl, the 'Board of Trade bird'. This is the name that all merchant seamen attach to this ornithological rarity that, only available from ship's-store suppliers, possesses one breast, two pairs of wings and about eight legs. This fowl is joined by substantial pieces of yam and thick slices of okra, the whole forming a creamy pale-brown concoction.

Once that is served, we add generous helpings from the tray of assorted 'small chop' that is circulated around the four of us. This mixed delight consists of roasted peanuts, sliced onions and tomatoes, dessicated coconut, crumbled hard-boiled egg and some more red pepper for the really valiant diner. Finally, a generous dressing of pure hot palm-oil pours its ruby-red and gold benison from the silver sauce-boat.

The chicken is never as bad as its provenance sounds and the multiple textures and flavours of the bowl of 'chop' drive the enjoyment, above all the unique flavour of the glorious palm-oil. Only the yam can sometimes disappoint. Generally it has an earthy potato-like flavour but, on occasion, there's a distinct impression of chewing on lumps of balsa wood. That small imperfection, and its rich and unhealthy beauty, are the only drawbacks of this culinary masterpiece.

After that, the only possible destination is bed, a haven that I occupy until I go on watch at eight. There is no need to relieve Don for his customary dinner break as there is a cold buffet laid out in the saloon for those gannets who need further sustenance after the palm-oil chop celebration. I'll probably call in there when I finish at midnight as there'll still be plenty left to eat.

For now, I find that Don has made use of a cloudless sky and a sharp horizon to come up with an excellent position from his evening star sights. We've crossed the Equator but are still an hour's steaming from the Greenwich meridian. This means that at nine o'clock we'll be back in both the horizontal northern hemisphere and also the western vertical hemisphere. It's completely fanciful, since it's pitch dark, but at that time I will go out on the port bridge wing and say that 'nowhere', defined as zero degrees of both latitude and longitude is just 'over there'.

In later years, this fanciful concept occurs to some smart marketeer in the company. 'Cruises to Nowhere' are advertised for our largest passenger ship, the *Aureol*, which then takes expatriates out from Lagos for what is essentially a boozy, well-fed weekend at sea. Whether the ship actually reaches its zero destination is the subject of much speculation in the rest of the fleet. However, all on board receive an attractive certificate confirming their visit to the official position of 'nowhere'.

I'm on watch again the next morning, the ship plodding uneventfully across a sparkling blue sea totally bereft of other ships, when I spot Hugo entering the chartroom with a mass of papers. 'OK if I use the chart table for a while?' he enquires, 'Only it's the best flat surface that I can find for this lot.' What he has are the ship's cargo plans. Alan has palmed him off with the job of preparing the fair copies to send home.

They show what cargo we've loaded, where it is stowed and details of its weight and any important shipping marks. Dave and I have been keeping a rough working plan that contains all this information. Now it's the purser's job to render it presentable and see that it is airmailed from our last port to both our Avonmouth agents and to the 'Kremlin' in India Buildings, Liverpool. As our last port will be Bathurst, a bit of a one-horse town, Alan is going to send some plans from Freetown with the Freetown and Bathurst cargoes pencilled in as forecasts. Hence Hugo's current activity project.

He's brought a calculating machine up with him and, since my lookout and other duties are minimal this morning, I go through the various tonnages that we've loaded while he cranks away and the little wheels whirr around. Bassey, on the wheel, comments, 'Dis machine, e say how much money for dese big men wey sell all dese tings for dis your people?' Freight, which is the money that the ship earns for carrying cargo, is always a commercial secret kept well hidden from anyone on board a ship. This means that I can happily tell Bassey to mind his own business and concentrate on his continuing indifferent steering.

Eventually we've agreed and balanced all the tonnage figures and decide that the total cargo on board is just under 4,800 tons. I know that we're expecting a final load of about five and a half thousand tons. We're very nearly there and, thanks to the copper cargo, not too worried about whether we still have space available. We also won't need to have any deck cargo. This guarantees that the work that the sailors are doing today in painting up the decks, denuded of rust by the Krooboys, will not be scarred by dragging logs and their heavy lashing chains across them.

Freetown welcomes us back with a stupendous downpour that has us searching anxiously for the fairway buoy as we approach and makes even the simple task of anchoring the ship a sodden ordeal for everybody.

Not least for the poor Krooboys who, having assembled their extensive baggage on deck for a smooth departure, then have to beg for an old tarpaulin from the Bosun to offer it some protection. To cap it all, rainwater has got into the VHF aerial connection and so Lawrence is out in the tempest trying to restore service. Then, as is the way so often in tropical Africa, the rain stops, the clouds part and all is sunshine and light and a return to steamy sweatiness.

As soon as the decks dry off a bit it's time to take the usual precautions against polluting the harbour as we're taking on heavy fuel oil for the passage home. Stan gets busy hammering wooden plugs into the scuppers that drain the main deck and a couple of sailors bring bags of sawdust for use around the bunker connections. Pretty soon a ramshackle bunkering barge and its smoky old tug will emerge from the fuel oil storage area at Kissy, just around the corner from our anchorage.

We also have cargo to load here and a large flat lighter is already in sight leaving the quay and being towed out to us. It must then wait a little while until the usual gang of official rascals have received their alcohol and tobacco tribute. It's all to come on board at number four hatch: large empty chlorine and arcton gas cylinders painted yellow or grey, other smaller empty gas bottles and a couple of hundred bundles of piassava fibre. Finally, an untidy collection of old lorry and car radiators as valuable non-ferrous scrap complete a very mixed shipment.

Now the Krooboys can depart by taking over the cargo winches for the last time and landing their voyage spoils onto the empty barge. Some small boys and other relatives arrive by canoe to help convey and guard this cargo. It's a necessary precaution as one or two other canoes, manned by some hulking desperadoes, are visible in the offing. After so many weeks of valuable hard work for the ship's benefit, we all feel sorry that their possessions, acquisitions and honest salvage are now to be at the mercy of both these floating rogues and the licensed plunderers within the Customs shed on the quay.

Now we're fuelled, we've read our last letters received from home, cargo work is finished and we have recovered our anchor from the mud of Freetown harbour. Then we're out again into the blue Atlantic Ocean and heading northwards and homewards.

It's almost 36 hours to Bathurst and thus breaking daylight as we turn eastwards out of the open ocean and look for the entrance to the great Gambia river that gives this last British West African possession its name. We sight the channel buoys as they emerge from a flat grey sea and, warned by the proximity of Stop-in-time Bank, turn southwards to find our destination.

Just ahead of us now, the ferry that crosses the river mouth is trundling along its route and we can clearly see Government wharf, our berth. I note from the chart that the area just south of there is called Half-Die and wonder about its derivation before I go down and welcome our cheery British pilot on board. 'Money for old rope' must be a description of his services, as the Old Man has been bringing ships in here for many years. This means that the two men have a lively and easy conversation as we execute an immaculate berthing operation.

The Gambia might still be a British possession but the usual squad of harbour officials are gathering almost as much loot from the ship as their colleagues in the new nations. With no Krooboys to do the work, our sailors have to set to and arrange the derricks before cargo work can begin. The Nigerians tell me that these 'Bathurst boys' are always up to no good but I take that advice with a pinch of salt as my previous visits have been pleasant enough.

I can still recall celebrating my 21st birthday here, a short enjoyable party on board that was followed by an extended indulgence at the Atlantic Hotel. This is a modest enough establishment but it possesses a fine swimming pool, into which I was ceremonially dumped at the conclusion of the evening. Then the police arrived, but not to chastise us, merely to act as our taxi back to the ship for the price of a few beers. I awoke mid-morning to find the ship at sea and my watch being covered by the Old Man, who very generously excused my dereliction of duty by wisely remarking that I had officially ended my childhood and could now begin behaving like an adult.

On this call, we are to load groundnut oil for Liverpool and groundnut cake for the BOCM cattle-feed mill at Avonmouth along with a small consignment of various hides and bones for the former port. We are also due to take two passengers. It's when I see a bright-red Sunbeam sports car coming down the finger pier and parking at the foot of the gangway, giving scant attention to the other wharf users, that I just have a feeling that they'll be 'trouble'.

Alan has also seen this noisy arrival and meets the driver at the head of the gangway. They have a short conversation before the car departs, again with a casual disdain for everybody else on the quay. Give it a little time, I think, then I'll pump Hugo for the details.

Right now I need to open a locker for the bones as they need to be loaded first. With that done, I call Stan to seal the locker door with flour paste and a couple of thicknesses of newspaper. This will ensure that all those exotic bugs living in the cargo can be kept safe to thrill the men from the 'Min. of Ag. and Fish'. They're always eager visitors to our ships in Liverpool, boarding with their official black briefcases and ample supplies of specimen bottles.

The big preoccupation of the Bathurst dockworkers is the English football pools. This means that I'm asked for help with next Saturday's coupon even more frequently than for the usual 'dash' of cigarettes. 'Please, sah, you play pools?' 'Maybe you get chance for help me with dis eight draws for big money for dis my family?'

I'm no football expert as I normally only glance at the results that Lawrence types up from listening to the BBC and then places on the noticeboard each Saturday evening. But the work on deck is easy and I'm feeling generous so I pick ten matches for his 'perm'. I also promise not to divulge this expert opinion to any of the other supplicants who have not yet realised that such a fount of English soccer wisdom is moving amongst them.

Since we're not here for long, we keep sea watches during the fairly relaxed hours of work that will see the day's loading end just before 10 p.m. This means that I can go ashore during the afternoon with a small party headed for a more civilised use of the swimming pool at the Atlantic Hotel. Bathurst is not a holiday destination yet so the pool is virtually empty and this makes an enjoyable afternoon.

On the way back to the ship, we have time to take advantage of the low prices that the mainly Lebanese tenants of a street of cramped shops are offering on alcohol, tobacco and normally highly taxed items such as radios and cameras.

My old Philco radio could do with a replacement but I don't want the bother of humping a shiny new Grundig set home from Avonmouth, so I just elect for a couple of 'docking bottles' and a carton of black Sobranie cigarettes. The second bottle will need to be concealed from Customs at home but the prices for both are much lower than those on board. The cigarettes are exotic as well as cheap and I'm sure that they'll add to my air of suave sophistication once I get back amongst those Liverpool girls. Such are the romantic delusions of the seafarer down the years!

Returning on board about four, we find that we've all been recruited into an *ad hoc* football team that is going ashore to play a match against some local schoolboys. I'm due to relieve Dave on deck in an hour but he's delighted to tell me that I can exercise my ball skills ashore instead.

Apparently our agency manager is very friendly with a local headmaster and has volunteered the ship's services for an impromptu soccer international. The chief has released Eric, Terry and Tommy from their engine-room duties to join Lawrence, Pete, Dougie, Hugo, Stan and myself. We will also have Essien and one of the Nigerian firemen as honorary British players.

A quick change into a variety of passable kit and a brisk ten-minute walk bring us to a pitch of sad brown 'grass' that is home to two very professional-looking netted goals. We also see a team of immaculately kitted teenagers supported by a small and very partisan crowd of their supporters. We've hastily agreed our line-up as we walked over from the ship.

Eric will goalkeep on the basis of occasional appearances for his local pub team at home. Terry and Tommy will be keeping the defence in engineering hands. Stan, Dougie, Pete and Essien will be our attack force whilst Hugo, myself and Ekpan the fireman will contribute what we can in the centre.

The headmaster is to be our referee (no obvious risk of bias there, then) and, within a minute of first blowing his whistle, two or three very fit and athletic Gambian schoolboys are deep within our creaking defence and Eric is showing his mettle with some very skilful saves. Nevertheless, by half-time, the local team is two very well-deserved goals up. We enjoy a can of lemonade, brought to us on the field by Mick, our chief steward, during the break. There's also time for a cigarette and we change ends fully recharged.

Despite the fact that both Hugo and I are only really familiar with the oval ball, we manage not only to rob the opposition of the round ball from time to time but also to resist the impulse to pick it up and then run. We're helped by the fact that we only have to cover the two wings as none of these schoolboys are going to go near the menacing bulk of Ekpan in the centre.

Suddenly, it's Hugo who's off down the other wing with the ball and skilfully retaining possession. The repeated shouts from Stan of 'Over 'ere, you public school wanker' eventually register and a surprisingly accurate pass allows Stan to rocket the ball into the net. I must have been inspired by that act as I also manage to elbow my way to the ball, keep hold of it and boot it up towards the front row where Pete manages to convert my clumsy clearance into a second goal to level the score.

As the second half progresses, I get the impression that the opposition are more fatigued than we are so it's a complete surprise when one of them goes weaving through our defence and manages to beat Eric's vainly outstretched arms. But what's this? The goal is immediately disallowed by the referee as the scorer had committed a foul in order to get possession of the ball. It's an amazingly honest and sporting decision that allows us to hang on for the last few minutes for a fairly honourable draw.

Mick presents the opposing team with a couple of cases of lemonade and the referee gets a replica of the company's houseflag attached to a miniature wooden flagpole. In return, we receive a souvenir banner from the school. Everybody leaves the field happy but I personally resolve to go into hiding when any future ship's football teams are being recruited.

The next morning, Don is busy with the loading of the groundnut oil into a couple of our deep tanks but he tells me to ensure that I leave a nice safe stowage in a 'tweendeck for the passengers' car and their three lift vans of household effects. I arrange both of these areas and then go looking for an old tarpaulin and some plastic sheeting to protect both the car and the bags of cargo that it'll be resting on.

I can then leave the actual loading to Dave while I catch a couple of hours of peace in my cabin before we sail in the late afternoon. When Dave wakes me to get the sailing preparations under way, he's snarling about that 'bloody jumped-up twerp and his fucking precious car'. I can't extract any further details before I have to trot along the wharf, fend off the last pools enthusiasts and read our departure draughts.

I take the official draught notice up to Don, who signs it and says to me 'Maximum draught 18 inches by the stern and upright. Now that's what I call "full and down" and a good job done by you all.' As he's showing an unusual degree of camaraderie, I risk the observation that he's going out on a good note and will enjoy his next voyage as captain.

Don is not so sanguine, however, and reverts to his normal demeanour by dismissing me with the thought that he might just be going on to another mate's job on one of our new ships that are coming out of the Clyde. His parting shot, however, is a little more encouraging, 'And don't forget to put up the Royal Mail pendant when we sail, show them that we're a mailboat as well.' It's true, but a little impertinent, as we're only a mailship by virtue of about thirty bags of the Gambian mails loaded a couple of hours ago.

9

Full and down, the passage home

Don's summary of our condition is accurate. We're carrying very nearly our maximum load of cargo, 5,512 tons, to be exact. This, plus about four hundred tons of fuel and two hundred tons of fresh water, means that we're full and we're down to our marks. Our derricks are all in the horizontal position once again and the sailors are busy, with paraffin and cotton waste, cleaning off any grease prior to painting. They're also carefully lubricating the blocks and wires so that they'll not only look pretty but will function smoothly when they're next required.

Looking down on the foredeck from my bridge eyrie, I see that Billy is doing some old-fashioned sailor work by making new manropes for our gangway which he'll later cover with white duck canvas. Stan is repairing some wooden hatchboards and Tommy has a neat row of mended clusters outside his workshop 'surgery' in the masthouse.

After all the log loading, a sorry set of these circular cargo lamps has been squashed into oval shapes or otherwise abused. Now they're a smart set once again with their protective guards fitted as well as replacements of those strange wooden connectors that serve as plugs. No doubt our apprentices will soon be adding the final paint touches.

It's a sunny morning as we steer due north off the invisible Mauritanian coast. This busy foredeck scene is because we'll soon be under the influence of the north-east trade winds, which begin to blow more strongly as the northern summer approaches. Any painting or cleaning here needs to be finished before the spray starts flying over our bows. It's already too breezy for a comfortable lie out in the sun in any of my usual locations but a deckchair at the end of the promenade deck should be sunny and sheltered.

Hugo has the same bright idea that afternoon and so we find ourselves a place nicely tucked away in the port corner of the promenade deck's verandah. Half-dozing and half consciously ensuring that our tans get their final polish, we're slightly aware that our two passengers have come out on deck nearby.

We're too comatose to acknowledge their presence but they seem happy enough to just lean on the rail and watch the after deck and, beyond it, our creditably straight wake. They don't stay long, as I note their absence when I come out of one of my intermittent naps, but I think no more about it. After all, lying out in the sun is not a universal pastime.

When I relieve Don for his dinner that evening, however, he rather sharply informs me that the verandah and its deckchairs are for the exclusive use of the passengers. Therefore, he goes on waspishly, I must find another spot if I want to lie around half-naked in the afternoon for the rest of the voyage. I know that he can't get me doing anything in the boats when I'm off-watch, as I'm up to date there, but he might well find other employment for me so I meekly accept his criticism. Later, when I'm on watch, Hugo arrives to fill in the full details.

Needless to say, he found a 'snout', who was a former Shrewsbury pupil, in Government House back in Bathurst. This means that he knows all about our two passengers. He's a Treasury expert who's been advising on Gambia's forthcoming independence and she's his accompanying ornament. 'I knew they'd be bother when I saw that car,' I remark, but Hugo ripostes, 'You're just jealous because of his Sunbeam Alpine – you know that's a car you'd want but you can't afford.'

He's right, of course. I'd love that car but it represents over a year's salary for me, so it's merely an aspiration. Anyway, what Hugo really wants to tell me is that they're already in thick with Don and they've nobbled him about our use of 'their' space on deck. We need to make alternative arrangements as there are still a few afternoons remaining before we reach the latitudes of dull skies and stormy seas.

By the following afternoon, we've found our new solar perch. On the top of the poop house there's the potato locker, empty at this stage of the voyage. With the aft-facing doors fully open and a piece of canvas to cover the louvred windward side, it's a fine little sun-trap for two people, albeit a little cramped.

Hugo reassures me, 'Don't worry about the intimacy, I'm quite aggressively hetero-sexual these days so you can nap in peace.' In fact we can only use the facility for a couple more days as we run under dense cloud cover once we pass the latitude of Gibraltar. Sunbathing and the luxuriance of tropical warmth are supplanted by an Atlantic chill as we resume our normal uniforms of long-sleeved shirts, black ties and brass-buttoned doeskin suits. We've not left our tropical routine completely yet as the little blue and aluminium container on the saloon table reminds us that we must take our daily anti-malarial tablet until we get home.

It's time to start enjoying that traditional experience known as the 'Channels'.

It's nothing to do with the geographical proximity of the English Channel. It wouldn't happen if we were sailing up that waterway, as I'd done once or twice in the past, bound for somewhere like Rotterdam or Hamburg to then sail out abroad again. It's the feeling of once again returning to these waters prior to enjoying our home leave.

We've been away for just over ten weeks, not long in comparison with other trades, but our only contact with home has been by letter. Calls from abroad are both difficult and expensive to make and, in any case, not every home has a telephone to receive them. A growing euphoria shows itself in a variety of ways that range from public horseplay and practical joking to odd rituals and quiet private anticipation.

Lawrence and Pete forge a telegram from the Port Health office in Avonmouth that requires Dougie's attendance at a venereal diseases clinic on arrival. Dougie has his retaliation by inking an impressive beard and moustache on the cherished portrait of Lawrence's fiancée. He then holds Pete's correspondence course work to ransom.

In contrast, the Old Man and Chief betray little outward emotion. Perhaps they recall those not-so-distant days when a happy homecoming could be forestalled by a bomb or torpedo in these waters of the Western Approaches?

The mate's homage to arrival is to hang his going-home suit, overcoat and sundry other items of clothing from a spar on the boatdeck. It's the traditional way to blow away any tropical mildew acquired while in a cabin wardrobe. It's just that nowadays it seems slightly bizarre to us youngsters.

BBC radio and the occasional newspaper have kept us in touch with most of the world's news while we've been away. Now the patriotic strains of 'Lillibulero', heard around the ship as people tuned in to short-wave, have been replaced by the first crackly snatches of pop music from Radio Luxembourg on medium-wave. It's also a source of some domestic news but only the arrival of newspapers after we dock can fill our inevitable knowledge gaps.

At the end of recent voyages we have had to learn the names of the minor characters in a row of espionage, financial, political and sexual scandals. Now we're in relatively boring times while we wait to see if a general election will bring a change of government and the need to recognise yet another set of unfamiliar faces.

About half of the British members of the ship's company are, like me, in their early twenties and still single. The staid social and sexual restrictions of the previous decade are relaxing and we men are the principal beneficiaries. Career opportunities for women remain limited. For example, one large Liverpool shipping company, not ours, will not yet employ married women. This means that girls seek relationships that will soon lead to the raising of a family in partnership with a husband.

Seafarers are rarely seen as fitting this template and so any romances this coming leave will probably follow the usual path. There'll be intense passion, mutual promises made at a tearful parting and then the gradual disappearance of letters, themselves of diminishing intensity, as the next trip to West Africa progresses.

I can look back on this voyage with satisfaction. We've all rubbed along pretty well as a crew and there have been no disasters with the cargo or the ship. We've fulfilled our commercial objectives and maintained our particular way of life.

We took a cargo of Britain's manufactures to distant lands and exchanged it for another cargo of the produce of those countries, conscientiously and efficiently. As seafarers, we will never know what profit we've earned for our employers and whether it represents an acceptable return on capital but we remain confident that our future is safe.

I'm looking forward as eagerly as anybody to docking in Avonmouth. After my own 8–12 morning watch, I forgo my afternoon nap to go out on deck frequently to catch sight of the picturesque coast of North Devon as we push against the last of the ebb tide. We're heading for the Welsh side of the Bristol Channel and the Breaksea pilot station. Then the flood pushes us the last twenty or so miles to our destination and it's the dusk of a beautiful early-summer evening when we're all done and dusted, berthed in Avonmouth's Royal Edward Dock.

There's no sign of the expected gang of waterguard rummagers, so it's a pity that I don't live locally because then I could rescue my contraband bottle and carton of cigarettes from their cache and leg it up the road. For now, they remain in the flag locker on the bridge, carefully concealed in the 'T' and 'W' pigeonholes. Sleight of hand will have to wait until tomorrow when the coast is clear and we pay off.

I'm therefore sitting peacefully in my cabin with a mug of coffee and reading the letter which my mother has sent to meet me here. Later, I'll go ashore and look for a telephone box in order to call home. Then, in comes Dave, saying, 'Come on, shift yourself, we've got to get that car up out of number four for those bloody passengers,' before he goes along the alleyway to stir the apprentices.

Out on deck, we're getting the hatch stripped while Billy and some of the sailors are getting two derricks ready, and we're all heartily cursing the inconvenience of this task. Then, unknown to us, our saviour appears. It's Alan, along with a uniformed Customs officer who's come on board to clear the ship inwards.

'What's going on here, then?' the Customs man asks Dave, who's directing operations from a point safely away from any actual activity.

'It's our passengers, they live near Bath, so they want to drive home this evening.'

'Do they indeed,' responds the officer, 'then they'd be well advised to wait until the ship officially breaks bulk in the morning.'

'They really won't like that,' says Dave, who is now thoroughly enjoying the situation, 'they're quite important people, I believe.'

'Well, let's see how important a figure they can live with for attempting to import a motor vehicle illegally,' is the brisk response as he lets Alan take him back inside the accommodation.

'Right,' shouts Dave to all hands, 'belay all this and leave it to the morning,' to the general approval of all.

We don't see our two potential smugglers in the morning. Apparently they had an early call, left all their baggage on board and took a taxi up to Bristol's Temple Meads station. After the morning's signing-off formalities, that is a destination that we all follow later in the day, shortly after our reliefs arrive on board. Clubbing together, four to a taxi, we pass over our baggage passes, each accompanied by the expected ten-shilling note, to the bobby on the dock gate in order to discourage him from giving our suitcases any kind of inspection.

Exchanging our travel warrants for rail tickets, we then make our farewells to each other at the station. As Dr Beeching's axe is still being sharpened ready to trim the rail network, this is one of the last times that all of us can be certain to get a train to a station that is close to home. Then it's only as my train to Liverpool is pulling out that I sickeningly remember that I've forgotten to recover my contraband from its cunningly contrived hiding place.

I'm not going to let someone else profit from my oversight, nor do I want someone to be brained by a bottle in the unlikely event that they want a 'W' flag in a hurry. That means a sly visit to the ship on a Saturday afternoon when it reaches Liverpool. The wheelhouse door is unlocked, as I knew it would probably be, so I trouser my loot.

I'm just leaving the ship without having encountered anybody at all when my old watchkeeper, Essien, comes into view. Any suspicions he may have as to my sudden return on board are soon allayed when I offer him a lift up the hill to the shopping possibilities of Mill Street. Now my voyage is really complete.

10

The Nigerian coal trade

I t's some time before I return to West Africa because I decide to go to college and study for my first mate's certificate. Ordinarily, I would wait a while to build up some more savings as, despite the fact that I will have three months' paid study leave, living ashore will be expensive. A holiday taken during my last leave has led to a relationship that I'm keen to maintain and a long spell ashore will help to ensure that.

I fill in the weeks until the term begins at the Liverpool College of Technology in Byrom Street by joining the relieving crews for our ships that turn around in northern Europe. The ancient Dakota aircraft that flies us from Liverpool to Rotterdam, taking nearly two hours to do so, gives me my first flying experience.

All navigating (or 'deck') officers in the Merchant Navy at this time have to sit three examinations in order to achieve the status of a certificated master. Engineers can get off a bit more lightly with just two examinations, but three are needed if they want be certificated as chief engineer for both steam and motor ships.

The first academic hurdle is the second mate's 'ticket'. This is usually taken at the end of an apprenticeship but it is also open to those who have satisfactorily served some time as sailors. The next examinations for mate and master are open to all who had have sufficient sea time as watchkeeping officers. Whereas the second mate and master's examinations are considered to be tough ordeals, those for mate are reputed to be much easier.

You still have the confidence of passing at one level, still remember much of what you learned during an apprenticeship and don't have too many new subjects to worry about. In fact, the usual strategy for tackling the examination for mate is very laid-back. It plans for failing the signals exam in order to scoop up another month's paid leave for a second attempt. This can, of course, backfire if either oral or written examinations are failed. Second attempts at these might well need a good helping of unpaid leave or even of some further sea service.

The strategy works for me and I use my second stab at signals to extend both my time ashore and my burgeoning romance. To add to my pleasure, my next three voyages to West Africa are short ones, all of less than 60 days with nearly a fortnight's leave in between. They do involve trekking down to and back from Tilbury Dock but the ship, which carries a few passengers, has a good company and we're both well-entertained and entertain well during our time in Lagos and Port Harcourt.

It's in the latter port that the second mate and the ship's carpenter take on board the stock for their parrot-importing business. Cages have been improvised, very effectively, from empty whisky cases and welding-rods, and are all made ready in the spacious carpenter's shop on the way south. A large canoe comes alongside on the night before we sail. Its feathered cargo is all trussed up in old sacks and, once we've left port, the birds are unveiled to form a freely squawking chorus.

Naturally, import licences are required for the UK even though any Nigerian formalities of export documentation have been avoided. This is not a problem as we all give our home address details to the parrot dealing team, in return for a small tip, and the licences are waiting when we return to Tilbury.

The birds don't suffer any fatalities on their journey and, although only a few seem to be potential talkers, there are equally few so-called 'growlers'. The returns must be pretty good as the second mate has recently treated himself to a brand-new bright-yellow Triumph Spitfire sports car. That represents several months' wages.

Before long I treat myself to a more modest new car which not only fully depletes my savings but also puts an end to my romantic attachment. My girl-friend realises that funds for a possible engagement ring and more ambitious plans have simultaneously disappeared. I'm also getting fed up with West Africa as it has become a rather boring destination and I now hanker for a return to more appealing routes.

However, it soon becomes clear that vacancies don't exist in either the Far East or Australasian trades, so I concentrate on gaining a promotion to second mate where I am.

The immediate post-war years produced some young masters and other senior officers as a result of the retirements and fleet expansions of the time but now we are in a period of stagnation. Some junior officers are either giving up the sea or seeking those few companies that are still expanding. Someone who stays put can expect the strict hierarchy of seniority to come up with a promotion fairly soon but it just isn't happening as quickly as I wish.

I manage to find a succession of short relieving duties around the coast in the hope that a promotion vacancy will arise while some of the more senior candidates are away at sea. This queue-jumping strategy still isn't producing any results when, going down to the docks to do a night shift on one ship, I make a reckless right-hand turn at a junction onto the Dock Road.

I'm not expecting traffic coming from my right to be going straight ahead but one lorry is. It pushes me and my motoring pride-and-joy aside with contemptuous ease. It's my fault completely but the lorry still speeds off and I'm able to stagger on board ship, do my spell of duty and then arrange to have the car towed away.

My stupidity is becoming the object of sustained parental criticism, so I go into India Buildings and volunteer to leave on the first available deep-sea sailing. This means that I'm still third mate and now back on one of our oldest ships. My bank balance is improved by a write-off cheque from the insurers and I'm determined to enjoy a return to the simplicities of life at sea and of boring old West Africa.

Therefore, here I am back in Port Harcourt but this elderly vessel can't offer the same level of hospitality and shipboard entertainment to those expatriates who used to come aboard my last ship. There are no invitations to go ashore for a swim or a meal at the club and we're left to our own devices.

Most importantly, we're also wondering what will happen to us next. The last of our cargo will be unloaded tomorrow and we have no indication yet of our loading ports or our destination. The galley radio is spreading wild rumours that it's us for the States run.

That'll suit me, as a quick return home no longer has any appeal. There's no cargo work going on tonight and the speculation flows freely as most of us socialise on the promenade-deck verandah. There we lash out at real or imagined insects, send cigarette ends curving into the black creek waters, then drop a carton of empty beer cans over the side to a canoe that has been chanting, 'Hey, my fren', any small dash for me?' for the last half-hour. That must have been an acceptable prize for the canoe, and its paddler swiftly departs without raining any curses on us as he goes.

Any similar satisfaction is noticeably absent on our part the next day when we learn that we're going into the coal trade. The message from Lagos is brought down to the ship from the agency and Charlie, our easy-going and likeable Geordie mate, soon has us all organised.

My job is to look after the hatch cleaning, being done by the Krooboys, and see that all the proceeds are landed to a 'gash' barge which is due alongside this afternoon. Andy, the newly married second mate and our two apprentices are to knock off and be ready for the night shift once we've moved over to the coal wharf, a decrepit structure at the other end of the port.

The story is that we've been chartered by the Nigerian government to ship coal from here to the Ijora power station in Lagos and also for the account of Nigerian Railways for an unspecified period. The government's own collier is out of service for repairs that are taking a lot longer than anticipated and it seems that our first load is urgently wanted if the lights are to stay lit in Lagos.

By nightfall we're at the coaling wharf and we've opened up our two principal hatches, numbers two and four, and are positioned so that the stationary loader can tip the coal into the former hatch. It would be hard to find a more unsuitable ship for this trade as we have 'tweendecks and long 'run-ins' at all hatches, which means that the coal will have to be hand-trimmed into so many distant corners.

My deck duty spell is over but, out of curiosity, I watch the first coal being tipped from the conveyor belt into the lower hold. The coal is from mines near Enugu, just over a hundred miles away, and it comes in by rail. It's shabby-looking stuff, more like lumps of dark grey slate but just as dusty and choking as the real thing.

I retreat and go to join the promenade-deck grizzlers, who are bemoaning this turn of events. We agree that, following so soon after independence, the country's infrastructure is crumbling because the British have departed. Equally, our employers are outrageous in accepting this dirty charter for which we'll get no extra reward. It seems that the slump in shipboard morale that occurs at this stage in any voyage is going to be a deep one.

The next morning we have to shift the ship forwards so that the loader can tip into number four hatch. This is a much better space and has the added benefit that each load can be aimed at the top of the shaft tunnel, which will have satisfyingly ear-splitting reverberations throughout the engine-room until it is covered in coal.

Up at number two, Charlie and I have a look at the overnight workmanship and don't find it too bad. The initial pyramid of coal has been partially flattened but is nowhere near the corners.

Charlie, who hasn't been mate for very long, admits that he's only got an educated guess at how much space we'll need to fill. We know the volume available and our company handbook provides what is called the 'stowage factor', which gives a figure of so many cubic feet occupied by a ton of coal. We also know how much coal we can load to keep within the restricted depth alongside at our destination. However, until we see some substantial tonnage loaded, we don't know if the theory will equal the reality.

Charlie has found a gang of trimmers, equipped with their shovels, who have been trying to avoid attention by skulking in the offshore maindeck alleyway. Ignoring their protests of 'We go stan by for wen e dun finish dis load,' he shoos them out of there and up to number two, where he and I both lead them down to the coal.

Charlie illustrates what needs to be done by slicing out a shovelful of coal and neatly spraying it into a far corner. Still reasonably immaculate, despite being in his white uniform and long white socks, Charlie then makes his exit and I have to start encouraging the trimmers to emulate his skill.

I should be leading by example, but I soon get tired of the effort and, much to the amusement of all, I retreat. I'm accompanied by a chorus of 'Dis young boy, he go tire too much,' 'Dis boy, e no get power like chief mate' as I climb up the vertical steel ladder and get back on deck.

The loading routine of shifting and coal trimming continues until we have the required tonnage on board. The crew replace the hatch beams and the main deck hatchboards (the boards for the lower decks have already been stowed out of harm's way). They then spread a tarpaulin on each hatch before we leave our berth and make our way down the creek.

We pass Dawes Island and then Bonny Town before following the dredged channel out to the fairway buoy, where we turn right and plod off at a sedate 12 knots towards Lagos under a sullen grey sky.

On arrival at our destination we pass through the whole length of the harbour to reach a berth alongside Ijora power station. The urgent need for this seemingly unimpressive coal is quite apparent as the usual sizeable heaps of the commodity have disappeared. A couple of yellow bulldozers are scraping together what's left into quantities that can be scooped up into a queue of lorries that are patiently waiting.

The Nigerian supervisor is also impatient for our load and tells us that both of his cranes will be unloading our cargo as soon as we've uncovered the two hatches. It's therefore not long before they are lowering their grabs into the cargo, biting it up and then depositing it in hoppers which feed a conveyor belt that takes it off to the hungry furnaces of the power station.

As the afternoon arrives there's definitely a denser colour to the smoke plume from the station's chimneys. The operator, Nigerian Electric Power Authority (NEPA), looks as though it'll now escape from the usual epithet of 'Never Ever Power Again', one usually given to it by expatriates.

It's some of those expatriates that we know here who, unlike their equivalents in Port Harcourt, soon seek us out. Our stay alongside becomes an enjoyable social mixture of entertaining them to drinks on board and accepting invitations to share the facilities, especially the swimming pool, at the Apapa Club.

In between these pleasant diversions, there's the business of getting all the coal out of the vessel and, it being an equally dusty operation to that of loading, all door and window openings have to be kept closed despite the oppressive heat.

We are, however, spared the palaver of any coal trimming because the wharf supplies a small bulldozer that weighs only three tons (and thus is no bother bringing aboard). It's small enough to operate into all the corners and push the coal out into the square of the hatch where the grabs can pick it up. Nevertheless, we need to keep an eye on these grabs as it's soon obvious that they're capable of doing substantial damage to our steelwork.

Charlie appears on deck at one point on our last day of discharge with an Indian man dressed in an immaculate white boiler suit bearing the NEPA logo. He, Charlie explains, is the cargo surveyor who will agree what damage has been sustained by the ship during the discharge and which will therefore be made good by NEPA as the ship's charterers.

When I point out some damage to the housing for one of the hatch beams, he notes it but then remarks that all damages will be made good 'at the end of the charter'.

Charlie replies, 'But that needs fixing now because we cannot ship the beam and this affects the strength of the ship.' The surveyor remains unmoved and witters on about charter party terms, quoting a document that we've not yet seen.

Before the unloading is finished, I find a beam housing damaged at the other hatch but Charlie decides that any argument with the surveyor will be pointless. It's just logged and he'll convince the Old Man that we can dispense with a couple of hatch beams as, in his words, 'It's not as if we'll be bouncing over the bar going into one of the creeks.'

Off we go for another coal cargo, washing the dust of this one off our decks and into the waters of Lagos harbour in our attempt to try and look as ship-shape as possible. That's because we have to sail past the mile-long length of Apapa Quay with onlookers on all its berthed ships evaluating our grubby progress. Then we're back in Port Harcourt and the tiresome waltz of tip, shift and trim to collect another three and a half thousand tons of 'nutty slack'.

Back at Ijora, however, there's some news for me. The second mate of one of our ships needs to get home for his forthcoming wedding but is facing a trip over to the States. The solution proposed by our personnel department back at the 'House of Laughter' in Liverpool is personally attractive to me.

Will I transfer and take his place on a confirmed promotion? I'm packing my bag immediately, but first I can enjoy a hastily arranged departure party and Charlie makes a nice gesture. He 'dashes' me a set of second mate's epaulettes (which he'd worn himself until only just over a year ago) so that I can 'look the part'. With my bar bill settled and my watchkeeping certificate signed, I head off from my coaly home to a rather more agreeable berth.

First impressions contradict that prospect, as I've agreed to sign on one of the ships that formed the 'Paddy' Henderson fleet, taken over a few years previously – a ship that began its sea life at about the same time as me and is thus the newest ship that I've ever sailed in. That I would never believe as I step on board.

Sad to say, she is the very ideal of parsimonious Glasgow ship-owning from her cramped accommodation to her skimpily equipped decks. The latter epitomised by her ancient steam winches, which are at least 30 years older than she is, having been recycled from the ship-breakers at Dalmuir.

Fortunately, I find out that there is a very welcoming ship's company. The chief steward is one of our own men and so I'll be spared that Paddy Henderson phenomenon of the quartered kipper. It is standard Merchant Navy practice that half a kipper can be offered at breakfast as stock dwindles but no smaller fraction. After all, how much flesh can be found at one side of the after end of a smoked herring?

11

Caught for a double-header

The West Africa to North America Trade

A British ship carrying cargo between the West Coast of Africa and North America is engaged in what is known as a 'cross-trade'. This term arises from the fact that the vessel is owned in a country that has not produced the cargo that it is conveying. Cross-trading is an important element in the sea trade of the world but it is often limited in order to protect the economic interests of the producing countries.

In the case of trade between the United States and West Africa, it was the American interest that had the legal safeguards. Legislation that began in 1920 with the passing of the so-called Jones Act continually limited the type of US exports available for carriage by foreign tonnage. Some cross-trade shipping was provided by a US–Norwegian consortium (the Barber Wilhelmsen Line) and Elder Dempster were their principal competitor.

Even Elder Dempster had reduced their North American involvement. Their postwar service between Canada and Africa as far south as the Cape, using ships under the Canadian flag but with mainly British crews, terminated in 1950.

Shipments of primary products such as cocoa, coffee, timber and latex were plentiful from West Africa. The return cargoes of manufactured goods and of food or development aid were largely reserved for the American-flag carriers Delta Shipping and Farrell Lines. However, it was British participation that allowed direct shipment of cargoes to the smaller ports on the Coast since American ships limited their itinerary to a few important destinations.

I always considered that a voyage to North America instead of returning home from West Africa was termed a 'double-header' since that involved the loading of two complete cargoes within a single trip. Purists maintain that two American voyages were necessary to claim that title. My personal view is that an absence of eight months instead of the more customary eight weeks was sacrifice enough to award myself the dubious honour of having earned that title for my trip.

I'm pleased to find that morale is so good on a ship that has just been handed the prospect of an extended voyage. My new fellow officers, even those four with wives and families at home, all seem to be happy to have a break from our usual trade pattern. I also learn that the African crew, all from Freetown on this ship, are quite pleased with the prospect of going somewhere new.

We have to finish unloading here and then complete our outward passage by calling at Victoria, Tiko and Douala before starting to load for the US on an itinerary yet to be decided. This voyage began in Tilbury so a large part of the cargo this time is cement rather than salt. On the coal trade, the dust and residue made the Nigerian dockworkers even blacker in their skin tone. Now I see the reverse effect as cement dust makes the gangs resemble Australian or New Guinea aborigines dressed up for a celebratory dance.

Out of some consideration for their grubby plight, the deck service line is charged at the end of each shift and at meal times so that the labourers can get some salt water out of the ship's fire hydrants for their ablutions. The ship, however, has to await our departure before the sailors and the Krooboys can start to tackle the mess on deck and in the holds with hoses and deck scrubbers.

Getting the ship clean is a priority, as we know that the States run means a large cargo of cocoa and coffee in bags. Both of these cargoes can only be loaded if the government produce-board inspectors declare the cargo spaces to be clean and hygienic. This means that whereas my last ship left a dirty black wake across the Bight of Benin, we now repeat the abuse with one of grey and white shades as we head for the anchorage of Victoria under the great bulk of Mount Cameroon.

The cargo for Victoria cannot be completed by the day shift so night gangs are called for by the mate. The formidable woman who supplies the labour declares that those new hands are on the way but we're amazed to see the launch carrying the day gangs ashore do a complete turnaround once ostensibly out of sight and return to our gangway.

Madam, with a staggering display of bluster, insists, 'Dese be new men, all be fresh from de shore.' When challenged that we recognise at least six or seven of them as old faces, she becomes alarmingly vocal and physically quite threatening at this impugning of her honesty. In the face of her monopoly, we have to concede to her. The 'new' labour, to their credit, finish the job ahead of time. They're desperate, no doubt, to escape from that violent termagant who probably has them earmarked for more work on the next shift later that morning.

Our next port of call, Tiko, is just around the corner but up a creek rather than facing the open sea. It's principally the outlet for bananas, and the smart white ships of Elders & Fyffes have priority there. We would have to quit the only berth if one of their ships was due. My father works for this firm back in Liverpool and has given me a contact name if ever my ship called at this place.

When I find that we might be staying in Tiko for a few days, I try to look this person up but, naturally, he's at home on leave. Nevertheless, his Camerounian deputy very obligingly arranges for his car to take me to visit Buea, a small town high on the slopes of the mountain.

Along with two others from the ship, I'm able to enjoy a fine excursion as we drive up into the clouds and then through them to reach our destination. Buea is a town that presents some recognisably Bavarian architecture dating from the pre-First-World-War days of German colonial Kamerun. It also has distinctly Scottish Highland views and a complementary almost lightly chilly dampness. After this temperate and very enjoyable afternoon, it's an anticlimax to have to descend 4,000 feet to sweaty sea level. I can then thank our host by treating him to dinner on board the ship.

Our extended stay here in Tiko is partially because we have to load additional cargo. That comprises about 50 or 60 iroko logs which must be taken to Douala for tranship-ment by another of our ships whose arrival here coincides with that of a banana boat.

Iroko is a very noble timber; it's also very dense and the logs therefore do not float as do those of other trees. We call them 'sinkers' rather than 'floaters' and they come alongside on a barge from the nearby sawmill which has prepared them to an extremely clean smoothness.

Despite each one averaging only around seven tons, loading them on deck is quite a performance due to our limited number of derricks and those cantankerous steam winches. We also have to lay out log-lashing chains because a roll of the ship as we cross the bar of the creek at Tiko or in the shallows around Douala could easily deposit these valuable timbers in the sea.

When I see 'Liverpool' painted on a couple of these logs, that invokes some homesickness, but it soon passes. Later, we have an uneventful stay in Douala and so the last of our outward cargo is completed. Now we're off to the bar crossing at Escravos and the tortuous creek passage up to Sapele.

As an empty ship we pass comfortably across the bar and, heading into the calm waters between the two stone revetments, we're looking out for the pilot. It's Sunday Kalaroo on this occasion, who very soon has himself, his scruffy canoe, his helmsman and his obligatory 'small boy' brought safely on board. The Old Man gets things off to a good start by 'dashing' Sunday a brand-new Elder Dempster houseflag with which to adorn his craft in future. Our pilot reckons that we cannot reach Sapele before dark and must pass the night at anchor before entering Chanomi Creek in the morning.

Darkness soon falls. Our deck lights illuminate the blackness of the tropical night and the rank perfume of the mangroves assaults our noses. Later, canoes are gathering around the stern. Soon the volume of excited chatter and giggling coming from the poop accommodation indicates that a good deal of 'business' is being conducted with our Freetown crew and, no doubt, more than a few of the Krooboys. For the rest of us on board, it's just another boring night in an African backwater.

On arrival in Sapele we're moored to buoys in the creek and are thus a canoe ride from the delights of the Ferry Inn and other top local 'nitespots'. As stories now abound of villainous canoe owners demanding outrageous return fares on pain of passengers being tipped into the creek, there's no great inclination to go ashore.

We can concentrate on the cargo, some seven hundred tons of rubber, both sheet and crepe, destined for New York. But first we must lower one of our lifeboats so that the mate and a couple of engineers can inspect the propeller blades as they are turned to become nearly fully visible at our very light draught. The good news is that they're undamaged by our trip up the creeks where logs that have broken adrift are an unseen or unavoidable hazard in these restricted waters.

The rubber comes alongside in its special lighters that protect it from the rain. Today, however, is hot and sunny and our ancient steam winches add to the furnace intensity on deck as net after net of rubber is swung aboard. We're into the usual talcum powder routine with the gangs of Hausa boys getting whiter by the minute but there's no interfering European here to put his oar in concerning the stowage.

All the rubber will have to go into the 'tweendecks as that is the only suitable place to stow it and, anyway, it's for our first American port of call. That makes us top-heavy but the tonnage is insufficient to cause any real stability concerns.

In between all this loading, the Krooboys are busy making sure that the holds are spotless since we'll be loading cocoa, the principal part of our cargo, when we get back to Lagos. There was some cocoa offering here but, in typical West Coast fashion, in the end it never appears and so we set off back down the creeks.

We pass a Palm boat on the way up and our Sparks is delighted to tell his opposite number there that he is, of now, the guard ship for Sapele. Sunday and his entourage, with their canoe now well-laden with goods from Sapele market and other sundries cadged from the ship, are disembarked as we pass their home village of Ogidigbe and then we're over the bar and pointing towards Lagos.

Tied up at one of the original berths on Apapa Quay which are rich with the odours of sewage and decaying spillages of groundnut cake and other produce, we await the survey of the Nigerian Produce Marketing Board inspectors. They prove to be both fair and efficient and issue the necessary certificates to allow the loading of cocoa to begin. We're booked for about 1,500 tons of this season's crop of cocoa beans, which are destined for Philadelphia, with a little for Baltimore also.

We have six gangs booked to load this to nearly all points in our lower holds and there are three cranes helping to overcome our lack of derricks. As our light condition makes us very high out of the water, these venerable machines, delivered over thirty years ago by Stothert and Pitt of Bath, will struggle.

This is because their low height means that their drivers cannot see into the hatch and so they'll not be as fast as they might be. Nevertheless, it's all hands on deck now, three mates and two apprentices all bent on ensuring that the cocoa stowage gets off to a proper start. It might be thought that banging in a load of cocoa sacks is light relief after the complications of loading logs but there is a considerable art to producing an effective stow of bags.

The secret lies in getting the first four tiers on the face of the stow absolutely right. The Krooboys have already prepared the hatch as part of the inspection requirements. They've laid two layers of wooden dunnage planks on top of the tank ceiling which is, perversely, the name for the bottom of the hold. The first planks are laid athwartships so as to lead any moisture to the bilges for drainage. The second layer is laid fore and aft and then the whole trellis-like construction is overlaid with brand-new hessian separation cloths.

Cocoa bags are sixteen to the ton so, if we look at our number five lower hold, for example, we're planning to have 4,800 bags in the forepart for Philadelphia and 2,240 bags in the after part for Baltimore. Time to get the gangs in this hatch cracking.

I call the two gang headmen together and explain the plan, pointing out that the two stows must stay apart by at least two feet and be absolutely stable. Happily for me, they both seem to be bag experts so I can confidently point out where I want the first rows of bags to run.

We'll take our time to start with since I want all the bags on the bottom to face fore and aft. I also need one well-plumped end of each bag to be lying on the line that I've made with the aid of a length of rope yarn stretching across the hold. With two fat frontages facing each other, the next tier will be laid athwartships but also plumped up to keep that all-important straight face.

Behind this immaculate dwarf wall, stowage can be a little more cavalier in the interests of speed but the gang must leave a three-foot-square space under each corner of the hatch. This will be the start of a ventilation trunk to allow fresh air to penetrate the cargo while we're at sea. Now I can pop along to make sure that the third mate has got his stowages off to a good start. Then I want to get ashore for an hour or two before I have a kip prior to taking up the night shift.

Where I'm bound to is Tugwell House, the Missions to Seamen facility, which will enable me to telephone home and let my parents know about my change of ship. I'm certain that our marine personnel department will already have informed them for posting purposes but I'd like to explain things myself.

I'm resigned to a good measure of palaver over the call being connected, so it's a pleasant surprise to get through almost immediately on a line that is clear as a bell. Once I've assured my mother that, unlike a previous tanker voyage, I won't be away for a year, we exchange brief news. I then pay for my call plus a small 'dash' to the mission clerk who so efficiently arranged it. Finally, with time in hand for once, it's a chance to enjoy a dip in the pool, a bottle of Star lager and a sandwich before my return.

Number 3 berth, Apapa Quay, is not a pleasant place at night. The purulent stink of the wharf seems to gain in intensity and the surface of the quay is patrolled by huge posses of substantial cockroaches which crunch very satisfactorily when you cross them in your standard-issue tackety boots.

As some compensation for this unsavoury environment, there's something very welcome about the labour tonight. There are just three gangs as we concentrate on the heaviest hatches and I'm gratified that they're not only maintaining a splendid loading rate but also carefully protecting the structure of the stow. This means that the front of the bags is neither retreating to a slope or advancing to an overhang. My further delight is that neither are the ventilation trunks narrowing to letter-box size as they rise.

The loading is all being done by cranes so we're also being spared the din of our museum winches. The only cargo attention needed is to make sure that plant fibre mats are being applied to the ship's frames before bags lie against them as a protection against any rust or sweat damage, and also that not too many of them are being abstracted for use as sleeping surfaces.

My apprentice and I can then join the duty engineer in the galley, which he has just fired up. Oil is the heating source on this ship with its minimal electric supply. We enjoy an undisturbed meal of bacon, eggs and copious rounds of fried bread. However, this greasy celebration proves to be so absorbing that I don't realise that the labour have left the ship. The cranes are parked, the hatch tents are rigged and secured and I only just catch the foreman at the top of the gangway.

'All de lorry done finish, no more work dis night,' he says, and then adds, 'Dis place, e go stink pass latrine, make I go now, drink beer and no fit smell kaka again.' So that's the reason for this exceptional work performance by an Apapa night shift that is usually more adept at finding sleeping places or otherwise misbehaving.

It's another day, another surveyor. This time, it's an Englishman in a bright white boiler suit who comes to survey our two lower deep tanks, which are booked for 500 tons of palm-kernel oil for New York. The hard work put in by the Krooboys results in the tanks being passed as fit and even our hard-pressed Scotch boiler has proved capable of raising the tanks' steam-heating coils to a satisfactory temperature.

At this berth we can load the oil direct from the quay and so that's done in a morning. The cocoa cargo finishes a little later and then there's just a miscellaneous collection of cases of sheepskins and bundles of other dry hides, all for New York.

We make an unhurried departure and then a short sail along the coast to Lomé, where we'll be receiving another eleven hundred tons of cocoa, this time all for Philadelphia. That takes us three days as we're loading it from boats and there's no work done at night. Hessian separation cloths are laid to indicate the change from Nigerian to Togolese beans and the gangs prove capable of both handling our clattering deck machinery and maintaining the established discipline of the stow.

Then it's on to Takoradi for bundles of sawn timber, principally for Norfolk and a hefty consignment of nearly 500 tons of logs on deck for the same destination. Out come the long lashing chains once again to lie athwartships at about ten-foot intervals along the whole length of both foredeck and afterdeck. This is the port of log experts and they soon make a very presentable job in both places.

Then it's the turn of our Freetown sailors under their bosun's direction to put in place the senhouse slips and bottle screws that tighten up the chains to keep the logs immovable as we cross the Atlantic. Some wooden gangways arrive from the company's store in this port and then a gang of local carpenters position them on top of the logs. This will enable us to reach both the forecastle and the poop in safety at sea.

Abidjan is our next call; this time it's for a mixed bag of sawn timber, cases of veneers, bags of coffee, of chillies and of kola nuts. Finally, we reach Freetown, where our coffee cargo gets us a berth on the quay, much to the delight of the crew. They can get a couple of nights at home and the Krooboys can get friends down to protect their loads as they depart with their voyage pickings.

For the Europeans, it's a last chance to post letters home for a while and we also manage to make a swap of our films so that we start our ocean passage with a full allocation of movie entertainment. As we cant the stern off the quay, go slowly astern and then turn our bows to seaward, we're the proud carriers of nearly seven thousand tons of cargo. We're looking forward, we hope, to a leisurely disbursement of this load on the eastern coast of the United States.

The crossing from Freetown to New York will take us fourteen days at our customary stately pace of between 12 and 13 knots. That's just fine as we're sailing through the pleasantest latitudes of the planet, the domain of the trade winds, flying fish and big blue skies under a hot sun. And that's the way it proves with just two diversions to interrupt a fortnight of quiet watches and sun worshipping. It's also the chance to practise some celestial navigation and to give a bit more dedication than is usual to the meteorological reporting logbook.

The first break in routine is when we find ourselves coming up on a pod of whales. The Old Man, an underwater and fishing enthusiast, calls down to the chief engineer for more speed so that he can get some cine-camera footage. Before there's any perceptible acceleration, the great cetaceans give him a dismissive flick of their splendid tails and are gone.

The next source of amusement is when we find ourselves in amongst the sargasso weed that is sprinkled liberally across the waters south of Bermuda. Our apprentices are not gullible enough to believe that we'll see the weed-encrusted wrecks of old Spanish galleons. They do, however, fall for the canard that dried weed provides a very satisfying smoke and an economical alternative to a spot of that other 'weed' that is beginning to fascinate in the 1960s.

An improvised grappling hook is sufficient, given our very modest speed, to gather in some substantial hanks, which soon appear in the officers' drying room for curing. It's planned for the mate to devise a drugs 'bust' on the two lads but they get their smoke in first and are later seen, gasping and retching, as they ditch their haul of 'Sargasso Gold' over the side.

It's not long after this that we're asked to make Norfolk our first port as the New York dockers will not board the ship while it has the deck covered in logs. That change will mean that the rest of the Norfolk cargo won't be accessible since it's overstowed by that for New York. When this is pointed out, we're told to revert to a New York arrival and so it is, on a gloriously sunny morning, that we embark our pilot near the famous Ambrose light vessel.

I came here on a similarly sunny day during my first voyage to sea. Then the skyscrapers of New York floated between blue skies and a shallow layer of sea smoke that seemed magical to a 16-year-old. That entrancing sight helped me to forget the pain of coiling ropes so frozen that they could be formed into squares.

Now I'm a seasoned visitor but can still be amazed by the scale of the Verrazzano Narrows bridge, which we pass under. It looks complete but we hear that the official opening is still some three months away. On my previous visits, the ship had berthed in the backwaters of Newark Bay. Now, however, we're bound to the Bush Terminal, lying almost in the shadow of the famous Brooklyn Bridge.

'Bush', in West African parlance, means primitive or unsophisticated, so it's an appropriate name for the berth where we tie up. Its single storey sheds on wooden piers are of such a collective dilapidation that they cannot withstand the pressure of contact with a large steel ship. We have to heave ourselves alongside steel pontoons and then a wooden drawbridge is lowered to span the gap.

Our dismissive perceptions of this terminal are matched by the reactions of the New York longshoremen when they see our steam winches. 'Hey, it's a goddam museum ship,' is one typical comment. It calls for a long huddle between the mate, a stevedore superintendent, the agency's port captain and some union representatives.

It turns out that they don't like the logs on deck, they don't like our heavy steel hatch covers and most of all, they despise the winches. It's an impasse that lasts all morning and leaves us wondering if we'll have to retreat to Norfolk to unload the logs after all. On the other hand, we might have a couple of days of peace in which to get across the harbour to the big city.

We're not party to the decision that's made ashore; however, the gangs return early in the afternoon and start sending out slings of coffee bags and nets of rubber bales to land on the drawbridges. These must be pretty robust as forklift trucks can cross them and carry the cargo into the shed. The dockers seemingly rediscover the art of handling our winches and, apart from the odd gripe about safety lines or sticky bales, all is harmony and we can plan our exploration of New York.

There'll be no night work and none at the approaching weekend because of the expense of hiring labour on overtime so plenty of opportunity to taste the city is in prospect.

We're a fair walk from the subway stations on Flatbush Avenue where trains will take us to either Times Square or Grand Central Station according to the line. Going ashore in daylight is no problem but is reportedly asking for trouble after dark so the solution to that is a taxi. I can split both the cargo work and the night on board duty with the third mate and that means it'll be budget rather than opportunity that will dictate my shoregoing.

I've already done the usual tourist sights more than once so my interest is in the nightlife and, on our first night in port, it's not long before a bunch of us have booked taxis that take us over the Manhattan Bridge and across lower Manhattan to Washington Square. Two of our number are quite recent visitors and reckon to have the Greenwich Village area all sorted.

After sampling a couple of forgettable bars, we arrive at a place on the corner of 10th Street and 7th Avenue that calls itself 'Your Father's Mustache'. Once inside, we're invited to clip uncomfortable black card moustaches to our nostrils. We can then quaff pitchers of gaseous beer and dig into large bowls of peanuts, whose husks we're free to scatter on the wooden floor before demanding replenishments.

The big attraction here are similar sized groups of girls with whom we soon strike up a rapport, although their fascination with English accents and mannerisms does fade when we suggest they come to a shipboard party and we have to reveal its Brooklyn location.

The free weekend allows me to visit some more of the tourist attractions of New York in daylight and also to renew acquaintance with one of the famous Tad's steakhouses. On offer is a substantial piece of beef, a green salad and a huge baked Idaho potato for about a dollar twenty (less than ten bob in those far-off days). It's a meal ideally suited to a budget which is starting to feel the strain of this place where spending is all too easy. I also need to remember that there are more ports to come before I can start repairing my savings once we're back at sea.

The first of these ports is Norfolk. It's principally a naval base and not much else, where our decks are stripped of logs and the rest of the cargo is unloaded by shore cranes. Then it's up the length of Chesapeake Bay, where the pilot, on being told that we can offer him a full speed of 12 knots, turns his baseball cap back to front and says to the Old Man, 'Wowee! Not bad for an old tramp like this. Let 'er rip!' It's a comment that none of us on the bridge could comfortably challenge.

Our shortcomings are of no concern to the longshoremen of the Erie Railroad terminal in Baltimore, Afro-Americans to a man, who seem perfectly happy with the winches. They obligingly rip out 800-odd tons of cocoa and sawn timber inside a single shift before despatching us the following morning.

This means that we enjoy an interesting passage through the Chesapeake–Delaware canal in daylight to reach the Delaware river. Here we pass below the spans of two massive bridges to reach our Philadelphia berth. This is where all our remaining cargo is destined save a small amount of rubber and cocoa butter for Halifax. We will also begin loading a cargo back to West Africa. The welcome news is that we'll be here for at least a week.

Another weekend is now in the offing and the third mate and I decide to split it so that we can both pay a visit to Washington as it's only an eight-dollar Greyhound bus fare from here. At the same time, our two American experts are busy reviving old ties. The result is a block invitation on Friday night to a barbecue in Germantown, a suburb to the north of the city centre.

It's a welcome invitation since my previous recollection of Philadelphia is that it lived up to its title of the 'city of brotherly love' by sending down cars manned by predatory homosexuals who'd heard that a ship carrying 30 young apprentices was in town. The Germantown excursion is a very enjoyable one and we organise a return event on board one evening.

As in New York, there's no night work on the grounds of cost, so we can set out our rather cluttered boat deck as a bar and dance area. When the time comes for us to leave, it's with a lot of regret since many of us have managed to create some passionate and enjoyable romances with the girls of Germantown.

We depart with the first of our cargo on board, nearly three thousand tons of steel pipes for the booming oil industry in Nigeria, and head back to New York. The cargo from here is much more varied.

There are bags of flour that bear trademark brands for Lagos and Monrovia. Other flour bags for Cotonou and Douala have the clasped white-and-black hands logo of US Aid and the legend in large letters 'Gift of the people of the USA. Not to be sold or exchanged'. Sadly, we'll too often see those bags in African marketplaces where this 'two hands' flour brand commands a premium price.

We're also loading desirable items such as confectionery, bourbon, tinned goods and tools that soon fill up our only two lockable spaces and this is where the bother starts. We are threatened with violence while trying to intervene when cartons are blatantly opened. We can but watch as the contents are pocketed by the gang working the cargo.

Pilfering of cargo happens in every port but the ship's officers are expected to keep it under control by acting as watchmen when any vulnerable items are being loaded. Nevertheless, prosecutions in court for theft of cargo are usually impractical. This means that dockers the world over can always outwit the ship's staff but they very rarely steal so blatantly as these examples of New York's finest.

An appeal for help to our port captain only produces the lame response that we should not expose ourselves to any serious assault. The ship will not be blamed since high cargo insurance premiums for goods shipped via New York recognise and compenate for this high level of 'shrinkage'.

Maybe I should have capitalised on the situation by issuing tickets to steal as my dollar budget is now nearly exhausted. Philadelphia and New York have proved rather too tempting in terms of shopping for books, records and other purchases in addition to entertainment. This means that I'm pleasantly surprised when George, our chief engineer, asks me if I fancy going ashore with him that evening to dinner and an organ recital, completely free of charge.

Thus we find ourselves in a taxi that has been sent to the ship to collect us and take us to an address in the Greenwich Village area. It's a converted warehouse that belongs to the man who owns the ship repair firm that has been doing some work on board and our invitation there is by way of thanks for the business.

After a meal with him and his family we are to hear the recital, a prospect that intrigues me as we are apparently not going out again. So it is that we are seated in comfortable chairs with brandy and coffee to hand in a large room while our host opens a sort of wardrobe and reveals an organ console.

As his performance begins, the room is flooded with the unmistakable sounds of Bach but it isn't at all clear where this music is being generated. After this initial piece, seguing into a medley of Broadway musical favourites and terminating with an arrangement of a recent Beatles hit, all is revealed.

The sound comes through large wooden grilles in the floor and we look through them to see the massed ranks of organ pipes below. This lovely instrument is a Wurlitzer organ that our host has rescued from a demolished theatre over in New Jersey and then installed in this converted warehouse.

The premises are not only large enough for this dedicated concert space but also for his family to be insulated from the performances if they wished. And, as he points out, there are no problems with the neighbours. Later, sitting in a taxi that has been paid for to take us back to the ship, I reflect that this has been one of the most unusual and enjoyable nights ashore in my seagoing life.

A reminder of recent nights ashore comes the next day when Andy, our third engineer, tells me that he's just had a postcard from our Philadelphia girlfriends. They're driving to meet us in Halifax and have booked into a motel for the weekend that we're expecting to be there.

'Bloody hell,' says Andy, 'that's a drive of nearly a thousand miles. This is getting to be a bit serious.'

It certainly is and likely to be expensive as well since we'll really have to offer something towards their petrol and hotel expenses. It was a great time that we'd had in Philly but this type of romance, however passionate, was supposed to fade on our departure.

'And what if they decide to fly to the UK?' Andy muses further, 'I'm supposed to be getting engaged next time I'm home.' It's certainly something to think about as we make our US farewell and plod our stately way up towards Canada.

In Halifax, we unload our small African cargo and take on board more bags of aid flour, several unboxed tractors and a large consignment of bales and cartons of second-hand shoes and clothing. We had been expecting to load much more cargo but our agents have decided that the additional bookings are too uncertain and plan to get us out of the port by Friday evening.

Those who've visited Halifax on earlier voyages aren't too disappointed as the local liquor laws are particularly restrictive and, anyway, we're collectively skint.

For Andy and I, of course, there's now a big problem. We don't know where the girls are booked to stay and they'll already be en route. We must ask the agency boarding clerk if he'll take a message from us in case they contact our only Halifax address. It's therefore with more than a slight sense of guilt that we leave North America and look forward to a couple of weeks of uncomplicated sea routine as we head for Dakar, our first port of call back on the Coast.

Back at sea, we're feeding well three times a day as usual although some of the items we stored in Philadelphia are not to our taste. Head cheese, which sounds disgusting, proves to be a reasonable type of cold meat. However, the bacon was not designed for British palates, and neither were the sausages and, with kippers finished, breakfast is not its usual self.

Salads are another surprise to us. The lettuce leaves are large enough to be used as roofing material back in West Africa. They're joined by radishes the size of golf balls and spring onions like young leeks. It's just a great disappointment that they inevitably prove one thing, the taste of vegetables varies inversely with size.

Into Dakar and, with our decks clear of any cargo, we're offered 60 head of cattle to take to Monrovia. These skinny beasts have walked down from the interior of Senegal and will be fattened up for slaughter at their destination. It's the first time that I've carried such livestock and the way in which they're loaded initially horrifies me.

A rope sling is passed under the animal's forequarters and then, with its rear legs kicking frantically, the cow is hoisted off the quay to land awkwardly on our steel after deck. However, despite the loud bellows of complaint being made collectively by those cattle awaiting their turn to be hoisted, the animals already on board go quietly and obediently into the straw-lined wooden pen that will be their home for the next few days.

Five Senegalese cattlemen soon have their charges safely tethered to a wire bridle rope within the pen. They're watered and being looked after really quite well long before we cast off and, fully fuelled, head for Freetown. It's just another port for us again, of course, but our Sierra Leonian crew are in a high state of excitement and eager anticipation as they pack their 'loads' and get ready for home.

In comparison with an arrival from Europe, they have little in the way of goods as America has been a place of little business. It didn't offer them much in the way of a social welcome, either. I recall that the Afro-American stevedores of Baltimore and Philadelphia were quite dismissive of any sense of kinship when greeted by 'Hey, my brother, I done salute you one time' from our crew members.

It was one of our sailors, on night gangway duty, who had the perfect riposte to the attractions of the USA. Seeing a group of us about to go ashore, he inclined his head towards the glittering skyscrapers of lower Manhattan, took out his chewing-stick and queried of us 'You go village now?' It was the standard question posed of anyone making a shore excursion in one of our many 'bush' ports in darkest Africa.

Alongside in Freetown, I see our Dakar cattlemen going ashore and, not long afterwards, they reappear with sizeable bundles of greenery festooned about their tall, skinny bodies. At least they seem to be husbanding their herd with consideration. However, it's not long afterwards that a black police Land Rover drives up to the gangway and about half a dozen constables and their corpulent and very angry sergeant come on board and start haranguing the herdsmen.

Pretty soon a cane is being used by the sergeant to chastise them during the pauses in his spitting oratory. I call the mate, who intervenes to find out what's going on. It seems that all this fresh fodder has been garnered from the gardens of the Harbour Authority and the adjacent grassy roundabout. It is a serious affront to the dignity of the senior port officials. I find out afterwards that a large donation of whisky and cigarettes has served as compensation. Nevertheless, the police sergeant takes a final opportunity to administer a little more valedictory caning on his way ashore.

Our next stop is Monrovia and here I'm pleased to see that the cattle are to be unloaded in a rather more humane fashion. Guided into a wooden stall fitted with four lifting hooks, they sail serenely and horizontally over the ship's side and then are released onto the quay. Soon the herd and its minders set off on the next stage of their journey and, although I know their eventual destination, I hope that their minders will find a source of fodder that doesn't involve the destruction of official property.

The afterdeck is left in an insanitary mess after the cattle's departure but we daren't risk washing it down in while we're in this port. This means that the 50 or so deck passengers that we're embarking for Takoradi will have to be housed under a tent on number three hatch, just in front of our accommodation.

The carriage of deck passengers is a declining trade as each new nation on the Coast becomes active in restricting any movement of foreigners. These people are Ghanaian citizens, principally traders and their families, who are choosing to return home. It's not a very regulated trade and I often wonder to what extent their safety was ever taken into consideration by the various national authorities.

Their names are recorded as part of their registration when tickets are issued in order that identities can be proved at their destination. Our lifesaving equipment doesn't take account of their numbers and, like our Krooboys, they're excluded from statutory lifeboat drills. I'm not even sure that we have enough lifejackets for them on board.

But then we sail in warm and normally calm waters and the risk of shipwreck is minimal. These passengers have access to drinking water but they have to share toilet facilities with the Krooboys unless they can make private arrangements with the rest of the crew. Food is supplied to them from the galley, a meat stew with rice twice a day, eaten in small family groups under their protective tent. It's this arrangement that leads one of the passengers to invade the saloon while we're at dinner.

It's a quite unplanned entry. Lacking any air-conditioning, our saloon window ports are wide open to allow the sea breeze to circulate in its stead. One of the ladies living under the hatch tent must have seen the bright lights and comes over to satisfy her curiosity. The first indication that we have of her presence is when her head and shoulders, crowned with a very impressive headscarf, emerge through the porthole immediately behind the Old Man.

He's oblivious of this intrusion but the purser, ever ready to enforce the decencies, springs to his feet and demands that she withdraw immediately. This the poor lady does with alacrity but, in going astern, she's trapped by her magnificent *embonpoint* and her struggles seem destined to result in an unplanned striptease.

It is then that the captain, ever the gentleman, rises to gently reassure Madam that she is not at fault and that she should take the utmost care in releasing herself from her predicament. This she does gracefully and we all return to our meal and begin busily embroidering the tale for passing on to those not present.

At Takoradi we are greeted soon after our arrival by a convoy of Scammell three-wheeled tractors, each pulling a flatbed trailer laden with ship's stores that has been landed here by one of our mailboats.

'Oh, dear,' says the mate when he sees this, 'this doesn't look too good, they've sent us the whole bloody indent. Looks like we're not going home for a while yet. Better call out the Krooboys and get this lot aboard, I'll go and get the papers off the purser.'

As we tackle this collection of cordage, paints, oils and greases together with sundry bales, cartons and cases, it becomes all too obvious that this is a shipment designed to keep us going for another trip back over to the States.

At this time, we've not been introduced to the financial discipline of a budget for maintenance and so the storing of a ship is a Levantine exercise in haggling. If you want, for example, two new mooring ropes, then you order four. You're confident that someone in India Buildings will happily chop that request in two. They look to be savage economisers and you get what you actually need.

There are some mates who delight in this ritual and quite enjoy the strategy of 'If it's listed on the stores indent book, then I'll have at least one of them'. This can backfire, of course. I recall that one erstwhile comedian was very brusquely (and expensively) challenged by a cable enquiring what he proposed to do with an additional Norwegian fog-horn, an esoteric item at the best of times.

We soon have this unexpected booty safely aboard and find places to stow it all. Now we look forward to catching up with the mailboat in Apapa, where we can replenish our refrigerated stores and get those familiar British items such as proper bacon, bangers and kippers back on the breakfast menu.

After Takoradi we have only very small quantities of cargo remaining for ports other than Lagos so that's where we're instructed to sail next. The plan is to unload or tranship all the remaining cargo there. Then it'll be back into the creeks, where we will load more rubber for American tyres and more cocoa for all those Hershey bars.

The mood on board has become subdued. I don't mind returning across the Atlantic, although I assume that there'll be a frosty welcome in Philadelphia for Andy and myself. Others, especially our small married contingent, are naturally a lot less happy.

Nevertheless, the voyage has to be prosecuted and we settle into the job of emptying the ship until the Old Man returns from a visit to the agency with the news that it's all change in typical West African style. Gradually the detail, other than the basic fact that we are now to load for Hull and Newcastle, leaks out via the usual medium of the 'galley radio'.

Our outturn in the US has proved very successful as there are virtually no cargo claims in prospect. The fact that we've not attracted any potential lawsuits from litigious American dockers earns us further head office approval. However, it also appears that our cantankerous steam winches and the woeful lack of derricks could cause our return to lead to a black-listing problem.

These details are interesting; however, the main impact is the general uplift of morale on board. This is followed by a mass excursion of whoever isn't on duty to the 'high-life' fleshpots of Apapa on this first evening after the news arrives. The ordering of several rounds of Star beers, followed by an energetic session of bottom-shaking to the music in conjunction with the bewigged belles of Nigeria makes for an evening of appropriate celebration.

Now we have to sort out what cargo need not be transhipped as our loading itinerary will begin with calls to Victoria and Douala, both of which are destinations for our American cargo. Then we'll be heading back to Takoradi, Abidjan, Freetown and Bathurst. It will be another cargo of bags and logs with the exception of a lift of manganese ore in bulk from Takoradi.

It's in Victoria that we have some simple entertainment with part of the cargo that we've brought over from Halifax. This is what remains on board from a larger

Above: Elder Dempster's Swedru *ready to load in Liverpool's Toxteth Dock in autumn 1963. Short and squat, she is built for sailing up narrow creeks.*

Below: The Degema *of Elder Dempster sailing through Chanomi Creek in the Niger Delta, a crowded study of derricks, pulley blocks, wires and ropes. However, on this ship, at least the hatch covers are now steel although still covered with canvas tarpaulins.*

Above: Another study of derricks, ropes and wires, here on the approach to Pointe Muzuku on the way up the Congo. The scenery is reminiscent of a Scottish sea loch. Some of the Krooboys can be seen under the forecastle, having just finished their 'chop'.

Below: The formidable Chaudron d'Enfer. The tree-clad sandstone cliffs rise to 800 feet and the eddies and whirlpools generated during the season of high river are clearly seen.

Above: The Hotel Metropole in Matadi. Despite independence, the Belgian King Albert I still occupies his memorial plinth, completely ignored by these Congolese passers-by.

Below: An Elder Dempster ship, with the agency launch alongside, moored off Lagos Marina and awaiting a berth at the crowded Apapa Quay beyond. Fishermen here in 1965 are able to hang out their laundry. Eviction to allow development is still in the future.

A busy scene on Apapa Quay. The first of six 14 ton AEI transformers is being loaded to a rail wagon for its journey north to Kaduna. Of particular interest are the massive block with eleven parts of lifting wire (it could lift 50 tons) and the cramped deck space filled with lorries, hatch beams, wires and interested spectators.

Above: Alongside the wharf in Calabar. A view from the tower of the Hope Waddell Mission church.

Below: A riverside village next to the coal berth in Port Harcourt, whose inhabitants use these large canoes to carry cargoes of mangrove logs. They cut the timber in creeks around the town and it is then used for pit-props in the Enugu coal mines.

*Not all cargo is delivered undamaged! This lorry is the casualty of a storm in Biscay
and it passes over the customary tangle of hatchboards and beams on the deck.*

This 24 ton earth-mover is discharged intact. Here at Douala, a wide quay apron is far superior to its crowded equivalent at Apapa. We can see the usual spectators and hatch beams on deck but someone has at least tidied up the ropes in the foreground.

Left: 'Swinging the lead' is nautical slang for dodging work. This is the opposite sense, here the bosun is 'heaving' (or casting) the lead and finding out the water depth as we cross the shallows at the mouth of the Calabar river. His Krooboy assistant waits to recover the lead and then make it ready for the next cast.

Below: Another ship's football team; this one is in Luanda. The author, centre foreground, uses his right hand to show the probable size of his contribution to the game's result.

This is the real business of the Coast, loading tropical logs. The winch-driver (seen returning to his post) has got into a mess here and has been arguing the toss with other gang members. Note the heavy chains used to make the logs secure on deck.

Above: The same scene, a little later. We are lying off Sinoe in Liberia and you can see the German vessel that took the only berth alongside. Note the dunnage timber on the hatch to protect the canvas tarpaulins from the logs that will be laid on top of them.

Below: The solitary water-boy waits patiently for the last three logs to be loaded on the deck.

Above: On our way home. Logs on deck get some more saltwater treatment as we meet the grey skies and roughening seas that lie northwards from the Canaries.

Below: Journey's end. A group of Tilbury dockers, standing on some 15 tonners of Gabon okoumé, decide their next move. You can see the broken bullrope lying beside them. Note also the shambles above in the 'tweendeck. Chalk-marks on the logs indicate that the barge Calder *of the Mercantile Lighterage Company is their destination.*

Left: Szczecin, Saturday, 7 August 1982. The Red Ensign is raised for the first time on the Lagos Palm *as a shipyard worker carefully folds away the Polish flag for future use.*

Below: Sunset on an historic sea trade. The Lagos Palm, *down to her marks and with a full deckload of containers, is ready to leave Liverpool's Canada Dock with her last cargo to the West Coast of Africa.*

consignment of bales and cartons of second-hand clothing shipped by a Canadian aid agency. There has been a considerable amount of rummaging amongst this stuff at the earlier ports but that had just resulted in a scattering of items that indicated some disappointment for the searchers.

In Victoria, we discover that the motley crew of scarecrows brought on board by that formidable Madam Stevedore is replaced at the end of its shift by a pretty sharply dressed crowd, albeit in the fashions of the mid-1950s.

At the gangway, we decide to confiscate their most obvious loot. That is the snappy black fedoras, the cool grey homburgs, the suave drape jackets and the brown and white co-respondent shoes. However, it's clearly impracticable to demand their shirts and trousers unless we are callous enough to send them ashore naked. It is, after all, an aid cargo and it can be argued that they've just jumped the queue. In addition, we do have some sneaking sympathy for them as they are subject to a particularly harsh taskmistress in Madam Stevedore.

Loading our homeward cargo begins with a consignment of palm-kernel oil for Hull which is delivered alongside by an incredibly ancient tank barge. It boasts a very smoky woodbine funnel and appears to have a lineage that probably dates back to when this anchorage was an entry to the German colony of Kamerun.

Then it's off to Douala for logs and timber and, from there, across to Takoradi where we go alongside immediately at a special berth and have 3,000 tons of black manganese ore tipped into our two principal holds. In complete contrast to the shambolic loading of coal that I'd recently experienced, this operation is a model of efficiency. The powdery ore is fortunately far less dusty than coal and is levelled off by small bulldozers. We then cover it with old hatch tarpaulins and are ready to load logs and sawn timber on top.

We can enjoy a single night ashore before we move off to a buoy berth in the harbour. While out there we also load bags of cocoa expeller cake and cartons of cocoa butter. Finally, our departure earns us salutes by the whistles of all the other ships in port. That's a traditional Takoradi offering given to ships heading for home at last, but we still have other calls to make.

The loading of a consignment of palm kernels from Freetown gives our Sierra Leonian shipmates the opportunity of a night at home with their families and then it's on to Bathurst to load more bags for Hull, this time they're of groundnut cake. A fairly straightfoward call is in prospect here and then we can point the ship towards home but, as you might expect in West Africa, that's not how it turns out.

A party of us have been celebrating the end of our extended African travels in the bar of the Atlantic Hotel but, when we get back to the ship, it's in total darkness, and there's an unpleasant surprise in particular for George, our chief engineer. About half an hour before our return, it emerges, our dear old second-hand Scotch boiler gave up the ghost and has thus removed just about our only source of power and light.

It's a sobering moment for all of us on board but there's very little that can be done until the boiler cools down. An uncomfortable and eerily quiet night follows during which the mosquitoes of Bathurst take full advantage of our vulnerability. I'm one of those fortunate people whose blood is apparently anathema to these insects but most people are scratching vigorously and heartily complaining the next morning as we eat a necessarily cold breakfast.

The engineers diagnose the problem which, insofar as amateur observers like myself can understand, involves the failure of several of the steel tubes that carry hot gases from the boiler furnace. These tubes are the means to heat water to become the steam necessary to power so much of the ship's equipment. True, there's still an auxiliary diesel generator available but that cannot cope with the total electrical demand, so priorities have to be decided.

The refrigerated stores will be protected and there will be a limited supply of power for hot water and a toaster in the galley. However, the main ovens are oil-fired and the fuel for them cannot be heated. Nor will there be any water pumped up for washing or for servicing the toilets. Everything on board now depends upon the skill of our engineers in salvaging the boiler.

The agency gets busy on our behalf as soon as the situation is explained. The loading of the remaining cargo has to be suspended as no mobile crane can reach our main deck, let alone into the hatches. The hatches can be tented but their large steel slab covers must remain where they are on deck.

We also cannot adjust our moorings but, fortunately, there's only about six feet of tidal range here. Nevertheless we put out extra ropes for assurance, pulling them as tight as 'Norwegian steam' (as hand-power is jokingly called) allows. One of our anchors and about a hundred feet of cable will remain in the mud until such time as we have steam power available again.

There's no means of removing us from the port's single berth but the harbourmaster is fairly sanguine about that for now. The government steamer is still away upriver on her 300 mile round trip to and from Georgetown and a coaster due in soon from Kuntaur can lie inside the T-jetty that we're using.

There is a Palm Line ship due here in a couple of days time to load and her master, on learning of the situation, has offered to come alongside and drag us into deeper water where we can safely anchor. It's a prospect that doesn't please the Old Man: 'No use leaving us stranded like some old hulk just so he can load his blasted cargo, plus how can we get the boiler fixed out there?' Then the agency hears that the Palm boat's call is cancelled and we're safe for a few days more at least.

Some generous assistance to the engineers in our plight is provided by the port's workshop and the chief engineer of the groundnut mill. On board, the bosun and sailors have rigged up tackle to lift items out of the engine-room. The chief steward puts on a simple catering service of hot drinks, cereals and sandwiches while the mates, apprentices and sparks accompany the purser on a shopping expedition ashore for hurricane lamps, insecticide sprays and mosquito coils.

The agency promises some hot food arrangements but our visions of being let loose on the *à la carte* delights of the Atlantic Hotel are extinguished when the news comes that a Lebanese-owned hotel in town will be the provider.

Meals for the African crew will be brought on board but we Europeans can sample the delights of the hotel's restaurant in the evening. To be fair, the offerings there are perfectly good but the ambience is not one to delay a return to the ship. In any case, it's not right to linger ashore while the engineers are so obviously under pressure on board.

What we can do, we learn the following morning, is to prepare suitable kindling for when the tubes are repaired or sealed off. That is when a fire will be laid in the furnace until the heavy oil can be warmed up to perform its fuel function.

Pallets, dunnage, and anything wooden that can be found around the ship is soon rendered down by a variety of implements into presentable firewood. Then it's bagged up and sent below. It's just about enough combustible material to get started but our white knight from the oil mill suggests that he can supply sacks of groundnut husks, which will guarantee a decent fire.

When we do get to that stage, the furnace's appetite proves so voracious that the husks have to be thrown in complete with their good hessian bags before the temperature reaches the point where the proper fuel can be injected. Success comes at last, the steam pressure is gradually raised and, on deck, we watch the top of our squat yellow funnel for signs of healthy smoke as avidly as any crowd of spectators at a papal election.

Once the engineers feel that the boiler can maintain working steam pressure, normality gradually returns to our moribund hulk. The lights begin to come on once the generators are started and then the alleyways begin to fill with the usual engine noises. It's time for backslapping and beers all round and, naturally, suitable 'dashes' to our many helpers ashore.

Our special ally from the oil mill is soon getting over his very obvious shock at being told the fate of his precious bags and joins us in celebrating the happy ending to one of Bathurst's more memorable maritime incidents.

It doesn't take long to load the rest of our cargo and then, the ship fully secured for sea, we pull ourselves off Government wharf and start to find our way out into the Atlantic, where we can turn right and head for home.

Just over a week later we're pushing up the English Channel, the waters a sparkling light turquoise under a cloudless blue autumn sky. Such a beautiful day can be expected to lead to misty conditions for our night-time transit of the Dover Strait. We're keeping double watches on the bridge (that is four hours on, four hours off) as it's necessary to have additional pairs of eyes on duty in the crowded waterways that lie between us and our Humber destination.

In the event, it's a crystal clear night as I come on watch at midnight with the huge light at Dungeness now on our port quarter and the lights of Folkestone and Dover just as sharply visible as those of Boulogne and Calais. In fact there are rather too many lights visible and the art is to decide which ones need watching. There is no traffic separation scheme here – that innovation is still a few years in the future – but neither is there much ferry traffic about. I'm soon familiar with what's happening and can plot our position frequently enough to keep the Old Man happy while relying on the apprentice to warn me of any fishing vessel that threatens to upset our stately progress against a strong tide.

The next day we dock in Hull without incident and the following day our reliefs arrive. We say our farewells on the platforms of the impressive Paragon Station and I eventually cross England with only two changes of train to be back home, virtually eight months since I last saw it. It's time for a nice long leave!

12

The bright hues of independence are fading

I manage to take all of my leave entitlement and this allows me to enjoy to the full my replacement car. Of course, with my insurance history, it has to be a modest family saloon rather than the sports car that I really want. However, it serves its purpose in impressing a new girlfriend and provides us with a private space for our enjoyment.

Our relationship progresses to the usual point where my coming ashore is discussed, so I know that when I say that I need to pass my master's examinations first, that front passenger seat will soon empty. I also know that my last voyage was a change of scene that has only served to heighten my dissatisfaction with West Africa.

At the same time, former shipmates tell me that the Australasian trade is also changing, and not for the better, as they now have to work at night and at weekends. My problem is that though I want to visit somewhere new, I don't want any more long voyages. This quandary is terminated when I get a call to join one of our ships for a guaranteed eight-week voyage out from and back to Liverpool.

This ship, built in wartime and beginning to show its age, is one of two which provide an 'economy' service to and from the coast for African passengers and is thus inevitably known by the racist tag of the 'Cherry Blossom Express'. The first-class passengers travel in reasonable style in cabins amidships whilst the others are accommodated in dormitories in a 'tweendeck.

On the way out from Liverpool, only the midships cabins are occupied and the passengers are mainly Nigerians who have completed their government-sponsored studies and who must now return home. In a few cases, they have acquired wives and families and it can be pretty noisy at mealtimes in the saloon since there is no separate serving for the youngsters.

Two of those wives are British and, as the trip progresses, it's interesting to see that, though they are pointedly ignored by the Nigerian women, they're keeping company with two other 'foreign' wives who, it turns out, are Jamaican.

One reason for this solidarity appears to be that everyone perceived as a 'foreigner' is being treated very differently by the Nigerian stewards who, like their passenger compatriots, clearly disapprove of them. It's an interesting anthropology on this particular ship.

Nearly all the British people on board have been there for many voyages. The ship's schedule means that it's always home for Christmas, often also for Easter and always during the school summer holidays. Besides myself, I find out that the doctor is the only new arrival.

Doctors, on those British ships that have to carry one, tend to be either newly qualified or long-retired and 'Whisky Mac' is one of the latter. Two impressive rows of faded medal ribbons on his shiny new barathea uniform jacket are testimony to a long military career. His army service is the basis of many a fascinating yarn that emerges so long as his eponymous tumbler is kept well-charged. Unfortunately, as the voyage progresses, his eccentricities become a bit of a liability.

His surgery is in one of the masthouses on the main deck and our stays in Apapa and Port Harcourt leave him bereft of patients and in need of a diversion. This takes the form of using a substantial syringe as a form of cattle-prod with which to scatter those unfortunates who cluster outside his door and enrage him with their constant chatter.

He eventually has to be 'confined to barracks' amidships and his bar access is severely curtailed by the Old Man. It means an end to us all being entertained by delicious anecdotes of when he was in charge of treating sexual diseases amongst the soldiery in pre-war Egypt. His engrossing tales not only involve several famous names but also, as he puts it, 'chaps whose infections were not always the result of relations with the opposite sex, not to say even with the odd beast of burden'.

During this voyage, I can recall two incidents of later significance. We call at Tema, a new port in Ghana that replaces the famous surf anchorages off Accra. Our cargo includes a mobile electric power supply control-room and its accessories.

They are destined for the presidential palace where Kwame Nkrumah, who has recently awarded himself the messianic title of 'Osagyefo', is hosting a pan-African summit.

A floating crane put the 75 ton principal lift on board in Liverpool but here we have to wait for a large mobile crane to crawl its way to the port from the site where it is usually employed. Our passengers are visibly disgruntled at this delay but for me, and a couple of others, it's a chance to catch a minibus from the port's lorry park and pay a quick visit to Accra.

From the port, we bowl along a fine motorway (the equal of any of the few we have at home) but it suddenly comes to an abrupt end just short of a line of tall palm trees. It's hard-a-port then and on to a dismally rutted and crowded ordinary road for the last five miles or so of our journey. Later, I'm able to hear the story of this road and its puzzling termination.

It appears that there was money remaining after the port of Tema was built, part of a loan guaranteed by our government. The contractors needed to use it up and so they offered to provide a modern road link with the capital. Unfortunately, the funds ran out before the road reached its destination. The contractors just tidied up what had been built, and departed.

Such, I suppose, were the realities of overseas aid at that time. It was the failure or the disappointing outcomes of other such grandiose schemes that would soon cause the downfall of Nkrumah. Afterwards, Ghanaian dreams at independence began their long slide into both public and private poverty.

Another event occurs, while we are loading in Apapa, whose significance completely escapes me at the time. Hindsight now shows me that it was my first glimpse of the end of my way of life at sea.

Two heavy lifts are presented on the quay for us to load and this time they are well within the lifting capacity of our heavy derrick. As the sailors go through the rigging preparations I am able to have a good look at them.

They are steel boxes, about 30 feet long, each with a slightly curved roof and resembling railway vans with their wheel bogies removed. They're painted a silver colour, with the legend 'African Container Express Service' stencilled in black on both sides and I'm told that they're both filled with bags of palm kernels and weigh just over 20 tons each.

It doesn't take long to get them on board and landed on wooden bearers, where they can be securely lashed once the normal loading of this hatch is resumed. 'Wetin dey for inside, my fren'?' asks one of the Apapa dockers and I tell him, 'E get plenty palm kernel for inside wey de Hausa boys go pakam small, small, better dan dis work for Apapa side.'

That should give him something to think about, I reflect, but he's straight back with, 'Dis be nonsense. We go fit pak plenty bags, proper, for since dis time you get plenty palaver with dis big ting.' He gives the container a dismissive snort and receives some cackling support from his mates as they stroll off.

I'm inclined to agree with him. It's been a lot of bother for maybe four hundred bags that we could have loaded conventionally in about the same time. None of us is aware that we've just seen the future, not only of this trade, but also of the world's seaborne commerce and a way of working that will eventually turn all our lives upside down.

We're not the only people on the ship who are being presented with change. Our new northbound passengers are also having to adjust each day to a very strange way of life. They're all fairly mature students or craft trainees who have been given scholarships by either the British or Nigerian government and are finding shipboard life to be extremely taxing.

Most of their travel possessions are stored in a baggage room below decks but they have a weekly access on Sunday morning. Number four hatch is opened and they can go up and down a special companionway with whatever they wish to take back to their cabins. The fact that some passengers are poorly briefed is soon apparent when one or two bring some very sorry packages on deck.

One man has a large plastic bag which must originally have contained a stem of bananas that has deteriorated into an unpleasant black mush. Yet another has a bundle of stockfish which has suffered during its hot storage although he cheerfully explains that he can scrape off the bad bits and then nurse the rest in his cooler cabin.

It would be cruel to tell him that such delicacies are readily available in Britain at an affordable price but our white second steward is perfectly happy to label the passengers as 'ignorant bush bastards'. It's an opinion that is unfortunately shared by some of the Nigerian stewards who are helping to police this access operation.

My own sympathy for them in their involuntary suffering is, however, soon reversed the next day when we have boat drill. As the canvas cover is removed from my lifeboat, an appalling stench arises. The source is a pair of plastic buckets that are full of sun-dried shrimps that are far from inert, in fact they are a heaving mass of pink maggots. The only remedy is to toss them briskly over the side while their anonymous owner tries to conceal his dismay.

Such is life with these Nigerians, however, that this anti-social behaviour is immediately cancelled out by the passengers in my charge proving extremely adept in putting on our clumsy lifejackets. They also prove more than willing to put their shoulders into the task of both winding in and out the lifeboats using our antiquated davits.

At the end of the voyage, instead of heading into our usual berth in Liverpool, we're directed to Bromborough Dock on the Wirral side of the river. This is a private dock belonging to Lever Brothers, owners of the rival Palm Line, and it's therefore an unusual destination for us.

The problem for our passengers now is that they're all headed for London and so a coach is hired to take them and their cabin possessions back over the river to Liverpool's Lime Street station. Or rather, under the river via the Mersey Tunnel, and the next day we hear of the consequences of that journey.

Our passengers have endured many painful discoveries since they left home; however, the concept of a tunnel under the river is just too alien to their knowledge. The sight of the great black maw of the entrance causes a near mutiny on board the coach. The two unfortunates from our passenger department in charge have to carry out some very delicate diplomacy and explanation before the coach can pass the toll booth.

My next voyage to West Africa proves to be my last visit under the Elder Dempster flag. It's a happy trip as I have at last met a girl who doesn't seem to mind the prospect of my continuing my career at sea. I also have nearly enough sea time to sit for my master's ticket, after which I could look for a job ashore without breaking a promise to my parents.

I'm back on one of our oldest ships once again but that apparent misfortune at least allows me to visit some of the lesser destinations in West Africa before they disappear from our use.

Sailing once again from Liverpool, our first port of call is Safi in Morocco, a colourful little place where we load tinned sardines. The tins are so small that a gross fits easily inside a small cardboard carton and this represents a fair weight. It's certainly one that proves to be too much for the shoddy glue that keeps the box intact.

The result, as we reach the sweaty tropics, is disintegration and the dockers are soon ankle deep in small red tins as they unload. Naturally, a good few are pocketed but more than enough survive. We then have a struggle to find enough old sacks and plastic bags to contain them before they can be accepted ashore.

Our next stop is Funchal on Madeira where we have, amongst other items, the unusual cargo of logs to be unloaded. These are of fine English oak, mere twiglets in comparison with the great tropical trunks that we normally handle. They're destined to be made into barrels to contain and mature the famous wines of the island.

Our stay in this very attractive port is prolonged by the need to carry out some main engine repairs and that gives some of us the opportunity for an afternoon ashore. We sample the wine in various bodegas and then induce some sobriety by taking one of those famously hair-raising toboggan rides that are another Madeiran speciality.

Later in the voyage, I find that my time that afternoon could have been more usefully occupied on board checking the hatches because we haven't actually unloaded all of our cargo for here.

What must have happened was that our cheery Liverpool dockers set up a handy little bar in one of the casing sides, that part of the 'tweendeck that runs along the top of the engine-room between hatches three and four. For their access, they removed a large steel plate that normally closed off the space. Once their impromptu hostelry closed, they slung in about a hundred car tyres for Funchal before carefully replacing the door.

Naturally, this cargo never appeared on the loading plan that we received from the stevedore but a check on the manifest would have revealed its presence. Happily, we get away with it since, as the purser points out, the ship's manifest was airmailed to the coast and so it wasn't in our possession at the time.

A further zig-zag across the Atlantic to call in at Las Palmas for fuel and to load baskets of Canary potatoes for Tema and Apapa pleasantly delays our progress towards West Africa.

Conakry, our first port on the coast proper, proves to be little or no attraction. The capital of Guinea, the only territory that had disassociated itself from France at independence, it is now totally reliant upon Soviet aid and is also the refuge of the deposed President Nkrumah.

Forbidden to go ashore, we unload Land Rovers and the ubiquitous Scotch whisky to a crowded and crumbling dockside that is dominated by a grey mountain of cement bags. Lying totally unprotected, these thin paper sacks of East German produce have not survived the onslaught of the last rainy season. Beyond this disaster there are glimpses of a line of heavy earthmoving vehicles, obviously long immobile. It all adds to an impression that development aid to Africa from communist as well as capitalist donors does not always do its recipients much material good.

Little foreign aid of any description reaches our later destination at any time, the small Spanish possession of Fernando Póo and its ramshackle capital of Santa Isabel.

On a previous visit, with a genial Irishman as master, we steamed into the anchorage to find a deathly hush only relieved by the mournful tolling of the cathedral bells. Impatient for service and declaring, 'Sound the whistle, will you, son, and wake the buggers up. Damned heathen, they should've gone to an early Mass.'

This time, just as then, the port administration takes its full time in allowing us to berth. The difference now is that it is chaos and confusion ashore rather than the traditional sleepy indolence that causes the delay.

The civil war in Nigeria is gathering pace and this island has become the principal conduit for aid to the new state of Biafra. The wharf is packed with the usual food and humanitarian aid from the UN and the well-known charitable agencies, most of which is in a poor state through lack of cover. In addition, the Spanish are on the verge of leaving the island to an independence for which it is quite unprepared.

We're glad to leave after only a few hours alongside, even if it is to go to the even more ramshackle destination of Bata on the mainland, capital of the enclave of Spanish Equatorial Guinea. Bata is probably the most primitive place that I've visited in West Africa and the labour there is quite horrifyingly inept.

We make sure that our Krooboys take charge of the unloading of a few precious Land Rovers to the very primitive wooden boats that come alongside in the anchorage to collect them. We feel that the labour can then be left to handle the odds and sods of construction materials that are the rest of the cargo. They are clumsy, fractious and sulky with one another in equal measure but the cargo is going out, the surf remains quiescent and they aren't actually damaging the ship.

Then they come to handle the last items. These are large bundles of steel reinforcing rods about 20 feet long that our helpful scouse dockers have pushed into the very outboard edge of number four 'tweendeck. It's the Krooboy headman who helpfully alerts me to the homicidal pantomime that is unfolding. 'Boss, you done come dis nummer for now, dese bushmen wey dey go kill someun one time for soon.'

His assessment is spot-on. Two substantial maindeck support pillars are an obvious obstruction to dragging the bundles into the hatch square where they can be safely lifted out of the hatch. The chain slings must be secured around one end of a bundle or two and then dragging them out will bring the cargo clear of one pillar.

Then these slings can be reconnected to both ends of the bundle and it all safely emerges. This is too laboured a process for these unsupervised and untaught hooligans to bother with, however, and they've simply secured both slings to the middle of the bundles and heaved away.

Out comes the centre of the bundle but both of its ends are still trapped behind the pillars until a further heave causes one end to spring clear. Now the cargo emulates an angry steel serpent. Only a breathtaking bit of choreography saves three or four of the labourers from having their feet bilaterally amputated. Amazingly, they apparently enjoy the spectacle before a bit of collective common sense kicks in and they allow the Krooboy headman to show them how it should be done.

On our homeward progress along the coast I come across the ship of my American adventure and I go over to see if any of my former shipmates are still there. Three of them are and they feel happier sailing in her now that she is exempt from the US trade. The ship is still proving to be a bit of a Jonah, I learn.

The ancient Scotch boiler is now behaving itself but a new diesel generator could have been more thoughtfully installed. Its exhaust uptake terminates where it is able to set the wooden awning spars on the boat deck alight after a couple of hours' running. Whilst Chippy and his big saw had remedied that, his resourcefulness did not extend to curing the rather prominent 'banana' derrick that I saw when I was coming aboard. This dramatically bent steel tube was another classic example of 'wawa' that was far from uncommon on the coast.

It happens after the crew set up the derricks to the dockers' liking on arrival. After an hour or two, the gang decide on some fine-tuning with the rope-positioning guys but forget to re-secure the back-up wire and chain preventer guy. The mate on deck doesn't always notice this fatal omission. Then a sling of cargo gets stuck somewhere down below and the call goes out for a further tug on the lifting wire, the cargo runner. The winch driver obliges, one of the rope guys finds it too much to bear and it breaks.

Off goes the derrick, gaily released from any horizontal restraint and it swings around until it's obstructed by the mast, or at least most of its length is brought to a halt. Sadly, the head of the derrick carries on its momentum just that little longer and a spectacularly bent steel tube is the result. The ship carries this badge of shame and becomes the target of friendly derision from others until it gets home.

Home once again and, after my leave, I'm able to get a few trips around the usual continental ports to complete my sea time before I head off to college to study for that last professional hurdle. During this absence from the coast, the excitement that I often longed for duly takes place.

Unfortunately, it's the tragedy of civil war that replaces the somnolence of West Africa. The Biafran secession is working towards its bloody conclusion and some of our ships are involved in various rescue missions of expatriates living in or near the creek ports.

The importance of a stable Nigeria to the whole of our West African trade is emphasised when hostilities become responsible for a substantial drop in business. That leads to the sale of two of our three passengers ships as well as the disposal of the oldest cargo ships without any prospect of their replacement.

Anne and I have decided to become engaged and we plan our wedding to take place as soon as possible after my studies finish. Conveniently, I manage to not only pass the examination as scheduled but also find that Anne will be a good sailor on the return from our honeymoon.

We have a ferry crossing from Boulogne to Folkestone in boisterous seas. The retirement party for the ship's chief steward had been held the previous evening so the catering staff were looking as pale green as the waters of the Channel. I'm very proud that Anne proves able to resist joining the vociferous suffering of both the crew and many of the passengers during a violent and extended crossing.

No sooner are we back and ready to start looking for a flat than the office is on the phone to me at my parents' home. I'm required to join a Blue Funnel ship in Birkenhead the next day and sail a fortnight hence. This change of destination for an Elder Dempster employee arises from the integration of the sea staff of our two very different companies under the new umbrella of Ocean Fleets Limited.

I'm able to negotiate a deal whereby Anne will be able to sail with me on what turns out to be a trip westwards right around the world with good opportunities for sightseeing and, most crucially, it saves us three months' rent of a flat.

We eventually find our first house and I go on to spend the next three years sailing on services to the Far East with Anne able to join me on further voyages. On balance, I'm quite happy to see the back of West Africa and, despite the continued closure of the Suez Canal, the voyages aren't that much longer than I am used to.

I also find that both work and shoregoing are more appealing. The cargo work in port is definitely easier in that more can be left to the care of the stevedores, although this advantage is tempered by the need to be less cavalier about health-and-safety issues.

My principal problem now is the effective cessation of promotion within the combined fleet. Despite a few temporary excursions as mate, it's clear that not only will things not improve but the talk starts to become one of possible redundancies. It's time to move on, to look seriously at the sailor's last resort of 'swallowing the anchor' or to find an expanding fleet somewhere else. I've quite enjoyed my years sailing to West Africa and I have a good store of memories to dine out on wherever I find myself in my next employment. I have little idea that I will find myself, before very long, back in Nigeria but under very different circumstances.

13

Sailing under the Nigerian Red Ensign

West African Merchant Shipping Companies

One economic injustice associated with the colonial era was the practice of exports to overseas possessions being priced on a c.i.f (cost including freight) basis whilst imports from those territories arrived under an f.o.b (free on board) tariff. This meant that all the transportation revenues from such trade accrued to the colonial power, in effect for the principal benefit of its ship-owners.

The United Nations Conference on Trade and Development (UNCTAD) agreement of 1965 was designed to correct this imbalance by allowing a nation to reserve 40 per cent of its overseas trade to its own transport operators. Some of the new West African nations, however, had already founded their own shipping companies, prior to this important initiative.

The pioneer was Ghana's Black Star Line, established in 1957. It was wise to take foreign assistance with such a project and Ghana, significantly, chose Israeli participation. This was a departure from the expected British patronage despite the fact that Elder Dempster had trained Ghana's first indigenous shipmaster.

Nigeria, on the other hand, took British partners and both Elder Dempster and Palm Line were responsible for launching the Nigerian National Shipping Line in 1960. The smaller territories of Sierra Leone and the Gambia eschewed indigenous ship-owning, although the former state was able to find new seagoing employment opportunities for its citizens on other than the traditional ships. Sadly, they were to be eventually displaced by Asian seafarers, principally those from the Philippines.

The former colonies of the other European nations were slower in setting up their own merchant fleets, mainly because they lacked any encouragement. French assistance and capital eventually saw the flags of Congo, Gabon, Sénégal and Côte d'Ivoire flying from the sterns of a motley collection of second-hand ships although only the latter country operated them for long.

It was the West Germans who took the initiative in putting the countries of Cameroun and Togo to sea whilst the Belgians eventually offered similar assistance to a Zairean shipping company. Of course, throughout the immediate post-colonial era, the ensign of Liberia graced the sterns of the world's largest merchant fleet but this was merely a fiscal and legislative fig-leaf to cover the ship-owning operations of American and Greek nationals.

None of these shipping operations directed by the independent nations of West Africa lasted until the turn of the century, but by then neither were the principal British shipping companies in existence.

It could be argued that the African fleets suffered the fate of so many other nationalised concerns in that they put the economic interests of their employees and the political objectives of their governmental owners ahead of commercial objectives. Nevertheless, there were similar failures of privately owned shipping companies in both Ghana and Nigeria.

My short service under the Nigerian flag was long enough to convince me that one reason for this failure was that so many nationals of these new ship-owning countries saw seafaring as an entry into the profitable world of private trading. In addition, indifference to the commercial fortunes of the company was compounded by the inefficiencies caused by too many placemen in the head office at home. In contrast, professionalism at sea was proved by the fact that there were very few serious incidents involving ships of the new nations.

The end of most of these African shipping enterprises did not come from marine peril, but from the age-old ritual of nailing a writ to the mast, which signified arrest against an unpaid debt.

Before parting from Elder Dempster, I managed to spend time sailing around some European ports as mate to my uncle, a master in the company. I had already had a similar spell on one of the firm's ships with my brother, then a junior engineer, so that nicely rounded off our family's association with the African Royal Mail.

It was because any promotion that I secured was still only temporary that I moved to a Glasgow firm of ship-owners who were busily recruiting for their new enterprise as ship managers. This was a growing sector of merchant shipping at the time, providing crewing and operational services for other ship-owners and I could see that further promotion was a realistic prospect there. Soon I would be marking fifteen years of sea service and so the early opportunity of command was an enticing one.

I was soon to realise that the price of this accelerated progress was one of long and extremely boring voyages. They consisted of loading oil or chemicals at one god-forsaken point on the globe and then delivering them to another equally unattractive place several thousand miles away. A good salary and generous leave proved to be inadequate compensation for what was a barren existence in both personal and professional terms.

What was the suitable alternative? Did the answer lie with the seafarer's long tradition of 'swallowing the anchor' and coming ashore? With a hindsight gained from periods in my later working life spent assessing candidates for employment, I can now see that I wasn't ready then for a life ashore. In truth, my attitude towards it was hopelessly immature.

My wife, Anne, to her credit, accepted my shortcomings in this and supported my decision to go back to the local office of the Merchant Navy Establishment (MNE), where I was registered, renew my contract, and see what was on offer in the way of shorter voyages. In this way I could remain at sea but still keep an eye out for any shore employment opportunities that might suit me.

So it is that I'm called in to the MNE offices on Mann Island, near Liverpool's famous Pier Head, and offered a job. 'It's as coasting mate for Nigger Nash,' explains the counter clerk using the usual casually insulting epithet for the Nigerian National Shipping Line (NNSL). 'I see you're a West Coast man so you should be all right with them lot,' he adds, compounding his disdain for such a destination.

I ignore his attitude and agree to go along to one of their ships to see if we'll be suited. But first I ensure that I'll keep my 'pool' contract and be able to contribute to the British shipping industry's pension scheme. The latter assurance is because this allows me to move freely between companies and yet maintain a single pension. Later I was to wish that I'd taken down that clerk's name, rank and serial number because his assurance proved to be worthless when I eventually left the sea.

That's well into the future and, for now, I find that I'm readily accepted into the Nigerian Merchant Navy. I soon find out the reason underlying that eagerness. Apart from the company's masters, all of whom are British-trained, the deck officers are of a new generation, trained within the company and rather less professional in some of their duties.

In fact it's become a common complaint that the stevedores in Liverpool and elsewhere can never find anyone on board an NNSL ship to make the decisions or give the orders necessary to expedite the working of the ship. There are still three British masters employed by the company as well as a British marine superintendent and I find that they're very happy to have someone along who understands the ways of West Africa in this particular environment.

It only takes a couple of coasting trips and a spell in both Liverpool and Tilbury to get me properly immersed in the task. Whilst we're at sea, all of the officers are both effective and diligent in their duties and the Nigerian sailors are also equally professional but things undergo a dramatic change once we're safely tied up in port.

The demands of a busy social and trading timetable take precedence over shipboard duties and this is applicable to all ranks. I soon understand what I need to do to manage this situation. Firstly, I need to have the ship's master key with me at all times so that I can 'access all areas' and secondly, I need to explain the new regime to my two junior officers and to the bosun. This policy has two imperatives, I inform them. Nobody will be able to hide from me on board if I require their services and nobody will be able to keep trade goods on board without my authority.

This apparently draconian change to their comfortable way of life is actually given a genuine welcome and I find that this is because I am an 'outsider' who is not gaining any competitive or personal advantage. I am not the one who will be busy elsewhere with my own social and commercial commitments whilst always expecting everybody else to be working and neither will I be monopolising the best personal cargo spaces.

Of course I don't have any leverage over the engineering and catering departments but I have negotiating power due to a near-monopoly on spaces suitable for the carriage of personal trading goods. So, early on in my time in the company, I cross swords with a chief steward who I find has bribed a dockside crane driver to land two second-hand cars on the boat deck while storing the ship one Saturday afternoon.

His arrogant assumption that he can do this, because he is the agent of 'big men' in our Lagos office, is soon deflated when I call in an equally 'big man' from our Liverpool office, who swiftly tells him to get his alfresco garage emptied without any further nonsense. Later, on another ship, I discover a handsome leather sofa and matching armchairs have been installed in the trunking above the engine-room escape hatch. No need to call the office in for this one, the chief engineer deals with the rascal who has put the lives of all the engine-room staff at such blatant hazard.

This strategy of keeping my Nigerian colleagues on board while on duty and also co-operating through my control of their trading activity has to operate in parallel with some management of their social programme. At meal times it is just the Old Man and myself enjoying a well-cooked and well-presented menu in the dining saloon.

The rest of the officers are being served by the hard-pressed stewards, who can be seen carrying 'chop' for several people to any one of many cabins throughout the day. I'm often having to use my invaluable pass-key to open doors that have remained closed to my urgent knocking, in order to extract one of the mates to help with some task on deck.

This is much to the chagrin of the multitude gathered within who can only see this troublesome white man who is making life inconvenient for them. Furthermore, he is having the effrontery to continue this colonialist attitude on what is now Nigerian sovereign territory, or so I am informed by one officer's guest, who finds my intrusion and removal of his party host to be quite unacceptable.

As ever, it's the Nigerian sailors who are much less troublesome. Even those ladies who they've managed to smuggle on board for the duration are kept usefully busy during the day while their hosts are at work. They actually do a very creditable job of both keeping the accommodation clean and looking after the ship's laundry.

They're not interfering with the ship's cargo work and so I can easily overlook their common trespass. But they don't always ignore me and, on one of our older ships where the crew quarters down aft are starting to show their age, I'm accosted by one of these ladies one afternoon.

She is endowed with an imposingly voluptuous physique that is struggling to stay within the confines of a sparklingly white NNSL bathtowel. Firmly, she hails me with a challenge, 'Oi, are you in charge 'ere?' When I confirm that I am, she delivers a stentorian complaint: 'Well, dere's no effin' hot water again down aft and one of der toilet's blocked.' As I murmur that I'll see the engineers about it, she delivers her parting evidence, 'and dey were all on the effin' repair list last trip an' all.'

I know one of the British masters fairly well as we sailed together once or twice in Elder Dempster. One morning, on a ship laying by and thus fairly quiet, he suggests that we should have one of our lifeboats taken for a spin around the dock. As I suspect, he's put a seamanlike eye over the boat and correctly thinks that it may have lain there undisturbed since the ship last had its statutory surveys.

I muster a suitable crew of sailors plus two Nigerian apprentices and a junior engineer and we're pleasantly surprised when the boat comes out of its stowage with ease. The Old Man lowers the boat himself and, once its engine has gurgled into life, we're into the black waters of Canada Dock and pottering along quite happily in the chilly sunshine.

The engine starts to splutter and our engineer states grumpily that he needs to fix something to correct matters. That's no problem, the engine is stopped and it's a chance to get the hefty wooden oars shipped for a spot of rowing. It'll be good exercise and practice for all except me – I can stay loftily exempt. They don't make a bad fist of it after a few crashing collisions between oar blades and I'm feeling rather proud of them as we move quite swiftly towards the entrance to the adjacent Brocklebank Dock.

Two dock gatemen shout down to us, 'Where yer bound, Skip?' and 'Africa's dat way'. We're not here to provide comic ammunition for them so I order a rest for the oars and then put the rudder hard over. The boat crew can then lift up and bring these heavy brutes inboard and stow them before I ask our engineer to fire up the motor. It's still popping and spluttering from time to time and he gets even grumpier when I ask him if it'll last out until we get back.

Fortunately it does and, as we approach the boat falls and I need to take the way off the boat, I say, 'Stop engine and then go slow astern.' There's no response so I slap him sharply on the shoulder to attract his attention over the diesel's noise. 'Do not pat me like that, I am not your dog,' is his vehement response.

All I can do then is to put the rudder hard over to port so that we grind heavily alongside the ship rather than slam into it head first. It wasn't the best of my many boat manoeuvres over the years. I couldn't be sure then, but I've often wondered since, if my unhelpful engineer might well have been the disgruntled sofa owner on that other ship, now exacting his revenge.

Eventually I'm asked if I'll sail to West Africa and I agree. This is because it'll be on the flagship express 4,000 mile direct route to Lagos from Liverpool, one replacing the old mail and passenger link and operating on a six-week cycle. Eleven days out on passage, eleven days sailing home with ten days in each port.

I sign a so-called 'running agreement' when we reach Lagos which commits me to six months of continuous service but that's fine as I will effectively be at home for ten days after each month away from Liverpool.

This is a prestige service and NNSL are rightly proud that their newest ship is proving equal in matching the performance of the two other ships belonging to our West African conference partners, Elder Dempster and Palm Line. The master, chief engineer and electrician, three key figures in ensuring this record, are all British.

My Nigerian predecessor is only leaving because he's a rising star who has gone to command another of our newest ships as an accelerated promotion. I need to get a strategy of supporting my colleagues in place as soon as possible. When I discover that I'm replacing somebody who not only ran a tight ship but who was also a major trader, I see something that I can turn to my advantage.

The bedroom in my suite of rooms is being used as a store for small and therefore highly pilferable items such as torches, batteries, working gloves, shifting spanners, paintbrushes and screwdrivers. I therefore break out half a dozen brand-new close-shackle Chubb padlocks and use these to secure the deck storerooms.

This means that I can clear out all that stuff from my quarters and I'm now also effectively in charge of a lot of potential private shipping space. I call on the bosun and carpenter and tell them that, since I am no private trader, most of this well-secured space is now at their disposal. What I don't mention is that I am also effectively ransoming their goods against their continuing to deliver a motivated crew.

I'm pretty sure that they'll cotton on to this and that I'll have their full co-operation during the voyage. The unspoken alternative is, of course, my inviting the Nigerian customs in Lagos to inspect their 'loads' or the goods having to lie sacrosanct until our arrival back in Liverpool.

To my chagrin, the chief steward and who is now also acting purser turns out to be the procurer of automobiles for the 'big men' in Lagos. Happily, that episode has been forgotten and he turns out to be an excellent feeder and the purveyor of a palm-oil chop of a very high standard *every* Sunday lunchtime. We enjoy an excellent relationship and I'm able to do him some favours later in the voyage.

The only four non-Nigerians on board will have to socialise during our stay in Lagos as we'll be the only real residents of the ship and I'm glad to discover that we can get along excellently. We can't leave this ship while it's in Lagos and I've lost contact with those expatriates that I used to know there. However, we do invite people from other ships to join us on most evenings to chew the fat over 'this Nigeria!'

The cargo work is a lot easier than I recall from my last trips to the Coast. For a start, our itinerary is simplicity itself; we fill up at one end and then empty at the other with cargoes that are also relatively simple and predictable.

In Liverpool we start with that familiar staple, salt, but nowadays the bags are wrapped in protective plastic. A lot of the cargo variety of years past is reduced to the uniformity of goods being shipped on wooden pallets, frequently shrink-wrapped for protection. The expertise of the dockers is no longer required to seek out items to suit the space. The emphasis is on speed of loading to aid a similar speed of unloading and we use forklift trucks and pallet forks at will. Even the cunning of the dockers in finding suitable refreshment is frustrated by the fact that Guinness is now bottled in Apapa. The product is now shipped securely in large round dark-grey tanks.

Containers are continuing their hesitant impact on our trade. ACE, the new African Container Express consortium, which is owned by the liner conference, is using a junior version, an eight-foot cube, for the carriage of goods such as whisky and textiles.

These containers are far from completely secure. If not watched, any gang can position a cube so that its door is invisible from the deck but accessible by some serpentine wriggling of one man across the top and down the hidden side.

Another significant change is that the troubles of the British motor industry in these early years of the 1970s mean that we are carrying very few vehicles with the exception of the trusty Land Rover and a few Minis for the expatriate market.

The cargo that we load homewards is also much simplified since the oil riches of Nigeria are causing a movement of people from the land into the expanding cities and therefore away from agricultural production for export. Bags of cocoa, of palm kernels and of groundnuts and groundnut cake are still the principal element and continue to be loaded in the traditional way. Gone, however, are such bagged exotica as calabar beans (rich in strychnine!), benniseed, cottonseed, gum copal, bones, hooves and horns.

No timber is on offer although we call once at Abidjan to load such a cargo. That port is now a revelation with its modern cargo-handling practices. So much work is done by forklift trucks. There are giants that rumble along the wide quay aprons with logs weighing up to 20 tons apiece in their embrace and smaller ones that rush bundles of sawn timber or pallets of coffee beans to the ship's side.

It's a far cry from the continuing sweaty confusion of Apapa Quay. There it is still possible to see those dear old mammy-lorries with their painted cab slogans such as 'God is my Brake', 'Man no go fit worry' and 'No fit work, no get chop' crunching the cockroaches underfoot as they bring rope slings of bags under the hook.

On one of my first visits back to Apapa, I'm in my office one morning when a very crisply attired man knocks on the open door and introduces himself. He says that he has the pleasure to represent both the Nigerian Merchant Navy Officers' Association and the Nigerian Merchant Navy Pension Fund. Happily, my second mate has already mentioned the possible appearance of this plausible gentleman.

We then proceed to have one of those circular and contrapuntal arguments so characteristic of the West African coast whereby each of us sets out a simple but opposing point of view and then we try and wring as many variations on the theme as time allows.

His proposition is that I freely 'chop' Nigeria's money whilst revealing my colonialist attitude by refusing to join my new brother officers in securing their conditions and their future. On the contrary, I insist, this is a very serious matter for me. If I join these two schemes then I will be thrown out of their British equivalents and I also risk losing my passport and my citizenship.

Claim and counter-claim are inflating theatrically when I'm rescued by a call to go out on deck to fix a problem. Seeing my interlocutor going down the gangway, my second mate tells me, 'That man is a rogue and should be punished but 'e get big friends for shoreside. No officer here go trust 'im one time.' He does revisit the ship on our later visits but never manages to make a sale other than to a few juniors.

In later years, when I receive suspect e-mails from Nigerian sources, I always enquire if these funds that need my help for clandestine export have any connection with these two Nigerian Merchant Navy organisations. I then enjoy receiving angry denials from the fraudsters couched in florid personal abuse.

While we're in Apapa we're very much under the eye of NNSL's head office in nearby Wharf Road and thus are the destination of a stream of various jobsworths and freeloaders. It's the latter, wanting food on visits that always coincide with our mealtimes at 0800, 1200 and 1800, that bring the chief steward to my cabin one day with a plea for protection from the parasitic horde.

Together, forgetting our past differences, we devise a remedy since we now share a common interest. It's decided that we'll introduce a register for every feeder to sign, giving details of name, position and purpose of visit. That register will be held in my office and all accepted signatories will be given a chit to present to the saloon steward in order to obtain service.

Naturally, the most important legitimate visitors will proceed direct to a table because they will be recognised as such by the chief steward as they enter. Equally, there are some unpleasant encounters in my office with a lot of angry shouting and some lively exchanges of ritual denunciation. Nevertheless, word soon gets around that the *River Ethiope* is not the free-and-easy office canteen represented by the other ships in the fleet.

Unfortunately, I'm unable to help with another hospitality problem that is taxing the chief steward. This is the fact that every lunchtime there are one or two 'big men' from the head office who invite themselves aboard, invariably accompanied by their smartly dressed and impressively coiffed secretaries or personal assistants.

After a substantial lunch, often with wine, and during which they completely ignore the ship's personnel, even those deputed to wait upon them, the high official will request some cabin accomodation so that he can complete some work with his secretary. This post-prandial work results in a need to renew the bed linen and towels and is beginning to represent a substantial inroad into the ship's store of laundered items.

All that I can lamely suggest is that these room bookings are unlikely to be complained about if the linen and towels are not refreshed. Any such palaver would soon reach the ears of even 'bigger men', those who had no need to use a ship for their assignations in working hours.

Every evening, once we've enjoyed our dinner in relative peace and the night shift is successfully launched, we gather in the comfortable day room of either the Old Man or the chief engineer and set the world to rights over a few drinks. 'We' are the British contingent on board, but we're also joined most evenings by Ben, the Nigerian third engineer, who seems to be on permanent ship-keeping duties at night here in Apapa.

When I ask him why he's stuck with this task, he explains, 'My wife and family stay for Onitsha but I never get chance to pass there from here because Army people or police will beat me any time I go.' It seems that, since he's ethnically Ibo, he's automatically suspected by them of being an active secessionist or worse.

Nigeria's conquest of breakaway Biafra is now some four years in the past but there's still this bitter legacy of those years of civil strife. Ben, meanwhile, is buying a house in London which is being looked after by his girlfriend and one day he hopes to reunite his family there. The girlfriend, it appears, will not be any impediment as she is a student nurse and will eventually 'go back Jamaica'.

The Old Man, the Chief and Sam the electrician are men in their fifties who have spent most of their seagoing years in tramp ships. They're a bottomless fund of good yarns from the war years and from around the world in post-war times. Sparks and I, some twenty-odd years younger, are a receptive audience as they compete to impress us with their memories. This yarning occasionally tempts Ben to recount some of his recent experiences even though they are clearly free from any rosy hues of nostalgia. It all makes for interesting evenings that compensate for the frustrations of our daytime duties.

I'm able to relax in the evening since Sunny, my aptly named second mate, is a more than competent guardian of the deck during the night hours. These are duties that he chooses because the daytime is then free for his extensive business interests ashore. I've already learned that he has two houses in London, one of which he rents out and now he's after a third property in Plymouth, where he will be bound soon to study for his master's ticket.

I'm naturally curious as to how he does this, given the hoops that I'd recently had to jump through to get a new mortgage. He cheerfully explains that he's a man of many names and identities. I don't get the full chapter and verse, naturally, but I hear that passports of more than one nation are involved and that he declares more than one paid occupation.

Maybe I should denounce him to the authorities, I suggest, but he tells me that that is not the way of an English officer and a gentleman. Anyway, he adds, he is my sworn best friend and always willing to help should I need an introduction to some informal and very profitable Anglo-Nigerian trade. I have to agree about his friendship as my third mate, appropriately called Prince, is quite Sunny's opposite. He manages to combine indolence, arrogance and windy argumentation.

On one visit to Apapa, we're alongside on Good Friday which is the only day, apart from Christmas, that the port comes to a holiday standstill. We've organised a trip to Tarkwa Bay to celebrate and the ship's two most senior figures have agreed to keep ship for the afternoon.

Sunny also wants to come along so I'm pleased to tell Prince that he will be standing duty on board. Our two Nigerian officer cadets are invited, as also are Sam and Sparks, and the former will not only persuade Ben to join us but has arranged that we will pick up some of his friends from ashore as well. A packed lunch is prepared and I explain to Sunny the mesh-vegetable-bag technology for keeping the accompanying beer cool at our destination.

Before we set off, however, a very large and impressive gentleman in striking white robes and a huge gold crucifix is at my office door. He's accompanied by a posse of ladies with their children of various ages, all of whom are wearing clothes of some finery.

It takes me a while to translate this vision into our portly bosun and I'm helped in this understanding when he lets out a huge roar of laughter and shouts, 'do you not recognise me today, sah? For I am come with my family to give to you the Easter greetings of your Saviour and to wish you long life and eventual salvation.' The only response that I can muster, once recognition has dawned, is to invite everybody into my day room and pass out beers and lemonade from my fridge.

The bosun hands me an engraved visiting card which tells me that he is none other than the Metropolitan Bishop of Surulere of the Church of Eternal Salvation or some such ecclesiastical title. Oluyemi, for that is the name by which I know him, is a fine, reliable seaman but this parallel vocation of his is a complete surprise to me.

I ask him if he'd like to show his family around the ship and offer him the use of the passenger lounge to entertain them but he tells me that he cannot stay on board long. He has already conducted a service for 'too many people' and now must return to his church, where he will conduct the religious observances of this sacred afternoon.

Nevertheless, we are all on board cordially invited to witness his episcopal installation on Easter Day. I tell him that, regretfully, I will be extremely busy on board on Sunday but I will pass on his invitation. In the meantime, perhaps I might make some small contribution to the Easter offertory? The gift to him of some naira notes in a discreet envelope concludes what was the most bizarre and entertaining supplication for 'dash' that I recall from all my years on the coast.

After that encounter it's almost an anticlimax to get the boat launched and off to our seaside destination for an afternoon of sun and sea that has all the remembered pleasures of so many previous visits.

The novelty this time is on the morrow when my two cadets are complaining of sunburn, obviously not wearing bright-red faces, but showing a lot of blistered and peeling skin. I assume that, because they're Northerners, they aren't accustomed to the magnifying effects of salt water and sea breezes. I find some treatment for them in the medical locker but that does not help them with the cruel amusement of their fellow countrymen who see their unfortunate condition.

NNSL is recruiting cadets from all over Nigeria to fill the officer vacancies that will arise from its planned expansion of the fleet, and these two young men are taking passage with us to start some basic training at nautical college in the UK.

These particular two are sons of important families in Kano State and I'm told that they should be allocated two passenger cabins, normally unoccupied on our northbound run. This I do but, a day or so later, I decide to have a look at the usual cadet accommodation for some reason.

I'm not really surprised when I do go in to find that Sunny has spotted the opportunity and has converted the cadets' bathroom into a snail ranch. There are any number of plastic buckets on the deck containing these giant molluscs and the more energetic are exploring the climbing potential of the shower curtain and bulkheads.

I need to move fast to exploit this opportunity so I find Sunny and explain the tariff that I'll need to allow his rental of the facilities and my help in ensuring that the space is kept off the weekly accommodation inspection route.

Once our two cadets have recovered from their unexpected ordeal in the sun, they soon show their mettle as potential officers. They both have a willingness to acquire both the academic knowledge and the practical experience needed to be successful in this unfamiliar environment. As long as I protect them from the sneering disdain of Prince and the craftiness of Sunny, they'll present themselves as good college students when we reach Liverpool.

Only occasionally does their ready absorption of new knowledge falter. For example, on one of their bridge visits when I'm explaining the magnetic compass. I find that they share my schooldays experience of that beautiful experiment where a sheet of waxed paper is gently heated, scattered with iron filings and then placed above a powerful bar magnet to produce an impressive force field that is caught for ever as the wax cools.

The earth, I explain, is a huge bar magnet and so the large iron filing that is the compass needle will always point towards the end of the magnet that is called a pole. Therefore, I continue, wherever you are, one end of the compass will always show the direction of the magnetic north pole.

Their strong nods of approval and understanding of the concept are, however, rather diluted when the younger of the two comes back to me a little later, peers again at the compass in its binnacle and enquires of me in a low voice, 'Excuse me, sir, but *how* does it really know?'

Our arrival back in Liverpool is always the signal for a mass boarding by the waterguard of Her Majesty's Customs, who are convinced that we have a sizeable freight of cannabis.

It's undeniably true that the drug is popular with some of our crew and I know that there are small personal stashes all over the ship but, to my mind, it's use is generally as innocuous as that of tobacco and alcohol, those other two favourite diversions of seamen from time immemorial.

However, the rummagers must have their way and so several bulkhead and deckhead panels are taken down at random and torches shone into dark corners in pursuit of the prohibited herb. One trip, I decide to have all the panels removed from the crew messrooms and left off permanently because, being made of formica, the screw-holes in them are now becoming worn to the point of uselessness.

The crew are unconcerned about the resulting nakedness of their public space and the message gets back to Liverpool that we're fed up of this intensive searching. I notice that the intensity of their inspections diminishes and, as the number of random dismantlings also decreases, I feel that we're getting a clean bill of health. I therefore feel a lot safer about my own small personal accumulation of cigarettes and whisky concealed in the void space under my cabin's wardrobe.

The recent quadrupling of the oil price, the continuing closure of the Suez Canal and the huge expansion in Nigeria's oil exports should have made that country very wealthy but the economy is in a mess for a variety of internal reasons. The exchange rate of the Nigerian naira is becoming unstable, which impacts on our salaries, but the introduction of new import restrictions opens up possibilities for trying some personal trading.

Sam and I decide that it is time to enter this informal international business. But with what? The hot item of the moment is Vaseline, principally used for hair-straightening and other cosmetic procedures; one-kilogram tins are the unit of preference. Batteries and razor blades are also in high demand and don't take up much space.

Unfortunately, we soon realise that we lack sufficient start-up capital for the venture. It's a time of high inflation at home and our shrinking salaries just don't have any surplus. Added to this is the fact that we lack a reliable agent in Nigeria. Of course, Sunny is only too ready to help but we're aware that his level of commission will most likely leave us with a very thin profit. Sadly, that is the end of our dream of becoming international entrepreneurs.

The financial problems of Nigeria are being replicated within NNSL and, one month, our salaries are paid several days late and this also happens the next month. Fortunately I avoid a bank overdraft on both occasions but I recognise the danger signals. It's clear that I could improve my earnings by a promotion to master but then I know that my circumstances would change very much for the worse.

As the only non-Nigerian on a ship, how much responsibility would fall to me? I wouldn't worry while we were safely at sea and I could sleep securely at night but in port it would be very different. I might be lucky and sail with a Sunny as mate but, more likely, there would be a brace or more of Princes. I decide that, for a salary of about £4,000 a year, it just isn't attractive enough a prospect.

I complete my time on articles, say farewell to some good shipmates and find myself back in the smoky hall of the Shipping Federation on Mann Island.

'See yer got fed up with the nig-nogs after all,' my racist counsellor remarks, 'Nobody lasts long with that lot, even their own.' I don't want to get into an extended discussion of my affairs with him so I adopt a look of studied weariness. I ask him to find me something else that will keep me close to home, even though I know that my prospects of finding a job ashore will be no better than they had been just over a year previously.

'Got just the thing for yer,' he says, 'Tom and Jerries are always looking for mates for their five-fathom club. I'll give you a number to ring.' I translate this to mean that T. & J. Harrison, a long-established Liverpool firm, are looking for chief officers who can take their ships around the land and supervise the work in port while the deep-sea staff take their voyage leave.

A telephone call and my subsequent interview confirm that is the case and, since the salary on offer exceeds that of a newly promoted master in NNSL, I join the company and make a second farewell to West Africa.

14

Return to a Coast in chaos

The Merchant Navy in the late-1970s

The shipping company that I left in 1976 was a publicity-shy and conservative family firm so it wasn't very pleased to find itself the subject of front-page headlines in the *Liverpool Echo* soon afterwards. The newspaper revealed that two of the company's ships were prevented from sailing from Birkenhead because of a shortage of deck officers. This was a surprising story, given that there had been a sharp decline of all employment in the Merchant Navy since the container revolution of the late-1960s.

All British liner companies had to adapt to the arrival of the ocean container, which allowed one container ship to replace up to six conventional cargo liners. They did this by investing in this new type of vessel and by declaring large redundancies amongst their sea staff. Many of those made surplus were fortunate enough to find employment at sea elsewhere, either with new expanding national fleets such as that of Kuwait or with ship management companies. The majority, however, decided that their best course was to take up a new career ashore.

The latter made what proved to be the wiser choice as wages and salaries at sea stagnated in this contracting industry and none of the maritime unions appeared to be effective in improving the situation. It was a decade of rapidly rising prices and eventually, despite inflation, the unions managed to obtain a real improvement in our conditions. My own experience was that my salary doubled between 1971 and 1975. Seafaring once again became an attractive proposition to those who had gone ashore and had not found the change to their liking. However, they were fairly slow to return.

The last years of the 1970s did eventually produce enough returnees to the Merchant Navy, admittedly largely confined to the officer grades, to enable the fleet under the British flag to reach its post-war apogee in terms of tonnage if not in manpower.

I am now getting close to having spent 20 years working at sea. It's high time that I find a company that offers the chance of rapid promotion to master and thus cap my seagoing career. I know that this will involve long boring voyages but if I manage a few years of that I can then present myself as more suitable to employment ashore in a role connected with the shipping industry.

I decide that another respected family owned shipping company, based in Liverpool, seems to be the right destination for me and I present myself for interview. The personnel manager, a formidable-looking man with a suitably piratical black eye-patch, soon establishes that I meet their recruitment criteria. He then picks up my discharge book, master's certificate and passport and leaves the room.

When he returns after a short absence, he announces that he is delighted to offer me a post and that I will fly out to Tokyo in three days' time to join a ship. This is all going rather too fast for my liking so I have to think quickly. I manufacture a story that my wife has a hospital appointment later that week and I want to find out the outcome of that before I go back to sea. My documents are now back on the table so I scoop them up and sincerely promise to give my interviewer a call back very soon. I can only hope that, some 30 years later, my dishonesty has long been forgiven.

Why then am I answering another advertisement in the monthly newspaper of the officers' union that announces that Palm Line are recruiting chief officers? Do I fancy the idea of adding another house-flag to my collection of those under which I'd sailed to the Coast, or was I perhaps becoming addicted to West Africa itself?

I take the early train down to London, find my way to Blackfriars Underground Station and then across the eponymous bridge to the head office of the United Africa Company. An interview in an office that overlooks the Thames is followed by lunch in a riverside pub and then I'm on the train home with a new employment.

My memories of Palm Line when I was with Elder Dempster were favourable ones despite the rivalry between the two companies. Although we gave them the epithet of the 'lavatory brush line' (alluding to their stylised palm tree logo), I think that we all secretly admired their sleek lines and good looks Their very colourful paint scheme was also much more attractive than our own drab and conservative livery.

When I join my first Palm Line ship, it's therefore a salutary shock to realise that its beauty is best seen from afar. I'm back in the world of timber and canvas hatchcovers and old-fashioned derricks. The company's fleet, rightly admired by all some 20 years ago, is now the victim of a block obsolescence. There's an urgent need for replacement ships which is unfortunately not being met due to the growing uncertainties of the trade with West Africa.

It might seem that I'd not made a very wise decision in my job choice but, as we shall see, that was not the case and Palm Line was an excellent berth for my last years at sea.

I'm sitting in a comfortable, albeit old-fashioned, cabin on board my first Palm Line and looking out at a forest of equally antique derricks. I'm also being briefed on a voyage that sounds like another souvenir of the 1960s.

The great Nigerian cement scandal, which resulted in several hundred ships being anchored outside Lagos awaiting unloading berths, has passed but the port congestion in Nigeria remains severe. This disruption to planned sailing schedules means that there is a backlog of cargo destined for the minor ports on the Coast. This ship is to operate a 'sweeper' service to call at around eight of these places and is expected to sail just before Christmas.

The date of sailing is important as I am now back in the world of British deck crews. In common with Elder Dempster, Palm always employed West Africans in the engine-room and in the catering department, but did not carry them as sailors. My knowledge tells me that any ship posted in the local office of the Shipping Federation seeking a crew and sailing on 23 December is only going to appeal to the desperate few. Their numbers can then only be supplemented by the delinquent.

Because the supply of dockers to load the ship frequently dries up, it's a few days into the new year when we actually sail. However, our crew is signed on, so they cannot be replaced with more attractive candidates.

The Old Man tells me that any crew with a Liverpool provenance is beyond the pale in his estimation and I'm a little alarmed to find that, as a scouser, I'm also a borderline suspect. This man has the disturbing habit of issuing equally dogmatic edicts using the third person style of speech so it looks as though, between him and my unpromising crew, I'm in for an interesting first voyage in my new company.

As we head southwards my misgivings melt in the warmth of the improving weather. My two mates are good workers and the engineers are a congenial group. It's a ship that has a proper officers' bar, regular film nights and all the usual social gatherings. I also discover that Palm Line people are equally fond of a palm-oil chop, so that's another benefit yet to come.

The sailors also have a bar, which they manage themselves, and seem willing to make their contribution to the happiness of the voyage. There are a few grumbles about the lack of overtime hours. This is because the ship has just had the statutory quadrennial inspection of all its cargo-handling gear, which removes the need for a lot of their immediate work. Nevertheless, they seem generally content to be exchanging the gloom of a Merseyside winter for the sunshine of tropical Africa.

One or two of the sailors, who've been to the Coast before and know that we'll be picking up the usual gang of Krooboys, ask if there'll be more overtime later in the voyage. I tell them that there's no reason why that shouldn't be the case. Now that I'm back work-ing with British sailors, the vexed topic of overtime will occur throughout the voyage.

The unavoidable truth is that the basic wage for seamen is low and something between 20 and 30 hours a week of overtime is regarded as the minimum needed to raise it to a worthwhile amount. Working on Saturday and Sunday at sea produces up to 16 hours and another ten to 15 hours a week is normally available, but the latter sum is dependent upon the necessary tasks being available.

On my last sailings with a British crew I was given an overtime budget which barely covered their minimal duties and I had a constant battle between satisfying the demands of the head office accounts department and the aspirations of the sailors. No such strict budget operates here but neither is the ship to be an informal charity for them. I fear that this overtime conflict will be a recurring theme over the coming weeks.

We have no Nigerian cargo on board which is a major disappointment to the catering crew. However, the engine-room ratings enjoy a night ashore in Freetown, where we unload some cargo and take on fuel. I also top up our freshwater tanks as I'm told by the Old Man that it's becoming difficult to get reliable supplies in many ports on the Coast.

He still produces occasional gnomic statements using his peculiar mode of address but I feel that I'm now accepted as a partially redeemed scouser since I told him that I was born elsewhere. I don't bother to expand on that by confessing that I came to the city aged four and have never left it since. It's sufficient that we seem to have a reasonable working relationship and, since he never patronises the bar or film nights, the other officers are barely aware of his presence.

Calls at Monrovia, Abidjan and Takoradi follow but it is when we reach Tema that we begin to see the effects of the Lagos congestion. The anchorage is crowded with ships, many of which have come here in some distress looking for water and other provisions after many weeks or even months of queueing for a Nigerian berth.

We should enjoy priority here as we have cargo to unload but we still have to anchor for a few days. During this period we are frequently warned not only by the agency but also by other ships, via the VHF, that we need to watch out for pirates. I've already taken the Old Man's sound advice before we arrived in Freetown that I need to scour the decks for portable treasure and remove it to a place of safety.

This means that our fire hoses, with their phosphor-bronze connectors and nozzles, as well as our lifeboat stores of food and distress signals, are out of sight in lockers fitted with new heavier padlocks. Our polypropylene mooring ropes are safely stowed below decks and the carpenter has replaced the brass caps to the tank-sounding pipes with wooden plugs and taken down the brass forecastle bell.

The standard compass on the monkey island has been reduced to its bare wooden case, emptied of the compass bowl, its brass binnacle and its magnets. We're probably contravening all sorts of safety regulations and all this equipment will later have to be put back into position. It's so much additional work but it's the new reality of life in West Africa.

As it turns out, we're left unvisited at anchor by the local criminals and our two days alongside have only the normal levels of theft to deal with. I'm more concerned about our sailors, who've enjoyed their first run ashore by leaving two of their number in the care of the Ghanaian police. The Old Man is doing his gloomy oracle routine but I tell the bosun to have a whip-round with the crowd and take some presents up to the local nick.

This has the desired outcome and the two miscreants eventually return to the ship. I duly accompany them to the Old Man for the ritual logging of the disciplinary offence of being absent without leave. Have they anything to say in their defence? Their protestations of innocence, involving the usual fairy story of being kidnapped by evil natives, don't wash in this summary court of justice that is the master's power under the Merchant Shipping Acts. Nevertheless, it's customary to substitute a log entry and a verbal warning for a first offence, so they escape the docking of a day's pay for their shoreside adventure.

Doing a quick round of the deck before I go to the bar that evening, however, I see some of Liverpool's finest in a huddle on the poop. Although they disperse when I approach, they leave behind them the unmistakable aroma of West Africa's herbal narcotic of choice.

It's apparent now that I'm in for a lively voyage, holding the ring between the Old Man and my fellow citizens, although I can still hope that they'll not be under the influence too much during their normal daytime hours of work. At least I have the insurance policy of a gang of reliable Krooboys to keep the job going if they fail me.

Our next port calls, at Lomé and Cotonou, provide further evidence of the effects of the Nigerian chaos. Both ports are beset by small armadas of anchored ships, spilling over from the Lagos roadstead. Neither port visit allows for any shore excursions. It also appears that the cannabis purchases have all been consumed, and consequently there's a welcome return of the crew's normal performance.

It's in Douala that the next temptation arises for them as we spend a night in port despite the fact that the amount of cargo to be unloaded is small. Lawlessness on the quays here is such that import cargo (unless singularly unattractive) can only be worked for a few daylight hours. We have textiles, whisky, batteries, machetes and Land Rovers as our cargo, so we can expect to be closely attended by the local criminals, especially at night.

I arrange to have as many lights hung overside as we can manage and have several charged fire hoses at the ready. The agency have supplied us with six 'bow-and-arrow' men. They are not only licensed to use their eponymous weapons but are also permitted to heave lumps of rock and other missiles at any canoes that are hanging about or indeed at any loiterers on the quay. Half a dozen of the sailors do go ashore but they return at a reasonable hour in good shape and ready to turn-to the following morning. It'a relief to me not to have another disciplinary tribunal up in the Old Man's cabin.

As we head on southwards, the purser catering officer (the two roles have been combined into one as an economy measure since I was last on the Coast) tells me that beer sales into the crew bar have slumped. When I treat this as good news, he warns me that this usually means that 'happy sticks' are now being used as the relaxation means of choice. For now, I'm quite content that the crew are staying out of trouble and are working well and in good humour.

For example, we're in our next port, Pointe Noire, when the third mate tells me that there's a lot of shouting going on down aft. This is because one of the shore labourers has just 'had a dump on the punt'. In translation, this means that the ship's workboat, which is in the water by the stern, has become the unintended target of a thunderbox customer. When I reach the scene, expecting to find two angry seamen, I'm greeted with, 'Orright, Chief, no bother, we're nearly finished this fleet (area) anyway' from one and, from the other, the more forthright, 'Missed us this time but I've got me long bamboo ready so's the next black arse I see's going to get a dab of red lead.'

Our final port of call is Matadi and we're heading up the Congo (but it's now changed its name to Zaire) when the Old Man calls me to the bridge. He has to take a radio telephone call and asks me to keep an eye on the ship's progress and on the pilot, especially: 'Chap's a communist.' Not much of a discovery, since he's Polish and would hardly be allowed to leave his country were he not a party member.

He's not bent on driving us into the nearest riverbank but remarks instead to me, 'Very nice, looks like Scotland,' indicating the passing scenery. I agree and say that, whilst it is nice and open here, the upper stretches of this great river will be known forever as the 'heart of darkness' thanks to the writings of his countryman. Maybe that view is not that of Poland today because I get an enigmatic response from the pilot of, 'Oh, yes, your Mr Conrad, a very English gentleman, I understand.'

When the Old Man returns, I tell him that I'll get hold of Chippy and we'll head up forward, ready for our transit of the Chaudron d'Enfer. We sweep majestically through the brown river eddies and pass under the telephone wires, which seem to be sagging lower than I remember, and then we're safely moored alongside in Matadi.

It's the season of low river. We hardly need a gangway since the main deck is almost level with the quay, but this also means that we'll be all too accessible to the local bandits as the port's name has become a byword for extreme lawlessness, even by contemporary West African standards.

Fortunately we only have a small amount of cargo to unload although it will be a major task getting it landed as it has been repeatedly ransacked in every port beforehand. I leave the task of that to the third mate to sort out with the agency discrepancy clerk and a brace of Zairean customs officials.

My priority is to see a heavy lift successfully landed. I first ensure that it's been correctly slung with four heavy wires shackled to strongpoints on the body of this large piece of machinery. It's described as a stone crusher and is consigned to a mining company far up-country. It weighs 37 tons, no problem for a 50 ton derrick were it not for its rig, termed 'rove to advantage'.

This is a method of threading the lifting wire through a pair of pulley blocks whereby the mechanical advantage of the lower block is maximised by having the greatest number of moving parts of wire rope passing through it. There is a major operating disadvantage of this routeing whereby the wire runs from the lower block back towards the winch. That is when the derrick is tending towards the horizontal for a maximum reach, as it must be here to reach the quay, the lower block and hence the load is always being pulled back from achieving that reach.

Two or three small groups of dockers on the quayside have attached pulling ropes to the crusher and are attempting to counter this adverse effect. Unfortunately the winch-drivers on board are being poorly co-ordinated and all that is being achieved is an angry shouting match. I call the bosun to get four of the sailors to man the winches so that we can produce a better semblance of a team.

In the meantime, our nearly empty ship is leaning steeply towards the wharf because of this great outstretched weight. We are in imminent danger of catching the shipside bulwarks under the concrete quay capping since the eddies of this mighty river tease us playfully.

My crew are quickly in charge of the heavy derrick and, after just one or two tentative and unsuccessful attempts, they succeed in dropping the crusher onto the waiting flatbed trailer. Loud whoops and ululations of delight from both black and white spectators congratulate this success and the ship, relieved at last of that weighty burden, itself does a roll or two of relief before settling upright again.

There's no copper on offer here these days to fill us up quickly and only some cotton, some scruffy-looking bales of rubber and a few logs to load for Liverpool. There is, however, palm oil to fill two of our deep tanks and we're instructed to fill the other tanks at Boma when we call there on our way downriver.

I learn that enough of this tasty material is already in our catering stores so there's no need to unofficially sample our cargo. However, I can tell our Krooboy headman that, while I'm not looking, he can remove a few kerosene tins' worth of oil as a 'dash' for the good work his boys put in to clean the tanks.

Only the oil is on offer at Boma and our next call is at Pointe Noire again. It's a Sunday the day after we arrive and the bosun tells me that none of the crowd want to volunteer for work that day. A lie-in is planned, followed by a beach expedition. In the afternoon I accept the responsibilities of rank by allowing the two mates to clear off to the beach as well. It's also a recognition of their hard work on board.

What later surprises me is that the Old Man emerges from his usual seclusion and offers to supervise the deck so that I can enjoy a dip in the ocean before dark. When I get to the beach, I see that an informal segregation is in force. A quartet of sailors have moved some 200 yards or so from the main party to be just out of sight over a sand spit. I contrive to swim in that direction and then artfully emerge to see what's going on.

I needn't have bothered with such a contrived approach as they're completely oblivious of who I am or where they are, being reduced to giggling enjoyment of some corpulent and extremely aromatic spliffs. There's no point in my making any comment other than reminding them to get back on board before dark. I'm now left wondering just how much new smoking stock they managed to acquire while we were up the Congo.

Nobody can go ashore at Port Gentil or Libreville since they're both offshore anchorages. We fill our lower holds with a mixture of logs and sawn timber and then start covering the deck with logs.

Stevedores in both ports bitterly complain about our 'primitive' ship, which they unfavourably compare with the modern French vessels of the Delmas fleet with their wide hatches and deck cranes. Even the French supervisor asks me when Palm Line will replace these museum pieces. Reluctantly and a little disloyally, I have to agree with their opinions since this ship really is now an unnecessarily inefficient workplace for our particular trade.

On passage to our final port of call, Abidjan, we enjoy the pleasures of the palm-oil chop although the Old Man doesn't participate in what he dismissively terms 'native food'. We're also promised a further feast once we finally leave the Coast. Most of the British crew also turn up their noses at this 'nig-nog grub' as they more crudely describe it and go for the steak-and-chips alternative.

I also learn, via the bosun, that they're not happy with the deck cargo, which is understandable as their accommodation is right down aft. When I get the chance, I tell them bluntly that the freight on these logs pays their wages. I begin to wonder if this new-found irritability is connected with them not having purchased quite as much narcotic as I'd earlier assumed.

We complete our loading in Abidjan with a cargo of both cocoa and coffee, which guarantees us a berth on the quay for a couple of days. There's no sign of the crowd turning-to on the morning of our departure. The bosun and chippy have also gone into hiding and I need to find out what's going on before the Old Man remarks on their absence.

When I do track down the bosun I'm pleased to see that he'll be getting the Krooboys to complete the hull painting by working from the quay once he has persuaded a couple of them to work from the punt under Chippy's direction. As for our 'jolly jacks', apparently they're parked in a bar somewhere in the squalid dockside suburb of Treichville and aren't coming back until all the logs are removed from the afterdeck.

I have to let the Old Man know about this ultimatum and he's incandescent about 'our' (meaning the first person plural him, I assume) betrayal by these scouse *untermenschen*. He insists that we'll use the Krooboys to manage our departure. These putative deserters can then take their chance with the Ivoirian authorities. With this hard line being taken, I advise the bosun to get a message ashore to the crowd.

In mid-afternoon, one of the junior seamen comes back on board sporting a prominent black eye and says that the crowd was set upon by a gang of locals when their money ran out in the bar. That change of story appears to have some veracity since more stragglers appear on board as the afternoon progresses, each one in possession of sundry cuts and bruises.

The bosun gets supplies from the medical locker and arranges a temporary surgery in the messroom but it's still a sorry-looking contingent who help to take the ship out to sea that evening. They are even sorrier the next day when I have to take them, one by one, up to the Old Man's office, where they are duly charged and fined a day's pay. The purser catering officer subsequently fills several pages of the official logbook with the indignant statements (expletives all included) of these very much less than contrite plaintiffs.

We call in at Freetown very briefly to land the Krooboys and start heading for home. The decks are covered in logs but all the hatchtops are clear so it's not really that difficult to get around the decks. With the Coast safely behind us, all the firefighting and safety equipment can be restored to its proper place, the lifeboats can be reprovisioned and the standard compass put back together again.

Stowaways are beginning to become a problem in West Africa but we've had regular searches of the ship at all our ports and, fingers firmly crossed, I've told the Old Man that we're free of any informal passengers.

The ship's derricks have taken a hammering at all the log-loading ports and are now the only scruffy bits left on the freshly painted ship. I prioritise their cleaning and painting, along with inspection and any needed overhaul of their heavy purchase blocks, as work for the last good weather before we reach the Canaries.

I'm told by the bosun that the supply of champagne paint (a very pale yellow colour that is particular to Palm Line) will run out before the blocks can be painted. I authorise his suggested use of the emerald green paint that is another company colour instead.

It all looks quite smart in my estimation but I'm rapidly disabused of that fancy when I'm called to the Old Man's office and the Company Handbook is hurled at me with the demand, 'Read what it says about the ship's colour scheme on page…'. I know that I've contravened this policy but I also suspect that I've been added to the company of scouse traitors that have infiltrated the ship. I can only respond, 'Sorry, but it's a done job now,' and retreat before he starts looking for the official logbook and the disciplinary penalties available to him.

I see that I'm going to enjoy an awkward homeward passage. I must avoid giving any further offence and just sit it out. My fellow citizens aft are not ones to be so generous, however, as I find out early one morning as we roll our way across the Western Approaches. Sparks appears earlier than usual on the bridge and says, 'I'll keep a lookout, you'd better nip down to the boatdeck and have a look aft.'

I take his strange advice and see to my horror that an earthy slogan has been painted in three-foot-high letters across the front of the poop house. It alleges that our named master enjoys sexual congress with a named species of domestic animal. That's 15 large grey letters that need obliterating in short order and I'm hoping that it can be done before its target becomes aware of the obscene allegation.

An application of white undercoat by roller is an effective primary camouflage and, if the subject of the slander later wonders why the poop house bulkhead is being painted gloss white so late in the voyage, he makes no public remark.

We enter Liverpool's Langton lock on a sunny May morning and my irregular paint scheme is sufficiently aloft on our topped derricks to avoid any comment by our marine superintendent as he watches our arrival from the quayside as we berth.

Nothing further has been said about my crime so it's probably the fact that I'm the most junior mate in the company that explains my next berth on the firm's oldest ship when I sail out of the Clyde a month later. It's widely hinted that this is her final voyage before going to the predictable Greek purchaser who will sweat her into her final destination on a shipbreaker's beach in Pakistan.

The crew this time is composed of Glasgow's finest and I soon discover that drinking is their preferred occupation once we reach West Africa's ports at the height of the rainy season. We're not in Banjul (as Bathurst is now called) long enough for them to get ashore so my principal problem is keeping our substantial whisky cargo intact as we test our cargo security in this first port.

This attractive cargo is again being transported in those eight-foot cubes. They offer some measure of protection but they're also difficult to handle within our antiquated cargo compartments. I have to rely on the Krooboys for most of the work on deck as this trip the bosun is complicit in the crew's anarchy.

His first, of several, entries in the logbook comes when he provides sick notes for three of his team who've asked to see the doctor in Cotonou. They return and advise me that they have all been declared unfit for duty but I suspect forgery. This is when the evidence that they produce consists of grubby pages torn out of the stock book in the crew bar and recommending 'three days of' (sic) for all concerned.

The bulk of our cargo is bags of malted Scottish barley destined for Nigerian Breweries, which we unload in Apapa before continuing our trek southwards, which will end in Pointe Noire.

We begin loading the usual mix of logs and sawn timber for the homeward passage. The crew's absenteeism now becomes persistent; they even manage to charter a local boat to take them ashore in Libreville and again in Owendo. I cannot imagine what they found ashore in the latter place since it's barely a clearing in the virgin jungle. Whatever unmissable attraction it boasts is not explained at the usual court appearance in the Old Man's cabin the following day.

I am fortunate in that he is an equally hard Glaswegian who takes a great delight in progressively increasing the fines with each repeat offence. The crowd, to their credit, just roll with the punches and accept the price of their indiscipline and I am also grateful that they remain quite unconcerned about the lack of overtime which is inevitable on any ship's final voyage.

It's in a bar in Douala that our inebriated Caledonians excel themselves by substituting bill payment with a brawl and end up in the cells at the police barracks. I remain unsurprised at their absence until the agency clerk comes on board with a handful of British Seamen's Identity Cards and reveals the location of their holders.

'Right,' says the Old Man, 'let's get ashore and sort this lot out once and for all.' I change out of my customary boiler suit and into white uniform complete with cap to join him in the agency car and we're taken to the bar to establish the amount owed by our crew members. The agent settles the bill then, on the way to see the prisoners, the Old Man tells me his plan.

The two of us, both magnificently uniformed, are introduced to our imprisoned shipmates, whereupon the Old Man roars in outrage:

'These men have nothing at all to do with my ship. They're all impostors.'

I then follow the agreed script by chipping in with:

'And I've never seen any of these people before. They're just trying to stow away on the ship to come to England. They're absolute rogues, the lot of them.'

Our jolly jacks are stunned into complete silence by this apparent act of treachery on our part, whereupon we make our indignant exit. The Old Man tells the police chief, who is a party to our little act of theatre, that the disputed bar bill has been paid in full. He adds that, unless the police wish to prefer charges against them, the sailors can be released at the police chief's convenience so that they can walk the several kilometres back to the ship.

My next trip dispels my fear that I've made a poor choice in sailing with my countrymen as sailors because it's a voyage with a crowd of Londoners who are only interested in the money. As we also don't embark any Krooboys for a change, that's one objective I can easily satisfy. The only drama of the voyage involves a stowaway cat from Tilbury which has to be declared as an import on our way back to the UK and which promptly deserts on our arrival in Hull. A search party ashore manages to kidnap a passable substitute to avoid a hefty fine from the port health authorities.

15

A modern ship is not a cure for the Coast's troubles

I had been reminding our marine superintendent that I was familiar with the most modern hatch covers and heavy derricks since I first heard the rumours that we were buying two modern second-hand ships. At last, this informal canvassing has led to my flying out to Las Palmas to join one of our new acquisitions on the way home from her third voyage to West Africa.

I open the curtains of my hotel room to see the welcome sight of the ship entering the harbour with a full deck load of containers. It is this, rather than her boxy shape that benefits little from our attractive colour scheme, that makes me confident that Palm Line is at last on level terms with its competitors.

The taxi from the hotel takes me to the ship berthed far down on the Dique del Generalisimo Franco and I'm gratified to see that I have to go up a substantial external staircase to enter the accommodation block. This'll be useful to fortify the ship against the hordes who invade the ship in West African ports.

I meet my mentor in a spacious dayroom that has the ambience of the living room of a Dutch barge. Its ruched net curtains, dark furniture and tapestry tablecloth are inheritances from the ship's previous German owner. I'm housed in a spare cabin, from which I emerge in my customary white boiler suit and deck boots. However, I now have the novel addition of a plastic safety helmet, coloured a striking canary yellow. It's time to explore my new home.

We're not working any cargo as this call is for fuel bunkers only. The decks are perfumed with the attractive aroma of cocoa beans courtesy of the powerful hatch ventilation fans. We're walking in the shade of the deck load of containers, which are gently creaking as the ship moves easily to the inevitable harbour scend.

I can see that the hatch covers are of a familiar type and that the derricks are a slightly Heath-Robinsonesque interpretation of another familiar rig. I note that I'll need to learn about the specialised container securing system in use and my learning curve becomes even more apparent when we tour the bridge.

Gone is the spartan suite of equipment of my recent experience, replaced by a massive control console that runs almost the full width of the wheelhouse. Ranks of switches and indicator lights in red, blue, yellow, green and orange are helpfully labelled. The engine-room telegraph, banks of internal telephones, external speakers, VHF set and a basic fax machine are familiar friends. However, the controls for the variable-pitch propeller, the bow thruster and the remote operation of the anchors are all new toys for me to learn about.

At lunch I meet the Old Man, a man of Polish birth who immediately observes that my surname is 'not very English, is it, Mr Goble?' I've had this comment many times before from people that I sail with. Therefore I give him my stock response that my forefathers have been British since at least the time of the battle of Waterloo and that I have the family heirloom of my namesake's campaign medal to prove this.

After that first exchange, we find ourselves in a happy working relationship that lasts for several voyages. He makes no secret that the deck equipment is so alien to him that he'll leave me in peace to look after it so long as I see that the cargo goes in and out with the minimum of fuss.

By the time of our arrival in Liverpool, five days later, I've been shown enough of the ship and have learnt as much of its operation and maintenance to know that I'm happy to take over from my knowlegeable instructor. Above all, I feel confident of enjoying a release from the world of canvas, timber and ancient cargo-handling.

We start loading and I find that I'm back on the prestige express service to Lagos and back. Both Elder and Nigerline (as they're now so called) have sister ships of our new purchase in operation alongside us on a fairly regular schedule.

I use the word fairly because the chaos that is Nigeria is now affecting all import services. Even the export cargoes have fallen away to the extent that we must go looking elsewhere to make up our homeward tonnages.

For now, however, we have a full cargo to load and we begin in the traditional manner with Cheshire salt. It's being shipped now in one-ton polypropylene 'bombs' that contain fifty or sixty individual cotton bags bearing the trade marks of old. These bombs can be brought aboard six at a time and then they're stacked in the lower holds by forklifts.

We'll have over two hundred 20 foot containers to load at another berth in the docks (we could accommodate well over double that number) once we've put all what is termed 'break-bulk' aboard. Our number one hatch is our 'dirty' stow, where go the bags of carbon-black, detergent base, drums of printer's ink and industrial adhesives. Just the kind of mixture that'll leave a heartbreaking residue for the Krooboys to clean up and then dump overside into the waters of the Gulf of Guinea in due course.

We're no longer calling at those smaller UK ports where we used to load goods bound for West Africa. Cargoes such as tinplate from South Wales, whisky from Scotland and sacks of polypropylene granules from Middlesbrough are all being brought to Liverpool by road. The wide open spaces of this modern ship are so easy to load in comparison to the nooks and crannies of her predecessors that I don't at first notice our lack of locker space and the limited opportunity to put hazardous cargoes around the decks.

It's only when the container stowages are being discussed that I realise that it's not just a matter of plonking them as and where. Containers of pilferables must be located door-to-door to ensure their security. There is a hazardous-cargo handbook, several inches thick, to consult when planning the distribution of containers that carry those items. And then I have to understand the method of securing the containers and see that it's carried out before I can sign off the rigging gang's endeavours.

At sea and keeping a bridge watch, I have to get used to the very different outlook from the wheelhouse windows. The prospect is of an expanse of corrugated steel in various colours that is the top of the container stow with the addition of Land Rovers, vans and lorry chassis secured on top of them.

Three sets of goalpost-type masts don't add to the clarity of a forward view. Neither does our location nearly at the back of the ship in place of the conventional midships placing. It's readily apparent that a small craft like a canoe would be quite invisible for several hundred feet ahead of us That'll be something to consider when we start mixing it with suicidal fishermen off the Ghanaian coast.

For now, however, I'm quite content to enjoy my expanded accommodation, the fixed swimming pool and the very effective air conditioning. I even discover that there's a sheltered corner on deck with a deck-chair, above which my predecessor has stencilled the notice, 'Private: Chief Officer ONLY'.

A modern ship, a familiar trade with a regular timetable and no fear of being diverted to a trip across the Atlantic, as Palm Line only serves the UK and northern Europe: it should be an excellent prospect but I soon discover that the ship remains vulnerable to the increasing anarchy in West Africa.

It's clear that the Nigerian civil war not only acted as a conduit for weapons that have found their way into so many neighbouring countries but also that the conflict was the precursor of other, similar bitter disputes.

They are the result of disappointing economic performances, after nearly two decades of independence, being blamed on minorities who live in these artificially defined countries. Continuing poverty and wider access to modern weaponry make a dangerous combination that impacts on ships trading to all the ports on this coast.

The number of ports that we visit is also in decline. Warri is the only 'creek' port still in business, Sapele is closed and very little is heard of Calabar. All the old surf ports are long gone into history as well.

Now, only we relatively old hands can speak of such minor destinations as Nouakchott, Bissau, Sherbro, Lower Buchanan, Sinoe, Cape Palmas, Bata, Santa Isabel and Mayumbe. Those lovely ports of Angola, Lobito and Luanda are now abandoned by the Portuguese and embroiled in West Africa's most extended and vicious internal strife.

It's true that Nigeria is still importing, although an increasing number of goods are subject to licensing, but trade into Sierra Leone and Ghana is greatly reduced. I begin to feel that we've started modernising our fleet just in time to trade into a declining market for our services.

I'm also aware that there's plenty of urgent work to be done on this ship in the intervals when we're not keeping pirates, thieves and other rogues at bay. This is because I'm starting to learn about this ship's pre-history.

She was built in Poland some five years ago for a Hamburg ship-owner who is an expert in arbitraging the shipbuilding market. He benefited from the Anglo-German Offset Agreement of the previous decade to build in Britain at a subsidised price and now he was exploiting the need for the Poles to earn some hard currency.

Our ship is the first of a class of six identical vessels. This means that she not only lacks any improvements made as the series progressed but also suffers from poor materials and equally inferior maintenance by her original owner. Fortunately, in contrast to the crews that I'd already endured sailing with in Palm Line, I find here a team of good seamen who return, trip after trip, and give good value for the abundant overtime that is on offer.

Nevertheless, we still need extra help and therefore embark the traditional gang of Krooboys in Freetown even though we lack the usual basic accommodation that they should expect. Times are hard ashore for them these days in Sierra Leone. This means that there's little complaint when they see that we're at least providing a generous space in which to eat and sleep, albeit with little in the form of toilet or washing facilities.

Chipping equipment is handed out to the Krooboys and I'm soon content to see lumps and layers of rust being removed from the deck fittings. I'm even happier when the hatches are opened and they can start attacking the hatch cover trackways.

It's one of the advantages of a lawless working environment such as West Africa that many aspects of health, safety and working courtesy can be completely ignored. Consequently, my team of metal woodpeckers can bang off and scatter rust as much as they like without attracting any sanctions. It's only when I see that the steelwork is much poorer even than I thought, that I have to restrain this chipping before we produce too much of a colander effect on the ship's fabric.

Chippy has already shown me that the use of sub-standard steel is causing serious deformity in some links in the two long chains that pull the steel hatch covers open or closed. This results in the two sides of the covers moving at slightly different rates. This crab-like motion will cause one side of the covers to jam. If the operator doesn't realise this potential danger, then one chain is likely to break altogether.

A further sign of a low quality of material and maintenance is apparent in the ship's cargo-handling gear. I find this out when we examine a pulley block that isn't running well. Grease that is applied via a lubricating nipple can't reach its destination at the centre of the block because a greaseway hasn't been fully drilled.

Furthermore, the steel sheave itself is worn away at its circumference to form a razor-like edge that one day will guillotine the steel wire running past it. It's another item for the end-of-voyage repair list since any treatment is beyond the capability of the engineers' workshop on board.

With the import cargo unloaded and the holds cleaned, the resulting rubbish is still hung overside in bags to dump once we sail. Now we're ready to take an export cargo on board. The main change in that process is that we're only receiving a small amount of cargo in the traditional way, amounting to a couple of thousand tons of cocoa beans and palm kernels in bags.

It's just as well we're only loading a small bag cargo. Despite considerable expenditure on new steel and rubber piping for the ship's hydraulics, enough of the old poorly maintained stock remains for us to be plagued by pipe bursts.

These invariably occur at places where a mist of hydraulic oil can spray over some nearby bags of produce. The duty engineer must be called out, often during his mealtime, to replace the defective hose while the duty mate and I surreptitiously turn over any affected bags to conceal any damage from the cargo surveyor in Liverpool.

Most of our homeward load is made up of the new blue-painted twenty-foot containers that bear the ACE logo. They're mainly empty ones and are being brought alongside in a steady stream. We're soon completed below decks and I can take a break from our eccentric hatch covers and start piling them three-high on deck.

By today's standards this is modest stuff; however, getting around and about a deck cargo towering some 25 feet above me is still hard work. It's made all the more so by because I'm perpetually seeking any of our light aluminium ladders that aren't damaged or missing due to their theft for use ashore.

I've educated myself in a new vocabulary of twistlocks, lashing rods, penguins and bottlescrews and the way in which they all come together to keep this lot safe in a seaway. All that remains is to see that our crew are keeping to the rules of their use. At least they enjoy this work since it earns them a good bonus payment.

Back in Liverpool, our container cargo is subject to close inspection by a gang of customs officers since the West African trade continues to be a suspect route for drug smuggling. At least they don't want to tear the accommodation apart any more. This is comforting since I've got my usual modest stash of whisky and tobacco safely concealed in a number of handy locations.

If a full container is landed, with all its seals intact, then it's soon on its way through the shed door for storage but all the empties must have their doors opened and the interiors checked. At one time these waterguard officers were busy with their tape-measures as they inspected. This followed one notorious incident where a twenty-foot container was found to measure only 19 feet internally. This was the clue to finding an ingenious design feature whereby a new steel internal partition allowed the concealment of a substantial amount of contraband.

The growing use of the container for cargoes to West Africa, some ten years after its introduction to the more sophisticated Australasian, Far Eastern and US trade routes, means that Palm Line have to acquire even more new ships.

We learn that two are on order, which is welcome news as our old ships are gradually being sold to new owners. A fleet reduction also means that any prospects of promotion have now disappeared. However, I'm not tempted to look elsewhere for employment since the whole shipping industry is slowly disappearing and at least there is no talk here of redundancies yet.

In fact, I'm soon on a flight to Venice to join one of these new ships on her delivery voyage from South Korea. I admire her modern lines as she berths with a full cargo of brand-new bright-orange-coloured 20-foot containers made by her builders, Hyundai. That name, although soon to be borne by many cars on British roads, is an unfamiliar one in 1979. By placing an order abroad at this time when the British shipbuilding is struggling to survive, Palm Line are being widely criticised in shipping industry quarters.

This criticism is unfair since we'll soon be accepting into service a very similar vessel from a shipyard in Sunderland. We're the subsidiary of a multinational firm and we have to earn our keep in an international marketplace.

This foreign purchase actually isn't an unusual event in Palm Line's history. As long ago as 1938, our ultimate owner, Unilever, carried away some of its blocked earnings in Nazi Germany in the form of ships for its own operation. Later, as we shall see, Unilever will be using dollars from its overseas earnings to benefit from Polish shipbuilding's continuing desire for hard currencies.

These new arrivals in the fleet are not exact sister ships. Being quite biased, I consider the Korean ship to be the better-looking one although, as workplaces, they are virtually identical.

My view isn't shared by the engineers, who complain that their workplace has been put together by men a lot more compact than those who now have to get into some very tight places for essential maintenance. Both ships, being brand-new, are a considerable improvement on our two earlier second-hand purchases in terms of operation.

This means that I can pay more attention to combating the depredations of the criminal element in every West African port. I begin to understand what Captain Cook complained about on his voyages to the southern seas when his ship was in danger of falling apart due to the theft of the nails that secured the hull planking.

We're in Tema and, as I go around checking on the day's work, I see a long bundle wrapped in plastic emerging from one of the hatch accesses. I grab hold of one end and receive a grunt of gratitude from whoever is holding the other. That is quickly followed by a cry of shock as my white face is associated with this offer of help.

Resisting the temptation to drop the heavy trapdoor on the miscreant, I angrily demand, 'Wettin you dey get nah, my brudda?' 'I dey find dis ting ay dey bring so to you, master,' is the man's unconvincing reply and explanation. By now, I can see that the package contains about half a dozen fluorescent lamp tubes so I confiscate them. I ignore the previous carrier's pleas for some reward and go off to tell the electrician that we'd better arrange to remove any further similar temptation from the hatches.

This will leave the hold access trunkways as well as the hold ventilation and hydraulic pumprooms in darkness. I can find padlocks to secure those rooms but the open areas will naturally become dangerous to use and also add to the informal lavatory space. There's no practical alternative as further thefts will render them dark in any case. We're still locking up our fire and safety equipment so this is yet another breach of health-and-safety regulations, were any such regime in existence here.

Of course, it isn't all nuisance and inconvenience in every port. In Apapa, in particular, we enjoy entertaining guests from shore and other ships of the company that are in port to a weekend barbecue. In fact it earns us the sobriquet that I later learn of the 'Barbecue Palm'.

For our expatriate guests this is an opportunity for them to enjoy the delights of British 'bangers' and a range of other domestic fare that import restrictions have removed from their local Kingsway supermarket.

On one occasion we're able to offer some tasty barbecued chicken. It's the proceeds of a chance confiscation when the deck officer on duty finds a large plastic bag of plump little carcases that are still hard frozen and slyly concealed behind a cargo winch. They come from a Brazilian ship that is berthed just ahead of us but I decide that a walk along the quay to repatriate them isn't justified. It's surely far better to park them in our store-room pending our next party night.

I had myself challenged a couple of dockworkers earlier the same day whose prominent codpieces looked to me as though they might contain torch batteries from our cargo.

When one of my suspects reached inside his waistband to show me three fine fat frozen mackerel, I felt that I had to let them go on their way. They originated from a small freezer ship unloading nearby and were good Cornish produce. They could have been added to the barbecue but I didn't exactly fancy their recent provenance.

Our hospitality is reciprocated by invitations to private houses ashore rather than visits to share the Apapa Club facilities. Those are suffering from more import bans and from the general bedlam of life in Nigeria. Evenings ashore are a welcome break from our shipboard surroundings although the journey from the dock gate is now an obstacle course of ill-lit obstructions and pot-holes.

The once-immaculate boulevard of Liverpool Road that led to the residential sections of town is now marked by a new central reservation. This consists of disabled lorries, many partially destroyed by fire and others being subject to informal repairs. People drive cautiously as the carriageway might suddenly be blocked by an unattended wheel axle or an impromptu blacksmith's forge.

Any party ashore is inevitably plunged into darkness at some point when the electricity supply fails but is soon resumed once the emergency diesel generator is started. Bottles of Star lager have to be carefully collected up as refills can only be bought according to the number of empties presented. However, there is no shortage of spirits since an efficient black market operates within the expatriate community. Unfortunately, mixers for drinks have the availability of the proverbial hen's teeth.

Conditions are little better in even the most luxurious establishments ashore, as we learn at one party on board. Some senior visiting UAC managers ask if they might enjoy a hot shower, a facility that the once-prestigious Federal Palace Hotel on the exclusive Victoria Island is unable to provide. We perform a similar service on a later visit for other visitors from our parent company and I have cause to be grateful for that intervention a couple of days later.

We're loading some containers of tin ingots on deck one afternoon and I'm on the scene ensuring that they're all stowed in a door-to-door manner in order to keep their valuable contents intact. One container has to be swung around to meet this requirement and it then comes towards me rather faster than I'm expecting.

I take a couple of precautionary steps backwards and find myself on my back, winded but conscious of a terrible pain. I'm lying in the narrow gap between our twin hatch covers. I'm also aware that my head is within inches of a steel girder that would have inflicted serious damage since I'm not wearing my customary safety helmet. I can move my arms and legs so I'm content to note that I'm not paralysed but then I'm not at all comforted by a cry of 'Chief mate, he done die-o !' which accompanies me into a brief unconsciousness.

I revive to discover that I'm now securely strapped into the ship's emergency stretcher and some ten feet above the deck, being swung ashore by a derrick that I'm pleased to note is being controlled by my reliable bosun. The whole quay is in a state of excited uproar as I'm equally professionally transferred to the back of a VW-camper-style private ambulance.

My consciousness fully returns as we join the traffic jam on the notorious Carter Bridge, headed for Lagos Island. The Nigerian ambulance attendant is gently reassuring, 'Massa, dere is no blood, you no go die now.' More to the point, by being at my side, he'll prevent the usual roadside hawkers, who gather around us when we make frequent halts, from making off with my nearly new pair of working shoes.

I'm also sure that my wife, as a nurse, will be pleased that I'll be presenting at the hospital in not only a fairly clean boiler suit but also wearing one of my more respectable pairs of underpants.

In fact my only worry, apart from the fact that my whole back seems to have solidified, is the mess that I've left behind me on board. Perhaps I can get back in time to finish the stores book, get the overtime account up to date, complete the cargo plan and deal with that bucket of dhobi left fermenting in my bathroom?

We arrive at a small private hospital close to Tinubu Square in the heart of town. I'm wheeled inside to learn that the lift is out of order and so I must use the stairs to get up to the reception ward on the first floor. That brief journey is sufficiently painful to convince me that I'll not be able to rejoin the ship before it sails. I might, however, be capable of being repatriated without too long a hospital stay.

We arrive on the ward where the sister, formidable in size and impressive in her crisply starched white apron and cap, directs me, 'You are welcome. No worry but please get in the bed for the doctor to see you.' When I ask for help in removing my work shoes, she briskly repeats, 'Don't worry of that matter, just get in de bed.' I'm in no mood to argue so I insert myself between the crisply laundered sheets and peacefully pass out once again.

I'm woken to find two strangers at my bedside. One is a Nigerian doctor who says that he doesn't think that I'll need an X-ray as this is probably just a case of very severe bruising. Comfortingly, he remarks that the pain will certainly increase 'until it gets better' but I'll get some pain-killers once I'm transferred to a private ward. This move has been arranged by my other visitor, whom I recognise as one of our barbecue guests from a couple of days back.

He is genuinely solicitous of my welfare, assures me that I'll get the best of treatment, and is quietly amused when I show him my fully booted condition. He also says that he will have some clothes brought to me from the ship and that my flight home will be arranged as soon as medical advice permits. Then I'm back out of the bed, noting in passing that I don't seem to have done the linen much damage, up a further three flights of stairs and into my new home.

It's a two-bed room, and the other occupant, a young Nigerian with severe facial injuries that require a substantial clamp around his jaws, mumbles as much of a welcome as his condition permits. I'm just glad to get out of my boiler suit and boots with the welcome assistance of a young nurse, and take a pair of substantial white pills that take me swiftly into oblivion.

The next day my back has taken on the nature of cast concrete and I can barely roll out of bed. I manage to stagger to the en suite bathroom for a minimal wash before I resume my prone position. Later, my companion is visited by his young wife and family. Through them, I learn that he is a driver for a manager of the big French trading house SCOA. His injuries result from a lorry smashing into his car, late at night the previous week, as he was driving home.

His wife generously offers to take my clothes home to wash but that kindly gesture proves unnecessary as I get a visit from the Old Man and the purser. They bring me a suitcase full of suitable clothes and other useful items. When the former assures me that he'll see to my undone work on board until a relief arrives, I tell him that he'd best leave the stores and overtime alone until then as he'll not be able to decipher my unfinished progress.

We cross swords on a daily basis so I'm not surprised when he remarks, 'You don't seem to have damaged your attitude muscles, maybe a good bang on the head might have been better.' It's good to get normality back, I reflect, as they depart and I settle into the novelty of being in hospital.

While my companion has his evening visits, I take the opportunity to slowly make my progress around the top floor and out to an open area where I can have a welcome smoke and watch the activity of the neighbourhood. Vehicles are using their horns in blatant disregard of large signs asking for quiet outside the building and a colourful throng of people weave in and out of the stalled traffic.

There's that unique and velvety mixture of woodsmoke, fermenting sewage and the occasional hint of jungle that characterises Lagos at night. Later I can hear some familiar strains of high-life music from a nearby 'nitespot'. Then it's back to the ward and the relief of its comfortable air-conditioning.

I wake just after midnight in a sweaty lather and am aware of my companion's urgent groans of complaint. The cooling unit must have failed and I limp outside to see what the problem is. The source of the fault is a typically Nigerian one. Someone has identified the exhaust heat as a drying opportunity and the ventilator is covered in towels and various ladies' garments. I angrily brush this lot to the ground and it's not long before our room temperature begins falling and our comfort is restored.

The next morning I ask the nurse to put a notice above the unit telling people that it's not a clothes drier. I know full well that this will have as much effect as my daily enquiring of the hospital orderly why my meal tray always has one item of its content missing when it reaches me. 'It has been stolen by these people,' is her stock response with never a clue as to who 'these' might be.

It's not worth making a fuss about since I now learn that the doctor (who I've never seen again after my initial examination) has left a message to say that, if I sign a release form, I can leave. I'm hardly agile but I'll get to Murtala Mohammed Airport if it cripples me. This I tell the agency manager who has come to collect me and offers me the hospitality of his house until I can depart.

First we need to regularise my position in Nigeria as I cannot leave until I receive an entry permit to legitimise my presence in the country. This document is never normally issued to visiting seamen. Happily, this matter is soon arranged and the agency representative is equally efficient as he roundly abuses one immigration official at the airport who questions my status in the country.

This man is busily searching my passport and discharge book looking for those customary detachable large-denomination naira notes that he expects to see. 'You are a very ignorant man,' the agency representative chides the hapless official, 'These documents belong to Captain Goble, who has already been gravely injured by the stupidity of idiots like yourself. Stop this nonsense immediately before I bring your incompetence to the attention of your superiors.'

With my departure cleared, it only remains to thank my guide appropriately but I have no local currency so I offer him some sterling, which he accepts happily as he's coming to the UK for some training in the near future. I never met him again, probably because such a man soon rose up through the ranks of the company bureaucracy ashore. At least I hope that he did, he deserved nothing less.

As soon as I board the aircraft, I swallow a double helping of pain-killers in order to guarantee a comfortable flight, during which I only surface twice. Once is to hear a round of applause when it's announced that purchases on board can only be made using sterling or US currency and that naira are not accepted.

The second occasion is to hear one of the cabin staff announce, with barely concealed amusement, that our landing at Prestwick is because Gatwick is fog-bound. She adds that we will soon be taking off again for our proper destination. Passengers, she nearly giggles, do not need to get into heavy clothing despite the outside air temperature being below freezing.

This causes a number of Nigerian passengers to be rather embarrassed at their scramble to find suitable garments in the overhead lockers. These two small episodes serve to illustrate just how community relations between these expatriates and their erstwhile neighbours have become strained due to the inconveniences and tensions of Nigeria's descent into a society in chaos.

My recovery from injury means that I fall out of my usual rotation of duty and I find myself flying to Amsterdam to join our second-hand German ship once again.

I know that taking a ship around northern European ports in the winter is an experience best avoided. However, I don't expect to endure the usual lengthy spells of standing by the anchors as we negotiate the Elbe and the Weser since on this ship we can let go the anchors from the bridge.

Both Chippy and I are annoyed that this Old Man, who is new to the ship, distrusts the technology and wants to stick to the old ways. We've tried to hide as best we can from a biting easterly wind all the way down the river to Cuxhaven. Now we're looking forward to being stood down once we pass the *Elbe 3* light vessel and the estuary opens up ahead. After all, we've still got the ascent of the Weser to look forward to.

When there's still no call from the bridge, Chippy expresses his frustration by grumbling, 'Bloody hell, is this old bastard going to keep us up here until fucking Bremen? It's not as if we're in the bloody creeks.' We've both forgotten, in our frozen misery, that the forecastle loudspeaker is still live so, once we clear the outermost *Elbe 1* light vessel, it duly springs into life. We hear the smooth voice of the second mate telling us, 'Compliments of the old bastard on the bridge and you may stand down for a cup of tea but make sure that you return in 20 minutes for standing by the anchors from the Alte Weser light.'

We're loading quite a lot of uncontainerised cargo from these ports so it gives me the opportunity to see just how many of Britain's traditional exports to West Africa have been replaced by the products of European countries.

Cases of machetes now come from the Ruhr instead of the Black Country, Mercedes and Peugeot replace Austin and Morris; MAN and DAF replace ERF and Foden. Generating sets and transformers are from Siemens rather than from English Electric, and so the list goes on.

One export that we've never produced in the UK for the West African market is evaporated milk since it appears to be exclusively sourced in the Netherlands. It's shipped in cardboard cartons each containing about a gross of the tiny tins that you see on every West African market stall. The cartons are much stronger than the ones that carry the sardines from Morocco. At this time of year, however, they're subject to a dramatic temperature change in a very short time.

Our usual practice is to load this cargo in an empty vegetable oil tank where the fitted steam coils can apply some gentle warmth. That inhibits condensation forming as, within a week or so, the ship travels from below freezing in Rotterdam to the heat of the tropics.

We have no such tanks on this ship so we can only secure the hatches well and hope that the air temperature of the interior will rise sufficiently as we head south. Otherwise it'll be that familiar spectacle. African dockworkers will be up to their ankles in drifts of tins that are not only rust-spotted but which have lost their paper labels as the humidity of the coast wreaks its inevitable damage.

Because the French are fiercely protective of their own trade with West Africa, we don't usually call at any of their ports. A contract to carry St Louis sugar to Nigeria must have escaped their attention since our final European call requires us to follow the twisting Seine up to Rouen.

The Old Man calls me on the forecastle to say, 'We're slowing up, mate, your old Niger-line pals are blocking the berth.' No further explanation is offered but, as we approach the port, I'm surprised to see my dear old *River Ethiope* coming towards us, smartly painted and nicely down to her marks. I give them a wave but it's unlikely that anyone will recognise me, although I hear a few jibes from my current shipmates as she sweeps past.

Once berthed, we learn of the reason for her tardy departure. It appears that a lorryload of carpets missed the ship in Antwerp. Therefore, when the pantechnicon arrived alongside in Rouen only a couple of hours before departure, all hands refused to consider leaving until their carpet investments were safely on board. Clearly, private trading has become a lot more serious since I left.

After the usual palaver of the coast, this particular voyage ends with a cargo of some novelty. We've arrived in Banjul, where we're to bring home the equipment of part of one of the Guards regiments that has been training in the country.

I'm looking at the shipping list that the agency has provided and trying to visualise what some of these military items might be when a fresh-faced young subaltern comes on board and asks to see the Old Man.

I take him up to the master's day room and, once he's seen the ship's register, an unusual request, I ask him about the cargo. 'Oh!' he dismissively responds, 'It's not my concern at all, I'm just here to ensure that you're a proper British ship. Some of our chaps will be down tomorrow with all the stuff and to tell you what to do.'

Not a problem, then, so it's a chance to go ashore to the Atlantic Hotel and see if it's still like the old days. It looks the same externally but it's all change inside and not the rather pleasantly tatty place where I disgraced myself on my 21st birthday nearly two decades ago. The drinks are definitely on the expensive side so it's just some of the junior officers who feel that it's worth staying late and entertaining some Swedish tourists in the hope of the usual dividend.

The Guards regiment 'chaps' turn out to be a burly regimental sergeant-major and three other NCOs. They've obviously put in many years of army service and are extremely helpful in seeing that their cargo is presented in intelligent order. There's enough space below decks for a jumble of ration packs, tents and other canvas structures and a set of large cases whose contents are, apparently, 'sensitive'.

The strangest items are the post-accident remains of two Land Rovers. They're both flattened and resemble bizarre outsize Peking ducks in their coatings of dried red jungle mud. Slinging these wrecks in order to load them requires some ingenuity on the part of the Gambian dockers. Once we have them on board, I ask the RSM why we're shipping this apparent junk.

'One's evidence for a fatal accident and the other's got to be shipped back because they've both been booked out of our depot and need booking back in when we return,' is his explanation. The precise accounting of the military, it seems, has to be observed and this explains some of the other weather-beaten stuff we've already loaded.

The hatches are covered over now and we're loading the rest of this motley collection on deck. I need to find enough space for several containers of unused ammunition and then a collection of vehicles comprising lorries, a mobile crane, a tar tanker and a road-roller. Those few unwarlike items have been used for some road- and bridge-building activity that was undertaken alongside their military manoeuvres.

Space on deck is getting tight and the last six trucks will be a close fit for the top of number four hatch. I'm now a little concerned, but the sergeant drivers say that they'll guarantee that the vehicles will fit into the allocated space.

They were earlier invited into our bar, where they enjoyed some substantial access to our draught lager. However, as the RSM assures me, 'Don't worry, sir, Army regulations demand frequent rehydration while in the tropics and these lads always know what they're doing.'

I'm happy to see that his confidence is well placed as the drivers park their vehicles just as I want. With that done, and while the sailors are lashing them in position, it appears that the soldiers are happy to enjoy another round of lagers 'for the road'. Then it's time to leave Banjul after what has been an individual experience even for this coast of surprises.

My next voyage provides much more novelty. I'm back on one of those ships whose Palm Line days are numbered. We're chartered for a single voyage to the Indian sub-continent for the account of the Anchor Line of Glasgow. We're bound from Birkenhead for Aden, Colombo, Karachi and Bombay via Marseille and the Suez Canal. It's an opportunity to revisit places not seen since my tanker days and also to see some new sights.

It's an old-fashioned cargo that we load and only includes a few containers. Even those are so decrepit that they're described as non-returnable from Aden. We have to spend a long week in that dry furnace before heading out into the welcome breezes of the Indian Ocean. I've found that Aden and Suez have changed so much.

Our Canal transit is marked by the absence of those habitués that I recall from past visits. Where is the 'gully-gully' man with his artful sleight-of-hand show? And where are the floating shopkeepers? I miss traders such as 'Jock McGregor from Aberdeen'. I cannot explore the delights of his scruffy stock of pungent leather goods, kitsch brassware and, above all, those marvellous 'dirty postcards' and books.

The postcards all appear to emanate from a Parisian brothel circa 1890 and the books seem to be printed using one of those 'John Bull' kits remembered from my childhood. As for the tiny phials of rose-coloured liquid claiming to be 'Spanish Fly', well, a naïve adolescent in search of an aphrodisiac and his money are soon parted, as many of us know. This time, all gone to memory, as well as the chance for a quick swim in the Bitter Lakes.

The Red Sea is as hot and barren of interest, apart from passing ships, as I recall and Aden has lost all of its former bustle. The harbour is quite empty of calling passenger ships and the whole port is slipping quietly into a sad obsolescence.

Colombo is as enjoyable as I remember. This is despite being one of the few nominated to keep ship while the majority of the ship's company, European and African, enjoy a coach trip to Kandy. Karachi holds little of interest but my treat in Bombay is to enjoy a splendid meal at the Taj Mahal hotel followed by a concert performance, the whole evening being a courtesy of our agent.

The work in these ports is on West African lines with the usual problems associated with our ancient cargo-handling equipment. The noticeable and welcome difference is a lot more competence and professionalism in the local authorities and their workforces. It's a potent reminder of just how far West Africa is now falling behind these other former British colonial possessions in its development.

Our cargo discharged, we head westwards in the direction of Suez again, looking for news of a new charter but expecting the worst. The inevitable news arrives: after Suez it's on to Piraeus, where the ship will go on sale.

A useful legacy of our charter employment is a couple of hundred plywood sheets, used as cargo protection, and which we were told could be dumped at sea. The bosun and I soon decide that, once attractively sorted and presented, they can be flogged to one of the many bum-boat men who will seek us out on arrival in Suez Bay. The proceeds will be split equally between the officers and crew bars for a suitably generous end-of-voyage party before we fly home from Greece.

This charitable plan is frustrated when, shortly after anchoring off Port Tewfik, we're boarded by a small party of men who claim to be the representatives of the new owners. Their noisy presence deters, and finally drives away, all of our potential Egyptian customers. It isn't until we reach Port Said, at the northern end of the Canal, that our engineer superintendent is able to board and he confirms the sale.

The next day we set up an impromptu incinerator on the after deck in order to burn all of the company's property such as old logbooks and stationery that is not part of the deal. We also have to safely destroy the confidential Admiralty papers that are carried on British ships for use in the event of a declaration of war.

It then takes nearly a week before we can leave the ship in a stormy Piraeus roadstead, transfer to a hotel in Athens and then be driven suicidally to the airport. There we are reunited with those goods that the Greek customs officers had taken into custody when we landed from the ship. Most of us can then leave to get on our flights but that means we have to abandon our West African crew. They are still noisily embroiled with the customs over the contents of their voluminous 'loads' while a hapless agency clerk tries to mediate.

This sale means that the fleet that I had joined only five years ago is now reduced to half its size. In addition, the whole future of the West African trade is gloomy. Why, I can only wonder as I hear the announcement, is Palm Line building two more ships?

16

Behind the Iron Curtain for more new ships

I soon find out a lot more about these new ships since one of them is my next destination. I travel with three others to the airport in Hamburg, where we're met by our shore bosun, who lives in the city. He leads us out to a large white Citroën estate car that will take the five of us to the Polish port of Szczecin by way of East Germany.

Today, I'm recalling another visit I made to Hamburg many years previously and a bus tour to Lübeck and Travemunde, organised by the padre of the port's Missions to Seamen. That day's sights included a glimpse of the Iron Curtain that has dramatically divided Europe throughout most of my life.

Now I'm about to cross that historic political dividing line for the first time. It's therefore a small disappointment that the border guards at Selmsdorf give us only the most cursory examination as we enter the DDR and head off down the prescribed route to our next international crossing.

We almost reach the Polish frontier when the near-deserted autobahn, half a century old but as modern as many new British motorways, suddenly ends with an earth embankment and the need for a sharp diversion. This leads us to the exit point from East Germany and the inconvenient reality of a Cold War border crossing.

The car, which we've christened 'The Hearse', is painstakingly searched with all the carpets lifted and the door panels removed (it's left to us to replace them all later). Then our baggage is rummaged through and we have to lay out all our foreign currency on an examination table. The Falklands campaign is only recently over and the guards ask us if the lady on the sterling banknotes is the famous 'Frau Thatcher'. They seem disappointed to learn that the portrait remains that of the same monarch as it's always been. The rest of the party know the routine here so we allow the confiscation of the tabloid newspapers and some magazines featuring a number of bare-chested girls. That allows our other reading material to pass undisturbed.

Then it's a very short drive to the Polish frontier post, where the same thorough process is repeated. This is despite the two sets of officials being in clear view of one another and any illicit crossing here surely falling into the 'frying pan into the fire' category. Do they, I wonder, as we drive off at last, share the modest haul of light pornography that we sacrificed?

Once in Poland, we're only a few miles from our hotel, too late for a meal but still able to unwind in the bar. Our hotel bill (drinks excluded) will be settled by Amex cards on a company account that we've been given. The daily tariff (excluding lunch) is around the £30 mark, which is about ten times what a Comecon citizen will pay but use of the local currency is virtually forbidden to us.

We will bypass the hotel bar by setting up our own arrangements so one of our first objectives is to drive back to the frontier, where there is a Baltona duty-free store that accepts only hard currency. That allows us to stock up on alcohol and tobacco. We will use the generous buffet at breakfast to compose adequate packed lunches and so we're soon organised in our new berth.

This Polish contract has missed the attention of the shipping press, unlike Palm Line's recent foreign purchase. This is partly because the British shipbuilding industry has declined to a point where it has lost its capacity for such an order.

We find our ship in the former Stettiner Vulkan yard, the birthplace of many famous German transatlantic liners earlier in the century. Her sister vessel is clearly recognisable at another fitting-out berth. These two vessels are to a design that is a larger and improved version of our earlier purchase from the Germans.

The Harald Schuldt shipping company of Hamburg is the original buyer of these two ships. They are selling them to us along with the service of superintending their construction, a facility which is principally of value to our chief and second engineers and our electrician.

My task over here is to become familiar with the cargo-working gear and the hatch covers and to plan their maintenance in service. I'm therefore hoping to see that the quality of workmanship and materials will be a lot better than I found on their smaller predecessor. The need for this reassurance is strangely echoed by a passage in a book that I've just finished reading.

There, the eminent naval historian Professor Michael Lewis explained that the shortage of timber suitable for the great rebuilding of the Royal Navy in the 1760s was partially overcome by imports of 'Stettin oak'. It proved to be a poor decision, however, as the Baltic timber had only a quarter of the life of the English oak, whose necessary replanting had been so shamefully ignored.

At the shipyard, I'm a latecomer as the others have already made a lengthy initial visit. I am, however, fully briefed on the dress code. The white cotton boiler suits provided by Palm Line have proved to be a diplomatic gaffe since, in this tightly rationed economy, such apparel appears to boast easy access to detergents, which are generally unavailable to the general population.

This means that I'm in a suitably drab dark-blue garment teamed with well-worn boots. Then, apart from a total inability to speak Polish, I hope that I can blend into the activity of the shipyard. Our German superintending team can speak good English and they smooth out any translation issues but I soon find that they have an unfortunately patronising attitude to the Polish workforce.

This is typified by the sneering remark, 'Look, handmade!' when they pick up some artefact that in a British or German yard would be bought in, not laboriously manufactured on site. When I criticise this attitude, one of the Germans proves to have a good command of British geography when he identifies my accent and asks, 'Well, how would you like it if we had won the war and now owned Cammell Laird?' I hope that he grasps the essence of my reply when I say that, as a proper scouser, ownership of anything 'across the water' in Birkenhead is of little or no consequence to me.

The Germans, whilst always helpful to our little team, consider that we live in un-necessary luxury compared to them. They are renting a house in the city and so are more exposed to the reality of the Polish economy. Our hotel, the Reda, which is operated by the state tourist bureau, Orbis, is French-built but is far from luxurious. We are undoubtedly victualled much better than any Pole but the eccentricities of a command economy are obvious in the menus.

We enjoy an excellent dinner of steak and chips on our second evening but the appeal of the dish has rather diminished when it is repeated for the next seven nights, only to be replaced with an equally acceptable salmon dish for another week. What is a small drawback to our stay is the weekend invasion from Sweden of parties of men looking to escape from their home country's restrictive access to alcohol.

The Friday overnight ferry from Ystad to Swinoujscie must be block-booked by these revellers, whose arrival early the next day disturbs our lie-in earned by the shipyard's closure. They've all gone noisily to their beds when we come down to a leisurely breakfast but the revels resume early in the afternoon and, as dusk falls, the city's prostitutes begin to arrive at the hotel.

We're well insulated from the raucous festivity in the bar since we're upstairs enjoy-ing our customary soirée but, in the small hours, I'm woken up by a fearsome creaking as if the hotel is in a seaway. It seems that, with the beds being secured to the room walls, the unmistakable vibrations of sexual climax are transmitted across the whole floor of the hotel. It's difficult to get back to sleep, or am I just a little envious of their enjoyable activity?

Before a return to sleep can be attempted, I take out my resentment on a few Polish mosquitoes who are whining around the room. They've been more interested than their West African cousins in biting me, so I vengefully slap a few of their blood-filled bodies against the wall. That'll also put next door's satyr and his partner off their strokes for a while, I console myself.

Not all the Swedes made it to bed last night. That much is apparent as we come down to Sunday's breakfast and have to step over a few recumbent figures as we make our way into the dining room. Even those who did reach their rooms seem to have had plenty of eating as well as sex on their agenda.

I hear the squabbling of seagulls as I open my window and there on the grass are a number of remainders of a local delicacy that consists of stew contained within a hollowed cottage loaf. The meat and vegetable content is enjoyed and the empty loaf is cast out for the birds. Peace returns on the Monday morning. We clamber into 'The Hearse' to make our way into town and to the shipyard, frequently delayed by having to patiently wait while the trams, running down the middle of the street, embark and disembark their passengers.

The Stocznia Szczecinska im Adolf Warski, to give our workplace its full name, didn't replicate the recent events in Gdansk which had brought the names of Solidarnosc and of Lech Walesa to international recognition. I suspect that this was because the city was emptied of its German population at the end of the war and then settled by 'reliable' citizens from elsewhere in Poland. Nevertheless, this relative docility does not spare Szczecin from being strictly patrolled, in groups of three, by members of the Milicja. Their potential threat is apparent in the way that everybody keeps well away from them as they saunter confidently along the pavements.

The atmosphere is more relaxed in the yard and, despite the language barrier, the ordinary workers are both amused by and interested in their foreign visitors. One young foreman, with whom I'd been working closely as I checked the maintenance points on the hatch covers, asks me if I can buy some cosmetics for his girlfriend when I next visit the duty-free store. He offers me two rather battered ten-dollar bills without explaining their origin and, since they look genuine, I agree to his request.

There is a foreign-exchange desk at the hotel but that only offers the official rate, which is about 150 zloty to the pound. I'm told that using the services of men who hang around the hotel or up at the Baltona store might get me three or even four times that rate but it's a high risk as many of these traders are police informants.

Even the official rate means that any goods that are available are extremely cheap but that is of very limited benefit. Prices charged in the food markets are close to those at home and the alternatives are the nearly empty shelves of the shops and supermarkets.

Every adult, male or female, carries a string bag with them just in case they come across a stock arrival in some shop, indicated by a queue forming outside. A sudden arrival of toilet rolls one day, for example, means that I see lucky shoppers wearing lei-like strings of these prizes around their necks as they hurry past.

Up at the Baltona, I find the necessary lipstick and perfume and take them to the counter before getting on with my own shopping. The counter clerk seems to be about to interrogate me about this purchase but I dab a spot of perfume from a sampler on the counter onto the back of my hand and ask him if he thinks that it suits me? Completely amazed, perhaps even horrified, by this gesture, he mutters some words in agreement and hurriedly completes the transaction.

When I deliver the contraband to my customer, he asks if he might get some more hard currency from me to fund further purchases and offers 3,000 zloty for ten dollars. It's less than the hotel spivs are offering but attractive enough. It's only later that I begin to realise that even this modest amount will be a problem to spend before we leave Poland.

The money is an encouragement to get out and about at the weekends and also to use these long, light summer evenings. It doesn't seem to bother the others, but I'm getting a little 'stir-crazy'. I also find that I want to return early to our hotel where I can transcribe, in peace and quiet, the notes for the maintenance plans that I'm making. I need to tackle the bus and tram system and I must buy a map.

One idea that I've already had is to write a postcard home every day because there is no other reliable means of communicating. An external telephone call cannot be made and letters are subject to long censorship delays. Postcards, however, are relatively immune. General Jaruzelski's 'little helpers' (as Anne was later to call them) neatly slit the four card corners to look for microdots and then send them on their way. A daily card home will build into a reasonable narrative for her.

The small kiosk outside the shipyard where I buy the cards and stamps also sells maps of the city and bus or tram tickets. I'm now in business!

A ticket costs 15 zloty and is good for ten journeys. It's validated on board in the usual European fashion and one or two of my fellow passengers show me how to tweak an additional two trips by careful manipulation of the validator. Out of courtesy, I follow them once or twice but it does seem rather ungrateful to perpetrate such a fraud when I can cross the city for less than a penny.

Szczecin, although its extensive wartime damage is largely replaced by some of the same dreadful immediate post-war architecture that has also been visited on British cities, proves to be a place worth exploring.

There's an impressive castle built when the city was a Swedish possession. Some typical Hanseatic buildings are the oldest survivors of the city's variegated past ownership. Now they stand alongside those newer ones that epitomise the swagger of Wilhelmine Germany when Stettin was the sea gateway to imperial Berlin.

A modest maritime museum in one of the latter edifices features a suitable West African connection with artefacts from a pre-war Polish expedition to the coast. Could it be that this expedition, I wonder in hindsight, fired the imagination of Ryszard Kapuscinski and led to his acclaimed reportage of the continent?

Armed with my map and bus ticket I can go into the immediate countryside. It isn't a very inspiring area, being just pine forests or sandy heath, but it's a peaceful alternative to the shipyard noise. It's also almost deserted, possibly because the DDR frontier is not far away. However, it lacks a sense of danger, despite warnings from the rest of the team when they discover what I'm up to.

When I tell them that I found a group of men and women practising some nude callisthenics one hot and sunny Sunday afternoon, they become a little more interested. They press me for details, but I can't remember more than a blurred glimpse of the flopping protuberances of both sexes. I do know that I waved a friendly greeting and then hastily lit up a cigarette so as to give the gymnasts the impression of an insouciant encounter.

The ship is now nearing completion and the need to sign off our hatch covers for watertightness provides the excuse for a short escape to the pleasures of West Berlin.

The Lloyd's surveyor and our own engineer superintendent have to be met at Templehof airport. There have been some previous exits made by our party but now it's my turn to get out and to telephone home. The price of that privilege is to endure once more the pantomime of the Polish–DDR crossing up the road.

Then it's the pleasure of being a front-seat passenger in 'The Hearse' hurtling down a deserted autobahn with Tommy the bosun at the wheel telling me to look out for signs of fresh venison heading for the windscreen. That's followed by a cursory search by the officials at Drewitz before we reach the bright lights and bustle of West Berlin. The day ends with a warm welcome from the rest of the team since our two passengers have brought with them both a hefty bundle of mail and the day's English newspapers.

This Berlin excursion somehow seems to revive a sense of isolation that I had managed to bury since my arrival and now I want to leave Szczecin. Therefore I'm pleased that our hatches pass their examination despite their unprecedented size. They're the largest yet fitted to a British ship; the two covering the main hatch each have to span an opening over 100 feet in length and 25 feet in width.

This success makes the handover date imminent; therefore more officers are brought over to Szczecin in order that we can start to move on board. They're followed soon afterwards by the rest of the ship's company and the equally welcome arrival of the ship's stores.

We leave the Hotel Reda and enjoy our first full British breakfast in the saloon followed by our first boat- and fire-drill before we all sign the agreement that signals the start of the maiden voyage.

The actual handover is on a sunny Saturday morning when the red-and-white Polish flag at the stern is lowered and the Red Ensign takes its place. It's a ceremony that is accompanied by a reasonably tuneful rendition of the two national anthems by the yard's uniformed brass band. The serving of Russian champagne and a small buffet, accompanied by much photographing and hand-shaking, completes the day.

On Sunday, I take my two new mates through some familiarising instead of roaming freely ashore. On Monday the whole ship is isolated from the quay with the gangway raised and everybody confined to their cabins while a large detachment of armed soldiers searches the vessel. The bosun and I, each carrying a substantial bunch of keys, take the search parties through the maze of underdeck spaces on a tour lasting several hours before the ship is certified clear of any stowaways and is free to depart.

Our maiden passage across the lagoon that lies between Szczecin and the short canal into the Baltic is unfortunately marked by a brief engine breakdown. This happily proves to be no bad omen as we roar up the Great Belt at 18 knots, round the Skaw at the tip of Denmark and dock in Hull after a smooth passage.

I'm going no further as I hand over to my relief and head home, where I have a hospital appointment. My gall-bladder has to be removed, not necessarily because of my love of palm-oil chop. It's for a lifetime of dietary lapses for which the surgeon gives me the usual chastisement and, after surgery, tells me that he took out my appendix while he was in there. I'm very grateful for that extra intervention as the only medical emergencies that I've seen at sea were both resulting from a burst appendix. I've often heard colleagues say that they'd happily volunteer for the removal of this seemingly surplus organ for peace of mind on long ocean passages.

My convalescence of about six weeks, followed by a couple of weeks' holiday in France, sets me up for a medical examination at Port Sunlight where the Unilever doctor confirms that I'll probably still be able to enjoy palm-oil dishes again.

Two days later, it's the train to London, a brief call by our head office and then out to Heathrow for a flight to Copenhagen. Our agent there entertains me at an excellent fish restaurant and delivers me to the overnight ferry for Swinoujscie.

A midweek passage in late-November means that my fellow passengers are mainly Polish traders who are economising by not taking cabins or eating on board. This means that, when I go to look for for an early breakfast, I find that the alleyways leading to the restaurant are filled with tyres, car batteries, motorbikes and sundry anonymous packages. This cargo is accompanied by its recumbent owners.

On arrival, I'm met by our agency driver and whisked off without delay to a car that is soon bowling down the deserted road to Szczecin. To my dismay, I soon see 'The Hearse' speeding in the opposite direction but there's no means of contacting Tommy, who's come to collect me. I offer up a large package of mail and newspapers as a gesture of apology an hour or so later when he returns to our usual hotel.

It's a cold, sunny day when I resume my duties at the yard and this pleasant weather lasts for several following days. This, nevertheless, cannot disguise the fact that the mood of the country is much darker since my last visit. The city markets that were previously full of summer produce are almost bare of anything for sale and the string baskets carried by all are rarely filled. I don't look for any black-market zlotys this time as I now know that changing a small amount of sterling, even at the official rate, will meet all my needs during this unpromising stay.

One day, after a brief early snowfall, the buses and trams are filled with shoppers taking home wooden toboggans after an unexpectedly useful delivery. On another occasion I'm prevented from getting off my bus because the gangway and exits are blocked by passengers carrying home their share of an arrival of wooden doors. I have to remain in my seat, powerless through lack of language to explain my plight, until it's clear enough to disembark in the middle of some glum housing estate. Then it's a long wait for another bus going back to my destination.

I can now manage conversations (mainly in simple English allied to fractured French) with various shipyard workers and tram or bus acquaintances. There is much speculation that the imminent death of that old Soviet waxwork, Leonid Brezhnev, might allow the Solidarity movement to flourish again. Apart from that, the mood is one of resignation that things won't actually change and, like the coming winter, will have to continue to be endured.

The days turn milder but that means fog and a lack of sunlight, and removes any pleasure from my weekend walks. Fortunately, I find an acceptable alternative escape route when I discover the concert pleasures of the Filharmonia Szczecinska. This is through the medium of some tourist information at the hotel which is written in French.

One of the girls in reception is highly amused when I ask her to write out what I need to say in Polish in order to book a seat. Her counterpart at the concert hall is equally entertained when I try to pronounce my request instead of simply handing over the paper.

For the equivalent of a pound, I enjoy the concert from the best seats in the front stalls, a programme and a surprisingly good cup of coffee in the interval. Had I used the black market I could have joined the nomenklatura by buying a box for the same price. However, I feel that would have been coarse ostentation indeed.

I don't feel quite as isolated here as before. That's partly because I now have the measure of the city and also, on the advice of the others, I've bought a 'military visa' which allows relatively unrestricted border crossings. This enables me to make two or three visits to West Berlin and therefore to enjoy a telephone call home.

My duties on board are a reprise of the summer so I don't have to clamber around this freezing ship quite so much. The hotel still offers its menu eccentricities but the Swedish weekend trade has folded for the winter. The only groups that we now encounter are sober party functionaries attending conferences, who don't go in for littering the lawn or making the bedheads vibrate.

It's becoming a little dull here, I reflect, and so it's all the more welcome when the time comes to go on board with the rest of the ship's company. The same flag ceremony, tuneful brass band rendition of our two national anthems and Russian champagne precede the traditional search of the ship by troops before we retrace our delivery route to Hull.

On our arrival there we learn that there's no immediate need for the ship, so I'm free to enjoy the unexpected bonus of Christmas and New Year at home. When I do return to the ship, there's an arrival in my office and I find that the new world of the computer has reached my job.

The machine is a small desk-top device with a keyboard and a strange green screen and it'll tell me all I need to know about the ship's trim and stability. That's to do with ensuring that the loading or unloading of the ship never leaves it in an illegal or dangerous condition. I'm partially resentful that my specialist knowledge has now been distilled into a machine that anybody could learn to use. I'm also very grateful that I'm now spared the need to cover fathoms of paper with speculative calculations.

That need is because there is news of our potential chartering by the German Woermann Linie, who trade to West Africa. They want to know how much cargo, if any, we need to have on board in order to leave Matadi and get under the new bridge there.

The existence of this obstacle is news to me. A Japanese company has built a bridge over the Zaire where the telephone line used to cross the river just above the Chaudron d'Enfer. This means that the air draught (the height of the very highest point on the ship above the waterline) must not exceed 39.5 metres if we are to pass safely underneath.

Needless to say, no instruction manual comes with this gadget shipped from its Swedish manufacturer so it's a case of switching on and seeing what happens. It's relatively easy to understand as a concept; there are lists of all the spaces on the ship where weight can be added or removed and, according to those weights, the computer will indicate the consequent draught, trim and stability.

The trouble is that it takes me some time to find out how information can be entered and then altered if necessary. I also struggle to learn how to preserve the results while going through a set of loading options.

Trial and error soon show me that whilst intermediate results can be printed out on a roll of metallic paper, these figures cannot be stored for later reference. This causes a good deal of backing and fro-ing and general operator annoyance before an acceptable result emerges. It appears that, by using ballast water and estimating where the fuel might be carried, the ship can be empty of cargo but still not risk losing the top of our radio aerials to the underside of the bridge.

I tell the Old Man that it looks good for our charter prospects but he's seen my earlier experimentation and has little faith in my manipulation of a winking computer screen and a roll of aluminised toilet-paper. I'm told to check my forecast in the traditional manner.

A combination of using a book of stability information written in German and awaiting English transcription, as required by the British ship regulatory authorities, allied to my rusty recollection of serious stability calculations, means that I use a lot of paper before coming up with an answer. It is comfortingly close to what my computer competitor has predicted. That result, however, was found a lot more quickly. I start to see the spectre of my obsolescence in this new digital world. For now, I can take comfort in the fact that no computer yet built will be able to deal with the reality that is the West Coast of Africa in its current descent into waterside anarchy.

The charter is arranged, it's only for one round voyage from Continental ports, but we're still to be renamed and will bear the funnel colours of the Woermann Linie to West Africa.

As we sail up the Elbe to Hamburg we must be pretty convincing in our new colours since the famous loudspeaker at the Willkommhöft in Wedel greets us with the German national anthem as we sail past.

We're also proud to be presenting ourselves around these north European ports in a ship that can look those of our competitors in the eye after our overlong allegiance to wood, tarpaulin and museum derricks.

Our loading proceeds without incident; most of the cargo is in containers and I'm especially pleased to see our derricks slewing, lifting and lowering with admirable precision thanks to their immaculately running wires. I'm equally happy that my time spent in Poland marking all the container lashings with an easily recognisable code of coloured paints allows for the quick and effective securing of the cargo.

A storm in the Channel forces us to shelter for a day in the Downs because pilotage for the tortuous route through the sandbanks to Dunkerque is suspended. Then we're eventually sailing south out of the wintry gloom of Europe and towards the welcoming sunshine of West Africa.

We follow an unfamiliar itinerary as we make a quick call at Dakar for fuel only and press on towards the equatorial ports of Libreville and Port Gentil. The continuing oil wealth of Gabon is evident in the small fleet of Mercedes limousines that we unload at the former port, whilst the parallel exploitation of the interior will be met by lorries from the same manufacturer discharged at the latter.

Again, I'm proud to see us despatching vehicles and containers with the same ease that I'd earlier watched from afar being the practice of the French ships. A call at Pointe Noire is partly to unload a number of heavy lifts for the previously unknown destination of Soyo in the estuary of the Zaire river but we're instructed to keep them on board as they will now be discharged at sea to other craft.

Soyo, which turns out to be an oil exploration base on the Angolan side of the estuary, isn't responding to either radio or VHF calls so we're advised from Hamburg to proceed to Matadi.

We arrive there after seeing that we had a comforting distance from the underside of the girders of the impressive new bridge. There's nothing new or impressive about Matadi, however, and I'm glad that I took the usual precaution of locking away all our portable items normally left out on deck.

Even so, we have some bruising encounters with the port's bandit fraternity, involving the stone-throwers of Britain forming an alliance with the archers of Zaire as we repel boarders. The main change now is that some of these exchanges are taking place in broad daylight.

Reaching the sea again, we find that Soyo has woken up and is answering calls. That allows us to make a rendezvous with a pair of large oil-rig supply vessels. Our sailors are able to skilfully land a small collection of strange pieces of equipment and a few containers onto their broad open afterdecks. They do this by completely ignoring the shouted advice from a vociferous American skipper and using their own expertise instead.

Then it's off back up the coast to Port Gentil and Libreville to start loading logs for the Continent. That soon takes the gilt off the gingerbread of my shiny new ship and its well-lit and freshly aluminium-painted underdeck spaces. We don't need the traditional apparatus of the bullrope to get logs into the holds but it's still a tricky business to get these 20-foot, ten ton monsters of the jungle into organised piles. A soundtrack of echoing bangs and vibrating bumps is inevitable.

A good tight stow is taking shape but the price is paid in muddy skidmarks across the paintwork and curtains of stinking bark festooned from any projections. Most serious is the damage to the container-securing arms, many of which now are hanging drunkenly distorted despite being carefully folded back out of harm's way.

'Should have taken them down, mate,' is the Old Man's helpful advice as we both survey the damage. That would have entailed having the sailors working out of a cage (the fittings being about 16 feet above the hold bottom) and trying to lift something weighing 40 or 50 kilos out of a tight shoe fitting.

And who would have been growling about the delay to loading while all that was going on? I just hope that we'll be able to swing the damage onto the Germans when we have the off-hire survey.

About 20 logs remain in the water once we've finished down below and so they must be carried on the deck. Unfortunately, we're not carrying any securing chains for this. I have to use an emergency plan, which is to construct two 'walls' using empty containers on top of the hatch. I can then plonk the logs in between these barriers and they'll just form a single tier. A consignment of bundles of sawn timber placed on top of them will act as an additional restraint against any movement in a seaway.

It's not the most seamanlike of stows but it suits our purpose, as even the Old Man grudgingly agrees. Then it's off to Douala, Abidjan and a new port to me, San Pedro, located near to the border between Côte d'Ivoire and Liberia. In those ports we complete our loading with more sawn timber, plywood and veneers and two large consignments of coffee and cocoa.

In this fine new ship there's not the need for any finesse in the stowing of bag cargoes, as our mighty cargo fans will force cooler air through the produce as we head north to our Hamburg destination. It's been a successful maiden voyage. I fly home satisfied to Manchester although I find out on arrival that my baggage has chosen to take a flight via Heathrow to Liverpool. That means it's the next day before I'm reunited with most of my possessions.

My next voyage is in the other Polish-built ship and we sail from Liverpool on Friday 13th, which doesn't lead to any immediate misfortunes but, a week later, we're in Freetown and I'm brought back to the deteriorating reality of West Africa. Our brief stay in port is one continuous battle with thieves desperate to garner something from this apparent treasure ship.

My time on deck is split between trying to anticipate their next assault and attempting to prevent the stevedores wrecking the cargo-handling gear. We're fully loaded with containers on deck and the winch driver cannot see what the rest of the gang is doing. Their job is to manage the container lifting frame, which is called a spreader, so that it sits squarely on all of the load's four corners and can then be locked in place, ready for lifting.

I've reluctantly allowed them to use the portable harness controls in place of the static control pedestals. The problem is that some drivers are using the dinky little eight-position joysticks like today's youngsters use their games consoles, juggling them in every direction and with no interval between top and full speed. They cannot see the winches and are thus completely ignorant of the effect that this type of driving is having on the wires coming onto or off the winch drums.

I can see the results, however, in the great loops of wire rope that have become trapped by this sloppy driving and are now mercilessly flailing the winch and its guard-rails. In the worst case, one of the buggers who was driving has found the system's over-ride button and the result is that one derrick has become completely inoperable and is lying drunkenly against the mast.

I call the bosun and a couple of sailors and we try to recover the situation by using another derrick to drag the victim out of its paralysis. Halfway through this long and messy process, I look down between the containers and see that a couple of idle gang members are forcing open a container door.

This grants me the extreme satisfaction of chucking a handy 5 lb weight of container twistlock at the thieves. It's a tricky shot for someone as inept at games as me; however, I'm more than pleased to hear a scream of extreme pain come up from 20 feet below as a result. I don't see the wounded victim or receive any outraged challenge to my fit of temper. There is, gratifyingly, a visible fall in this type of larcenous activity in the hours leading up to our departure.

As we're a new ship, we don't embark any Krooboys. It's just as well, these ships lack any accommodation for them but this also means I'm grateful to have a reliable crew. Most of them are familiar faces and some of them are 'company's men' which is a new development.

They're paid a salary that now contains an element of 'consolidated overtime'. This means in effect that they can be required to do work considered as essential without extra pay at times that would normally qualify for overtime. This is a welcome improvement on the previous system, which all too often led to 'make-work' tasks in order to reward good seamen with a worthwhile wage.

It's when we arrive in Apapa that I become aware of developments that don't bode well for the future. We've previously had to spend a couple of days steaming slowly and well offshore to keep out of range of the armada of pirate canoes that infests the normal anchorage for ships awaiting a berth.

Our VHF, throughout the night hours, is breaking into regular life with the distress calls of those ships that have decided to anchor. Their pleas for help are being stonily ignored by the harbour signal station.

When we're eventually called in to embark our pilot, the Nigerian who comes to the bridge happens to mention that he's just come off a small ship that is chartered to our parent company, UAC. This vessel has brought in cargo that is being unloaded at an unofficial wharf in Badagry Creek in order to avoid the congested main quays. If that is the future, then how long will UAC put up with Palm Line having to play under the ineffective official rules?

Then, on an evening ashore at the Apapa Club, our small party falls in with a trio of ex-London dockers. They're working for a German shipping company bringing in a new kind of ship that neatly and legally sidesteps the chaos of the port.

This vessel is called a barge-carrier and it arrives each month with a cargo of containers and some loose goods that are contained in a number of special barges. These barges can be floated out of the ship and taken to a variety of destinations around the metropolis to be unloaded. Before the ship sails, it floats in an exchange load of barges from its previous call.

This means that its day-and-half turnround accounts for twice the weight of cargo that we will handle in over a week's unloading. It's an interesting concept and a couple of us gladly take up an invitation to see the next operation later in the week.

Before that promise of a look at the possible future, it's time to tackle the problems of the present, the principal one being that it is no longer possible to unload the ship in any kind of an effective manner.

The bureaucratic effects of import restrictions and the NPA's new security measures against the rise in waterside lawlessness have destroyed any semblance of a smooth supply chain between the ship's holds and the receivers of the cargo.

If a commodity is one that can be stacked in the open, for example, drums of chemicals or bundles of steel rods, then a sort of normality prevails. Should those drums contain lubricating oils, or if the steel is in an easily portable format, then the destination must be the dock shed along with everything else deemed pilferable.

Receivers that can't or won't take delivery of their goods mean that space and order within the sheds is eventually destroyed. The only response is to announce a closure while 'compression' takes place. Not that any kind of official announcement is made; we're just left to infer that from the fact that the shed doors are resolutely locked throughout the day.

Unable to unload the greater part of our cargo directly, we employ the gangs to sort and shift cargo in order to uncover the kind of stuff that can be sent to outside storage. I'm fortunate that I've only agreed to book two night gangs but even that small workforce runs out of work soon after midnight. That leads me to cancel night working for the present. It's a decision that proves wise as the next day the sheds are still 'compressing' and therefore remain closed off to us.

Even when access is restored, our progress is so slow that I feel no guilt in leaving the deck to my two juniors and the impatient oversight of the Old Man. This is while I nip off in a Jeep provided by my new friends and go along to see their barge-floating operation.

We transfer to a launch at the end of Apapa Quay and head off up the adjacent creek to see the great grey bulk of the barge-carrier, open to the sea at both ends. I'm just in time to see the last few barges depart.

It impresses me as a smooth operation conducted by the German crew with the assistance of a trio of small tugs manned by Nigerians. I then see the start of the unloading of a cargo of containers from the ship's upper deck to a queue of pontoons that have been towed alongside.

Finally, I'm invited to enjoy a refreshing glass or two of German lager in the mate's spacious cabin on board. I have no difficulty in agreeing that this might well be the future, especially when I have to admit that his ship has probably unloaded more during my short visit than we've achieved during the previous two days. At the same time, I know that Palm Line will never have the funds necessary for this kind of ship and my suspicions are growing that our parent company of UAC also lacks the will to invest in the future of this visibly disintegrating coast.

17

The end of an era, the end of a historic trade

I can put my concerns to rest, it seems, when I rejoin our newest ship and find that she has regained her Palm Line name, lost her German charterer's funnel colours and is booked for a record cargo to West Africa. Later, I'll find it significant that we have to load this cargo by making visits to both Liverpool and Tilbury.

Now we're ready to leave the latter port. Our holds are full and there are three complete tiers of containers on deck. That edifice is then capped by a collection of Land Rovers and a selection of second-hand commercial vehicles which includes a brace of ice-cream vans. It all makes for a very satisfying sight on this grey day.

The shipboard computer tells me that we're at our maximum permitted draught and have adequate stability so, just four days before Christmas, we're ready to sail. The dock pilot says that he's not seen such an impressive load on deck. Thus we're all taken a little aback when, with two PLA tugs and our powerful bow thruster straining at their limits, we move sideways off the quay and then perform a series of lazy but alarmingly large rolls.

Have I put too much faith in that little green screen in my office? Perhaps we were merely sitting in the mud alongside, hence the strain to leave and then the ship's floppy reaction. Does this mean that we might be officially overloaded?

There is no further evidence of any 'tenderness', the sign of too much weight too high in the ship, as we proceed towards the river lock. Once inside, I see that the forward draught is unchanged from its legal maximum. The post-mortem that the Old Man and I hold as we go downriver concludes that dock levels must have dropped just before we left the berth. That would sink us into the dock bottom mud.

When we arrive in Freetown a few days before the year's end we find that part of our deck cargo is more than eagerly awaited. We have six 20 foot tank containers of Octel and this is urgently needed if the whole country is not to suffer a New Year without petrol.

Octel – the 'tel' suffix stands for 'tetra-ethyl lead' – is an essential ingredient of leaded petrol. It's a liquid, which comes in either blue or orange colourways and is not one that I would like to see in order to check on its hue since it kills via skin penetration or inhalation.

It used to be shipped in large grey drums with substantial belly hoops for protection and we always carried a couple of sets of special protective clothing to wear in case of a spill. No protection is offered with these containers. However, I keep a wary eye on the discharge of these potential hazards before returning to my cabin for a short break.

My release is curtailed when I spot a couple of ruffians up on top of the container stack, busily removing the hardboard cover to the back of one of the Land Rovers. If I can get down below fast enough, I decide, I can waylay them and recover their loot.

I reach the maindeck at the forward end of number three hatch just in time to hear a lot of scuffling and to see one thief legging it with part of the haul. His companion is still on the way down. This gives me the opportunity to land a hefty blow to the backs of his legs with a handy piece of timber that I've picked up en route.

It doesn't have much effect on him as he's wearing a decent pair of trousers and I also notice a smart pair of black boots, before my attention focuses on a sheath knife that he's now waving fairly menacingly. He shouts, 'Go way ! Make I pass now!' I accept his instruction and step aside but, when his gunny sack of plunder catches momentarily on some obstruction, he stumbles. More enraged than sensible, I land another blow across his back as he prioritises his escape and abandons his haul.

I chase up the deck after him but he's over the side and into the harbour and despite his heavy footwear he's swimming powerfully towards a waiting canoe. I fling my makeshift weapon after him. It's a useless gesture, and a risky one at that, since I see that one of his companions is waving what looks like a rifle at me in response.

I turn on my 'bow and arrow' men in frustration, 'Wass matta, why you no take dese tiefmen for me? Why you no shoot your ting one time at dis canoe wey get dese people? Why for dis place wey dey get no law?'

'Aha, massa,' is the guarded response, 'Dese be very bad men who savvy we people too much. Dey be dat policemen who no get any pay for dis long time. Dey come shipside and say make we no make palaver if we fit go see dis our wife an pickin dis night. So we get plenty fear and we no fit stop dem pass.'

I don't know what annoys me the most after this exchange, the futility of trying to protect the cargo or the fact that this once sleepy, almost boringly quiet place had now become so corrupted that even the policemen were turning into active criminals.

Our next calls in Abidjan and Tema reduce our deck loading to the point that the security visibility necessary for our stay off Lagos can be achieved. We're about twenty miles offshore (to be any further out would reduce our VHF listening ability too much), nevertheless the dawn still reveals half a dozen canoes hovering around in the off chance of a lightning raid.

Once alongside, we're into the familiar ballet of shifting cargo around instead of unloading it because of the vagaries of the sheds. We unload the last of our vehicles but some comedian has been playing with the controls of one of the ice-cream vans and soon we're being treated to a painful rendition of 'Greensleeves' over and over again.

The only way to shut the noise off will be to disconnect the battery, as the erstwhile driver cannot remember how the tannoy was switched on and none of us can find anything to act as an off switch. 'You cannot do dis ting,' says an NPA supervisor as I open the bonnet, 'You must wait, de man e come soon for fix am.' Sod this, I think and shut the bonnet, get into the driver's seat and take the van to the vehicle security compound which is only at the end of the next shed. I lock up, give the keys to an official there and come back on board. The next day we're still getting audible snatches of the melody from time to time.

Now the ship is nearly empty and it's time for our first visit to the creeks. With such a large ship, it's a relief to know that the bar at Escravos is still being effectively dredged and the training banks maintained. Plenty of water under our keel but more water from above makes the crossing hazardous in a typical creeks downpour.

The pilot and his entourage board with a tale of woe: 'Too plenty teefman wey dey get dis place now, good man never get chance for life,' is the gist of their complaint. We have to anchor nearby overnight as there is no berth free at Warri, our destination.

Mooring ropes are the major attraction to thieves here but I'm reluctant to stow them away as they'll need to be handy for tomorrow. However, they can be lashed down with wire and we'll have hoses rigged and charged, ready to repel any boarders. We do have one visit in the small hours. The canoe is initially repelled by giving its complement a good rinsing before it emerges that it contains two of our stewards coming back from a spot of 'jig-a-jig' in the nearby village.

We've a parcel of a thousand tons of palm kernels to load here which is useful to fill a large space in our number two hatch that can't be used for containers. It does unfortunately mean an overnight stay and we're advised to lift the gangway as a barrier to unwelcome visitors even though cargo is to be worked through the night.

All goes well until a rainstorm at about 4 a.m. causes cargo work to cease and the duty mate and his two sailors take sensible shelter once the hatch is closed. Unfortunately this gives a gang of thieves the chance to get on board up forward and nick two of our mooring ropes by cutting them off close to the bitts and throwing them overside to a waiting canoe.

Fortunately, we have spares but it makes us more than glad to be leaving this sodden nest of thieves for what we hope will be a slightly more law-abiding Port Harcourt. Here we load containers that are said to contain bales of rubber. This is certainly an improvement on the old days of clouds of talcum powder and encounters with grumpy shippers.

It's good to see that the container, now that its use is established on the coast, is being used for return traffic. Of course, you'll never get logs inside one but it's perfectly possible to fill them with plywood or even sawn timber, as we do in our next port of Abidjan before back-tracking to Takoradi.

Here, the Ghanaians are experimenting with carrying cocoa beans loose in the type of container used for shipping brewing grain to Nigeria. These boxes can be distinguished by having small ventilation flaps that are left open to cool the contents on the passage north.

Other containers are declared as carrying parquet flooring blocks, timber doors or furniture parts. This is a welcome sign that Ghana at last is adding value to its raw primary products. Loading of containers is a welcome simplification of our work in port but there's still a little sadness at no longer being able to see just what we are carrying as cargo.

There's still some traditional work left, of course, and I've left space for 2,000 tons of cocoa to be loaded in the usual manner. Our powerful electric cargo fans will keep this cargo in good shape and wash warm chocolatey breezes from the stow around the decks on our way home.

I fall into conversation with the grizzled old 'Pa' who is in charge of the cocoa gang. I've admired the battered Elder Dempster cap that he's wearing and he tells me that it's a souvenir of his Krooboy days long ago. His surprising view is that the country should go back to being the Gold Coast.

'Big men' and their families and friends have done well at the expense of ordinary people, he continues, and it would be much better if the British returned and sorted things out as they did in the old days. We share a smoke as he explains his disillusion. He's so passionate, but not embittered, as he speaks that I feel that this is a genuine complaint and not the precursor to an appeal for more tobacco.

There are only a few cigarettes left in the packet, anyway, so I 'dash' them to him. My sad conclusion is that his story confirms my outsider's view that nearly a quarter-century of independence has provided most of the inhabitants of this coast with little material benefit. What little capital endowment that was carried forward from colonial days is now exhausted and too much of its potential replacement has been unsuitably spent or even dishonestly diverted.

We call at Las Palmas for fuel bunkers on our way back to Liverpool and here a vigilant duty watch disturb a gang who have managed to get on board and are in the process of removing several bags of cocoa beans to a waiting boat. No violence is offered and the thieves flee. Nevertheless it's a new development in this port.

Naturally, as in every bunkering port around the world, there's an opportunity to sell off scrap, empty oil- and paint-drums and old wires and rope for cash when we visit Las Palmas. However, this move into actually stealing stuff seems to be a case of the West African disease spreading north. I spend the last few days of the voyage gloomily wondering if my twenty-odd years visiting the coast in various guises has come to its natural end.

As it turns out, this has been my last voyage to the West Coast of Africa since I fly to the other side of the globe to join my next ship after an extended leave. Two long flights from Heathrow and a long run in from the airport bring me to the ship, berthed in Melbourne's Victoria Dock.

I remember this place from my apprenticeship days but, a quarter-century on, I can barely recognise the city apart from its broad thoroughfares, the ornate Flinders Street railway station, the old trams and the 'narra Yarra' river at its heart.

The ship is here unloading a cargo brought from Brazil because she is on charter to the state-owned firm of Lloyd Brasileiro, as is her sister ship and another. That means the Brazilians are now employing half of our dwindling fleet. We have this business because the Brazilian company cannot manage the service using their own ships. The Brazilian seafarer, it would appear, has neither the taste for extended sea voyages nor the patience to deal with the Australian stevedores.

From Australia we return to Brazil via Durban, which means a pleasant crossing of the Indian Ocean and the opportunity to enjoy the novelty of a sea passage of several days. Another novelty is that I'm now spared the need to practise my rusty recollection of stellar navigation.

The ship has been supplied with a satellite navigation system as part of the charterer's conditions, presumably because they don't want us wandering around the oceans and wasting their expensive fuel.

The satellites that we use are not the geo-stationary ones of today but their predecessors, which wandered across the sky like all other heavenly bodies. Once above the horizon, they can provide us with our latitude and longitude via a bright-green digital display. However, when they're out of sight, all we receive is a bus-stop type rolling banner advising when the next two arrivals are due.

After our Durban call, we enjoy passing the coast of South Africa at a speed well in excess of twenty knots, skid around Cape Agulhas and head into the grey skies of the South Atlantic. A fortnight or so in Brazil proves an enjoyable introduction to our new trade.

Some of our company fly home from Rio de Janeiro when we arrive, having done their tour of duty. Their replacements are all well known to us since Palm Line, now a very small firm, has even more of a family feel to it.

Our berth is in the centre of town, one of the perks of being operated by the national shipping line and, once unloaded, our first weekend is free of work and allows us all to enjoy the sightseeing and other pleasures of this famous port.

After our recent experience of West African destinations this is a welcome facility that the ship's company exploit to the full. The local currency, the cruzeiro, is depreciating daily due to inflation so whatever money we draw before going ashore needs to be quickly spent. On later calls we will see prices that are marked in US dollars as restaurants and shops try to keep abreast of a rate that soon reaches several thousand to the dollar.

We load our cargo from here, then from Rio Grande, Paranagua and finally Santos, a process which goes fairly well although our loading instructions are a bit confused at times. The only visible items, in this almost fully containerised trade, are several hundred bundles of small-bore stainless steel tubes.

The invisibility of container contents inevitably leads to problems. For example, at Rio Grande, I'm expecting containers of shoes so, at just six tons; they can be stacked high and that's how they go. Fortunately the third mate proves to be perceptive when one container appears to be on the heavy side as it's being hoisted to the third tier on deck.

I have it landed back on the quay while the stevedore's clerk checks its serial number from the loading list. It proves to be full of diesel compressor sets and is booked as being nearly twenty tons, along with half a dozen others. After a quick session in my office to adjust the master plan we find these boxes a better home.

This is the big difference to our familiar trade, where all this was sorted out by our colleagues in West African Terminals in Liverpool and Tilbury. Here, it appears, I'll need to keep a beady eye on the stevedoring and none more so then when I'm dealing with containers of dangerous goods.

The United Nations manual, some two inches thick, normally gathering dust on my office bookshelf ,will now become extremely dog-eared and grubby. It's a list of all dangerous goods and the rules concerning where they must be carried and how far apart from each other must be each category. They're classed as inflammables, explosives, corrosives, compressed gases or by any other harmful property that they represent.

It's a far cry from those days when we sailed out to West Africa with a fairly haphazard distribution of a container of aerosols here, a drum of inflammables there and the odd caged glass carboy of hydrochloric acid in another corner relying on a bed of straw for its protection.

We sail from Santos with a full container complement on deck and a full load of fuel for a marathon non-stop passage of 25 days to Melbourne. Apart from the possibility of a short glimpse of Tristan da Cunha (which doesn't materialise) we'll not see any land as we follow a great-circle track to the parallel of 40 degrees south. We'll only leave that latitude when it's time to head up towards Cape Otway.

A grey sky is our companion for the first week, and thereafter the only blue sky appears when a gale blows holes in the clouds and speeds us along the upper edge of the 'Roaring Forties' of sailing-ship days. It's a chance to renew acquaintance with that aristocrat of the Southern Ocean, the great wandering albatross, a pair of which fall in with us and stay around for nearly a fortnight, inspecting our wake after mealtimes to see what the messroom and saloon might not have consumed.

From time to time they fly parallel to the bridge wing and inspect me with a basilisk stare. I'm not sure whether they welcome me or, as I've seen in the past, are deciding at what point to casually drift inboard and then deliberately and accurately deposit a message on my nice wooden decks with a white splatter the size of a dinner plate.

I can also watch these magnificent birds from the panoramic windows facing aft that belong to our gymnasium, a room some 60 feet across by 20 feet deep and 15 feet in height. Fitted with wall bars, basketball nets, exercise bicycles, rowing machines and with a sauna room attached, this fine facility has been under-used during those busy voyages on our West Africa run.

A space like this, on a Nigerline ship captained by my old shipmate Sunny, could easily be converted into a small profitable supermarket. However, this lonely ocean passage offers us an opportunity to use it for its intended purpose. Most afternoons I try to enjoy half an hour of imagining myself rowing across these stormy latitudes before I opt for my mandatory afternoon nap. My more athletic colleagues have a more effective enjoyment playing either basketball or some type of football.

There's also plenty of time on this extended oceanic route for the Old Man and I to pass most of my afternoon watch recalling past times on the West Coast of Africa or speculating about the future. We both agree that this pleasant change of route cannot last for long as the charterers will always be looking for a cheaper ship and our employer is unlikely to want to stay engaged in tramp shipping.

The Old Man is only a few years from retirement so the prospect of taking that entitlement a little early is an attractive one for him. However, I still have nearly 20 years to serve before I can collect my pension. The situation should force me to start thinking about my future and try and revive my efforts to find employment ashore but, as too often in the past, I'm just drifting with the tide of events.

Far sooner than I had imagined, we're picking up the Port Philip pilot at the end of our 9,000 mile passage and are crossing the bay of that name to our berth in Melbourne. The unloading goes well here and another weekend in port without work allows me to enjoy the hospitality of a former fellow apprentice who I first met when we both began our seagoing nearly 30 years earlier.

He now works for a stevedoring firm in the port and can provide me with a few tips on keeping work going by foreseeing some of the tricks employed by Australian dockers to engineer a walk-out. The containers for Melbourne are mostly on deck and, although the bundles of steel tubes lead to some grumbling, we clear all the cargo without too many problems. Then it's on to Sydney, where my friend's warnings turn out to be only too horribly true.

We have a splendid berth in Darling Harbour, within walking distance of the town centre and the night-life of the Rocks quarter. It was a seedy neighbourhood during the 1950s but now it's been sanitised and decorated as a 'Sailortown' for tourists ahead of the Bicentenary celebrations to be held in 1988. Sydney dockers, however, have not been reconstructed and the bleating and bickering soon begins.

I have to confess that providing a safe workplace was never a real concern in West African ports, where negotiation, genial bribery and crime prevention were pre-eminent. Here I have to recognise that need and so we've rigged all those safety nets, handrails, lights and ladders that are required.

It might seem boastful, but my documentation of all the ship's cargo-working equipment is immaculate. This is, of course, thanks to many quiet watches on our long sea passage. Now, my ability to produce the exact piece of paper certifying the qualities of every last hook, wire or shackle in use will surely bring pleasure to the most demanding of bureaucrats.

Unfortunately, it's not enough for these sensitive Sydney watersiders, as I'm clearly not playing the game of presenting them with enough excuses to stop work. A lifting wire is judged damaged as it keeps twisting when the load comes off it. It must therefore be replaced and that's an hour's delay at one end of one hatch. Then the safety wire along the hatch opening somewhere else is found to be two inches too low as it sags between its stanchions. Fortunately, a gang of ship-repairers is in the vicinity and they cobble up some extra fittings to everybody's satisfaction except, no doubt, our London office when the repair bill is presented.

Then there's a 'bad smell' reported to me in one of the underdeck spaces so that needs a few buckets of disinfectant splashing around and the inevitable wait until the union representative finds the atmosphere satisfactory. Someone 'might have a serious accident' when a miniscule pool of hydraulic oil is spotted in some almost inaccessible underdeck corner by 'Hawkeye'.

This is the name that I'm using to myself as suitable shorthand for the chief whinger representing such a delicate constituency. Then, to cap it all, there's a total walk-out when somebody takes exception to the fact that we're booked to load some containers for discharge in Durban.

That's not the ship's fault, for once, so all on board gratefully accept the complete cessation of work for two days and I can give the sailors a day off as well. Those of us not detained by ship-keeping duties can head off wherever we wish, and I take the chance to introduce a few of my shipmates to the remembered pleasures of the Manly ferry.

This elderly vessel takes us from its terminal in the shadow of Sydney Harbour Bridge across the harbour to Manly. A short walk down to a magnificent beach, backed by those distinctive Norfolk Island pines, allows some of our party to try their luck impressing the local girls. Those of us not quite up to that formidable challenge can retreat to the main street, where we call up large plates of fish and chips and equally large glasses of frozen lager.

There's more bother about our intended South African destination when we reach Brisbane. However, that merely provides us with additional opportunities for sightseeing. This boycott and protest action is continued during my next visit to Australia because we now call at Durban in both directions and thus provide a full service between Australia and South Africa.

The odd day or two off work as a result is always welcome, as the long sea passages are beginning to pall and the news from West Africa about our future is becomier gloomier than ever. Palm Line is now reduced to two ships on that route, one of which is our vegetable-oil tanker which is actually taking palm oil *to* Nigeria, such is the collapse in the country's domestic food production.

Our oldest ship has been sold to new owners and, whilst Lloyd Brasileiro's trade with South Africa and Australia is flourishing, their agency in Sydney tells us that a larger ship has been offered by a Greek ship-owner for a slightly lesser daily rate than we have been fixed at.

I spend the last of many Christmas Days away from home in the little port of Risdon, near Hobart in Tasmania, where we've come to load billets of aluminium. Then it's not many days into the New Year when we learn that the name of Palm Line and its shipping conference rights have been sold to Elder Dempster.

Our two green-painted steel palm trees, now adding to the ambience around the ship's swimming pool, will never again grace the sides of our funnel and another minor chapter in the history of the British Merchant Navy has come to an end.

When we arrive in Rio de Janeiro our charter ends once we are unloaded. We enter a drydock in the port to await a pre-sale inspection from the Black Sea division of the state shipping line of the USSR. Then my relief arrives in time to save me taking part in this sad process. I walk down the gangway to a waiting airport taxi, fly home from the sunshine of Brazil to a freezing British February and never go to sea again.

Epilogue

My redundancy cheque duly arrives from Palm Line once my voyage leave ends. As might be expected from the subsidiary of a major multinational company, it's a generous sum in view of my service of less than ten years but it only buys me time to consider my future. My search for shoreside employment takes on a new urgency and sense of purpose that had been lacking in earlier times but, for now, I do have some leeway to exploit by returning to the fold of the 'pool'.

The shipping industry is contracting rapidly in 1986 so it's no great surprise when I receive a second redundancy payment within a few months. In contrast with its predecessor, this payment is for an amount that barely reaches four figures. When I challenge this meagre compensation, which allegedly covers nearly twenty years of unbroken service, a weaselly letter informs me that my sojourn under the Nigerian flag counts as 'broken service'.

My protestations at this adjudication are met by a catalogue of responses that steadfastly refuse to acknowledge that I had actually been recruited for NNSL by the Merchant Navy Establishment. They also ignore the fact that I maintained my British income tax and national insurance payments and also my contribution to the shipping industry's pension scheme. A bureaucratic wall and the stated inability of the officers' trade union to pursue my case mean that I end my sea career on a bitter note.

The demise of Palm Line is the end of William Lever's dream of a vertically integrated manufacturing empire within which his oil palms produced oil and seeds to be carried in his own ships to his various soap and margarine factories. His corporate successors are embracing the new business model of outsourcing everything outside tightly defined 'core' activities.

However, the ownership of his maritime trading brand by his traditional rival Elder Dempster, yet another enterprise dominated by a charismatic Victorian entrepreneur, Sir Alfred Jones, did not last long. It was the French shipping company of Société Navale et Commerciale Delmas-Vieljeux that finally inherited all the British shipping interests in West Africa, in 1989. It is an inheritance that lasts to this day.

Part of this French company's success in maintaining a presence in the sea trade to West Africa is due to the dynastic dynamism of the founding family (their British counterparts disappeared long ago), although continuity of the actual name of a Vieljeux is unlikely to last much longer.

Another factor has been the continuing influence in West Africa of the former imperial power by means of frequent French government interventions. This meant that the old French colonies avoided for far longer the military coups and internal strife that bedevilled their formerly British neighbours since the general arrival of West African national independence.

The West African trade was a very distinctive one throughout its history. Its particular complexities and specific practices even caused it to remain apart from the global hegemony of the sea container for over a decade. The operational cargo work that my generation of seafarers learned from our first voyages remained valid there for almost of all our working lives at sea. This gave rise to a false sense of security because the arrival of the sea container meant a transfer of many of our traditional skills from ship to shore.

In addition, British ship-owners in the West African trade were always much slower than their continental rivals to adopt the type of ship that could be worked less expensively in port. The final blow to those of us serving on their ships was the cruel economic reality that we could be replaced by seafarers of other nations who did not require the wages and service conditions that we enjoyed.

Our replacement, redundancy and dispersal to other work was undoubtedly traumatic. However, it was much less damaging to us than the destruction of the high hopes raised at independence was for those Africans we worked alongside. Nevertheless, we were all victims of a complex interaction of factors over which we had no control.

In Nigeria, the economic endowment of the value of huge oil reserves led to reckless spending, monumental theft of government revenues and the abandonment of primary production due to a flight from the country areas to chaotic urban slums.

In Ghana, the use of foreign aid was heavily skewed in favour of prestige projects that either glorified the president or failed to earn enough to repay increasing governmental debt.

In Liberia and Sierra Leone, the resolution of tensions, originating as far back as the founding resettlement of freed slaves, was only found through the medium of horrific civil wars. Similarly, other West African nations suffered from internal violence that owed much to the colonial legacy of artificial state boundaries.

It is only in retrospect that we can see how damaging this inheritance was. To expect and to try and enforce loyalty to an artificial 'nation', one that must ignore its inhabitants' wish for a communality based on kinship and ethnicity, can only have an unhappy outcome.

Many factors, many sources of blame, make for a sad story of West Africa since the introduction of Ghana to the United Nations forum in 1957. Those of us who visited West Africa by sea have many good memories of our time spent there and many of us have been fortunate to follow that by enjoying very different lives.

In my case that meant being able to graduate from university in my home city and then to find rewarding employment ashore until my retirement. For 12 years I worked closely with the crews of the Travelling Post Offices of Royal Mail. This was another group of men (and a few women) with a strong work ethic of getting the job finished, whatever the obstacles, and enjoying an equally strong suspicion of all outsiders. In short, it was my ideal social environment. I was very privileged.

A very final note:

While I'm writing this book, I hear from a former colleague in Palm Line. He tells me that the last ship that took me to West Africa has made her own final voyage. During September 2009 she arrived at the ship-breaking centre of Alang in western India. By now, her fabric has been recycled into steel reinforcing rods for the concrete that is needed for that country to become one of the dominant economies of this new century. The economic history of the world continues…

Further Reading

I hope that this book will encourage readers to seek out a lot more information and reportage about West Africa, its peoples, its history and its cultures. I'm sure that this short list will provide a helpful start for those who choose to begin such exploring.

Meredith, Martin. *The State of Africa, A History of 50 years of Independence*, The Free Press: London, 2005.
  A very readable account of the period with a comprehensive and useful bibiography.

Kapuscinski, Ryszard. *The Shadow of the Sun: My African Life*, Penguin Books: London, 2002.
  A modern literary classic with a large West African content of masterly essays.

Forsyth, Frederick. *The Making of an African Legend: The Biafra Story*, Penguin Books: London, 1977.
  Unashamedly partisan for Biafra, this book nevertheless remains the best account of the Nigerian Civil War from its origins to its aftermath and the foreign involvement.

Green, Lawrence G. *White Man's Grave*, Stanley Paul & Co. Ltd: London, 1954.

Mott-Smith, May. *Africa from Port to Port*, Harold Shaylor: London, 1931.

Taylor, Harold Robert. *Jungle Trader*, Jarrolds Ltd: London, 1939.

Young, T.Rex. *West African Agent*, Heath Cranton Ltd: London, 1942.
  There are few accounts of West Africa that contain a strong maritime element. Time in the more spider-infested corners of second-hand bookshops introduced me to these four works. Very much of their period – written in the colonial era – they nevertheless capture the flavours of the 'Coast' and still make for an enjoyable read. Nowadays they're probably available from a more comfortable internet search.

Tanneau, Georges. *Un Novice Au Long Cours, Sur Le Robert Espagne*, Éditions Coop Breizh, 29540 Spézet, 1997.

Claeyssen, Hervé. *Carnets De Voyage Au Long Cours*, Éditions du Carabe & Louis Dreyfus Armateurs: Dunkerque, 2005.
  These French accounts of trading by sea to West Africa are well worth finding if the reader has a reasonable command of the language. The first book relates two voyages made in the 1950s, the latter recounts the period 1989 to 1991 and includes photographs and superb pen and wash illustrations that capture the essence of the loading of logs and the navigation of the creeks of the West Coast of Africa.

Birkett, Dea. *Jella: A Woman at Sea*, Victor Gollancz Ltd: London, 1992.
This is the story of a voyage home from West Africa by a woman who delivers a very individual insight into shipboard life in the final years of the British Merchant Navy.

Lane, Tony. *Grey Dawn Breaking, British Merchant Seafarers in the Late 20th Century*, Manchester University Press: Manchester, 1986.
Finally, at the risk of being accused of some 'logrolling', anybody who wishes to have a sympathetic and readable yet rigorously honest account of the whole post-war life of those who worked on merchant ships needs to read this book.